D1273133

THE RISE AND FALL OF T. D. LYSENKO

The Rise and Fall of

T. D. LYSENKO

Zhores A. Medvedev

TRANSLATED BY

I. MICHAEL LERNER

with the editorial assistance of
LUCY G. LAWRENCE

COLUMBIA UNIVERSITY PRESS

NEW YORK AND LONDON

I. Michael Lerner is Professor of
Genetics and former Chairman of the
Department of Genetics at the
University of California, Berkeley.

*Frontispiece: Bronze monument of
Lysenko and Stalin, in the central
square of Ostrog, in the Rovno region
of the Ukraine. Erected about 1950,
and removed in 1961.*

Copyright © 1969 Columbia University Press

First printing 1969
Second printing 1970

ISBN: 0-231-03183-1
Library of Congress Catalog Card
   Number: 79-77519
Printed in the United States of America

THE STORY OF Soviet genetics in the period 1937–1964 is, perhaps, the most bizarre chapter in the history of modern science. In a society devoted to the betterment of the lot of peasants and workers, an illiterate and fanatical charlatan was allowed absolute dictatorship and control over both research in biology and practical agriculture. This event not only stifled the development of science, but also had a far-reaching and destructive influence on the national economy of the Soviet Union. To the outside world, it was completely incomprehensible that a country capable of developing a nuclear potential rivaling that of the United States, and of establishing itself in the forefront of space exploration, could have entrusted its fundamental agricultural resources to exploitation by an obvious quack. Geneticists and agriculturists of the West have long speculated about the machinery of the Lysenko take-over in biology and about the situation that made it possible. This book provides an answer.

As Zhores A. Medvedev states in his Preface, the three parts of the book represent the author's three points of view: as historian; as a witness to the events; and as an active participant in the last stages of Lysenkoism, which he helped to topple. The book is not only a history; it is also an indictment of a system of centralized control of science. We can all profit from its lesson.

Although I know only a few personal facts, I should like to recount the history of my connection with this book. In 1961 I received a copy of a book, in Russian, by Y. M. Olenov, for review in *Science*. It dealt with population genetics and evolution, and its main purpose seemed to be to present the developments in these areas to the Soviet scientific community which, under Lysenko's regime, knew nothing of them. It was a good book: Engels was mentioned in it only once, and the whole tenor was not one of demagogic style (described so vividly by Medvedev) but rather that of an objective and scientific spirit. My review was entitled "The blossoms of a hundred flowers of Soviet genetics," echoing the statement of Chairman Mao. In response to my review, a postcard came to me from the Laboratory of Radiobiology in Obninsk (some 110 kilometers from Moscow), informing me that I was talking through my hat—for every flower there are still a hundred weeds, it said. The writer of the card, Medvedev, turned out to be a young man of high intelligence, spirit, and courage, a Soviet patriot, and an active participant in the struggle against Lysenkoism described in this book. I later learned that he is forty-three years old and is in charge of the laboratory at the Institute of Medical Radiobiology, from which he wrote. He has an identical twin who is also a Soviet scholar, in the humanities. Their father suffered in the political purges of 1938 and perished in 1941 in a Polar Circle mining camp. He was rehabilitated posthumously in much the same way as were many of the persons whose stories are told in this book.

Medvedev has published nearly one hundred papers, mainly on molecular aspects of development and aging. He is currently interested in the genetic and molecular problems of gerontology and, as might be expected, in the social aspects of international scientific cooperation.

Medvedev and I struck up a correspondence and, at the Mendelian Centennial celebration in Czechoslovakia in 1965 (described in Chapter 10), managed to meet each other. He told me that he had been working since 1961 on a history of the whole sordid affair and showed me an outline of the book. I immediately volunteered to translate it when and if it was published in the U.S.S.R.

Subsequently Medvedev informed me that publication was to be delayed, because the powers that be had decreed that 1967, being the fiftieth anniversary of the Revolution, was not a suitable time to bring out books critical of the Soviet regime.

In the fall of 1967 I was instrumental in bringing to the United States a delegation of four Soviet geneticists (this was after Lysenko's fall), and at that time I discussed with them fully, frankly, and without reservations, the prospects for doing the translation. I afterwards learned that the discussion provoked some consternation among my colleagues. Later, Medvedev wrote suggesting that I request a copy of the manuscript from the publishing house of the Soviet Academy, with a view to translating it into English, and that I point out the obvious advantages of an authorized translation, with royalties accruing in dollars, and some guarantee of accuracy. After several months of silence, I received a letter from the publishing house which indicated that the manuscript was not publishable in the U.S.S.R. and therefore I could not have a copy of it.

Meanwhile, through unofficial channels, I came into possession of a microfilm of the typescript. The author had circulated many copies of preliminary versions throughout the Soviet Union for the purpose of checking the accuracy of his account of the events described. The final Russian text, which provided the basis for the present translation, resulted from numerous revisions by the author, and has been approved by him as representing his current views. For obvious reasons, he did not see the translated, abridged, and edited manuscript before publication. It is hoped that he may one day see a copy of this book.

After reading the microfilm and consulting with a number of colleagues in genetics and with persons informed of the current intellectual climate in the U.S.S.R., it became apparent to me that, if the book was to be banned in the Soviet Union, it is all the more important that it be published elsewhere. The decision to do so was not an easy one. Regardless of the route by which the manuscript reached me, the possibility of reprisals against its author exists. It appears, however, that Medvedev is willing, in the light of his circulation of the manuscript in the Soviet Union at the height of Lysenko's last surge of power (Chapter 9), to take whatever risks are involved in publishing the book here, for the good of his country. (At this stage there is the problem of transmitting his share of royalties, which Columbia University Press, without having to do so, has agreed to hold for him in escrow.) Full exposure of what happened in the course of Lysenko's rise and fall can do nothing but good for Soviet science and the Soviet economy. Indeed, as Medvedev attributes patriotic motives to Vavilov, Pryanishnikov, and others, so it is obvious that his own manuscript was written out of concern for the welfare of science and the national economy of his fatherland.

The book is written in an uneven style. In my task of translating and editing I wanted to preserve the tone of the original. The lapses into first person, and the personal reminiscences, although producing unexpected changes in key, reflect the author's approach. I have tried to preserve this tone at the risk of failure in uniformity of style. Unevenness in accuracy and incompleteness of bibliographical citations is also to be explained on these terms.

To me Chapter 6 is one of the highlights of the book. It presents the terrifying picture of the methods of the Lysenko take-over and the consequences of it. The courageous story of the struggle waged by Vavilov, Pryanishnikov, Tulaikov, Sabinin, and others in the earlier phases, and by Medvedev himself, Sukachev, and still others in the last stages, represents as glorious a chapter in defense of scientific freedom and human dignity as can be found in the annals of civilization. But the events of 1948–1952 are portrayed in so vivid a manner that the specter of Orwell's *1984* haunting our society becomes convincingly real.

Some apology is perhaps due for failing to meet the standards of the professional historian, and for possible inaccuracies in the specialized terminologies of agronomy and forestry. Miss Lawrence and I have tried to convert the original manuscript into a readable and understandable account of what can only be called a fantastic episode in the history of mankind. We consider that it has meaning, not only as a history, but also as a warning of what could happen in any country that relaxes or suspends its vigilance over concern for scientific freedom, for whatever reason.

Just as the author has dedicated his book to his courageous and patriotic predecessors, so we dedicate the work of translation, abridgment, and editing to Zhores Aleksandrovich Medvedev for his valiant fight in the cause of scientific principles and the welfare of his native land.

I. M. L.

Berkeley, California, 1968

THIS BOOK CONSISTS of three parts. The first two were written in 1961–1962 and augmented in 1963–1964; the third was written in 1966–1967. Each part, for various reasons, differs from the others in syle and method of analysis of the facts. In the first place, the existing situations in science described in each section differed, and the problems around which the debate was carried on were changing, even though genetics remained the center of attention. In the second place, the different parts of the book were written under different conditions. In 1961–1962 Lysenkoism still occupied a dominating position in the biological and agricultural sciences and was fully supported by the higher authorities. Criticism of its positions was actually banned in the press and was mercilessly eradicated by all means of press control. By 1966 Lysenkoism, as such, had already disappeared from Soviet science, not having survived even one year of open discussion. The first parts of the book therefore are active, aggressive, and polemical in character, while the concluding part is by and large descriptive, especially when dealing with the events after October, 1964. And, finally, I appear in different capacities in each of the three parts: in the first as historian; in the second as an onlooker; and in the third as participant, since the first version of the manuscript itself became, after 1962, one of the elements of the debate, and developed in the course of it. The manuscript was used as ammunition, and hundreds of men attempted to make that ammunition effective.

Many scientists have aided me greatly, particularly the following comrades, who supported me from the very beginning of my work and who helped to collect and analyze the factual material. Although many of them are famous scientists, I list them without their degrees or positions since, in the struggle for the triumph of truth which we all carried on for many years, neither post nor standing played any role. It is good to realize that many of them became my personal friends. In citing their names here I once more recall these men with pleasure and gratitude—their honesty, nobility, high principles, and courage in the defense of scientific truth, as well as their patriotism: V. P. Efroimson, Y. N. Vavilov, V. M. Klechkovsky, A. I. Atabekova, N. A. Maisuryan, A. A. Liubishchev, B. L. Astaurov, V. V. Sakharov, F. K. Bakhteev, P. M. Zhukovsky, A. R. Zhebrak, V. V. Alpatov, V. J. Mirek, V. D. Dudintsev, V. Y. Aleksandrov, V. S. Kirpichnikov, L. V. Breslavets, N. R. Ivanov, D. K. Belyaev, V. I. Tsalkin, N. V. Timofeev-Resovsky, I. L. Knunyants, D. V. Lebedev, I. A. Rapoport, A. M. Smirnov, A. V. Sokolov, E. M. Murtazin, M. K. Chailakhyan, L. Y. Blyakher, A. Efeikin, A. A. Lyapunov, R. A. Medvedev, M. G. Tsubina, P. M. Smirnov, and many other comrades.

Z. A. M.

January, 1967, Obninsk

THE CATEGORICAL condemnation, by the XXth and XXIInd Congresses of the Communist Party, of the theory and practice of the personality cult was met with enthusiasm by all the Soviet people as an event of historical significance and as a turning point in the development of our country and of the international Communist movement. Everybody can now see clearly how many-sided and burdensome were the consequences of the personality cult, and how timely and courageous were the actions directed toward restoration of Lenin's principles of democracy, the socialist law, a steadfast observance of the right of Soviet citizens, and the methods of collective leadership.

The long-time failure to observe these principles was not reflected solely in political events. The cult of personality also had a serious impact on the ideological and scientific spheres of our life and violated those conditions of free scientific creativity which should be basically inherent in the socialist system. The environment of the personality cult seriously influenced the development of a number of natural sciences, and above all, biology and agronomy. A study of that influence is required with pressing urgency.

This book attempts to analyze, from that point of view, the widely known biological-agronomic controversy which began at the end of the twenties and continued, with periodic intensification, until very recent times. Understanding the responsibilities behind this task, I drew on a great number of Soviet scientists for discussions of the preliminary versions of the book, and also tried to take into consideration the comments of comrades whose roles in the events described were, in my view, far from positive. Leonardo da Vinci's observation that opponents hoping you make mistakes are more useful than friends trying to conceal them is not entirely true in this situation; as a rule, friends did not try to conceal the shortcomings of this work, and I am grateful to them for much.

The first version of the book was prepared in the beginning of 1962, but it was changed and augmented many times as a result of numerous discussions. I wish to express my sincere appreciation to all comrades who, by their comments, considerations, and additions, aided in the preparation of the book in its present form.

Z. A. M.

October, 1962

CONTENTS

PART II. THE NEW PHASE: 1946–1962

PART III. THE LAST PHASE: 1962–1966

ABBREVIATIONS

AIPB	All-Union Institute of Plant Breeding
AS	U.S.S.R. Academy of Sciences
CC	Central Committee, Communist Party
CP	Communist Party of the U.S.S.R.
LAAAS	Lenin All-Union Academy of Agricultural Sciences
NKVD	People's Commissariat of Internal Affairs
R.S.F.S.R.	Russian Soviet Federated Socialist Republic
TAA	Timiryazev Agricultural Academy

THE RISE AND FALL OF T. D. LYSENKO

Dedicated to the memory of outstanding Soviet scientists,
participants in the events described:
N. I. Vavilov, D. N. Pryanishnikov, N. K. Kol'tsov,
and D. A. Sabinin.

Zhores A. Medvedev

Part I

The First Phase: 1929-1941

We shall go to the pyre
we shall burn but we shall
not renounce our convictions.

—N. I. VAVILOV

CHAPTER I

The Historical Background of the Controversy

THE CONTROVERSY on problems of agronomy, genetics, plant and animal breeding, and general biology initiated in the early thirties by T. D. Lysenko, V. R. Vil'yams, I. I. Prezent, and others had a strong influence on the development of many branches of Soviet science and of agriculture, medicine, and some branches of industry. Great international repercussions resulted in the adoption of certain attitudes toward our country by the foreign intelligentsia. The dispute also gave rise to analogous currents in a number of socialist countries, where it provoked similar struggles between different scientific trends.

The controversy directly affected the fates of thousands of Soviet scientists and the character of secondary and higher education in biology, agriculture, and medicine. Thousands of scientific works, school textbooks, masses of popular pamphlets, philosophical works and encyclopedias, newspapers, fiction, and even the cinema reflected the dispute. Teachers, philosophers, students, collective farmers, statesmen, writers, and journalists were drawn into participation in the debate.

The controversy is a historical event, but at different periods of its development it was interpreted from diverse and contradictory positions. It is natural, therefore, that under the new and currently prevailing conditions there is need for an objective analysis of the history of the dispute, its goals, methods, results, and consequences.

POLITICAL ENVIRONMENT
AND SCIENTIFIC DEBATE

The issues herein discussed cannot, of course, be properly
understood independently of our country's history. In considering some of the problems of biology, medicine, and agriculture, the political and historical background against which
the struggle of the scientific trends developed must be taken
into account. The great October Socialist Revolution gave
birth to a new social system and was the beginning of the
creation of a socialist state of workers and peasants. This new
state, founded by the great Lenin, should have become a world
center of constructive work in all areas of creativity. It should
have become the model of the new, true forms of democracy,
social justice, and technical and scientific progress. The new
state expressed the hopes of the overwhelming majority of our
people, and the most important feature of the revolution was
that it was being realized on a scientific basis. Karl Marx,
Friedrich Engels, and Vladimir Il'ich Lenin were, above all,
great thinkers and scientists: they were creating communism
as a science concerned with the forms of development of
human society. They were establishing the doctrine of communism as a social and economic system, acceptable to all
mankind, guaranteeing the equal, just, rapid, and friendly
development of all nations on earth. The scientific method of
Marx, Engels, and Lenin was the method of proofs, the
method of analysis of facts and of arriving at truth. It is precisely because of this that Marxism has always attracted the
minds of progressive scientists.

Marx, Engels, and Lenin aspired to the creation of the democratic forms of socialism, whereas Stalin, finding himself in
power in the then solitary socialist state, took another path—
that of concentration of power in the swollen apparatus of

repression, personal dictatorship, arbitrary rule, and personality cult. In the absence of opposition parties and of class struggle, and under the sociopolitical unity of the Soviet people, the establishment of an arbitrary regime of lawlessness, in the guise of protecting the people's interests, and screened by unrestrained eulogizing of Stalin, led to a grave and tragic situation.

Stalin came into power as a successor to Lenin, the beloved and recognized leader of the October Revolution. He came to power under conditions of enormous authority on the part of the Communist party and an upsurge of creative enthusiasm by the working people. It was as if he had inherited part of the prestige and confidence that our people and our party felt toward the great Lenin. History has shown that this confidence was misused by Stalin to create a cult of his own personality and to repress and destroy all who were not inclined to support and inflate that cult.

For the duration of the cult, Stalin was ceaselessly called the greatest scientific genius of all times and all nations. In fact, of course, he was no genius, and his creative theoretical legacy is rather small. As a person, Stalin had a number of negative qualities: a hypertrophied thirst for power, suspicion, cruelty, treachery, vanity, envy, intolerance of brilliant individuals of independent character, and megalomania. These qualities created a very difficult situation not only in the country's political life but also in those areas of science which came within his sphere of interest.

An unprecedented number of discussions took place in 1935–1937 in all fields of science, the arts, and literature. As a rule, because of the historical conditions, they all were harsh. Differences of opinion, approach, method, and evaluation of facts are completely natural occurrences in science Truth is born from argument. But in the environment of the massive repressions of the thirties, the spy hunts and centralized inflaming of passions, and under the conditions of a feverish search after the "enemies of the people" in all spheres of human activity, any scientific discussion tended to become a struggle with political undertones. Nearly every discussion ended tragically for the side represented by the more noble, intellectual, honest, and calm men, who based their arguments on scientific facts.

In that period, making political accusations was the easiest and most tempting method of vanquishing opponents who could not be subdued by the force of scientific argumentation. There were some who took that road, which often led not only to a rout but also to actual physical elimination of scientific opponents.

Unfounded political accusations were commonplace in the discussions of the period, and many debates had tragic denouements. Many scientific trends (now rehabilitated) in philosophy, economics, education, history, jurisprudence, literature, natural sciences, technology, and other fields were declared to be the work of saboteurs and enemies. The controversy in genetics and breeding did not escape. The history of the controversy is a description not only of scientific debates, but also of human fates and of the tragedy of Soviet science under conditions of the personality cult.

GENETICS AND BOURGEOIS SCIENCE

The 1935–1937 biological controversy, like some other nationwide debates, had a prehistory. To some degree its way had been paved by outbursts of sharp scientific discussion in 1929–1932 that gradually took on a political hue.

The scientific polemics of 1929–1931 were at first progressive in character. They were started under the influence of the party slogan regarding the developing socialist attack on the scientific front, as contained in the resolution of the XVIth Congress of the Communist Party. Some, however, especially among the younger scientists, broadened the front to include "bourgeois tendencies" in science, extending it to many areas of the natural sciences. They attempted to apply the class approach even to problems that could only be worked out experimentally, under either a socialist or a capitalist environment.

It was exactly in this connection that certain leading scientific schools, whose work later rightfully became the pride of Soviet science, were temporarily declared to be bourgeois, idealistic, and anti-Marxist. This was the characteristic fate of the teachings of such noted scientists as the psychiatrist Bekhterev, the psychologist Kornilov, and Pavlov, the great physiologist.[1] Many prominent physicists and mathematicians, including Ioffe, Landau, Tamm, Luzin, Fok, Frenkel, and others, were placed in the category of idealists. The tone of many scientific, and especially philosophical, journals became sharp, clamorous, and sometimes plainly vulgar. By 1933–1934 the turmoil raised by the search for bourgeois reactionary theories in the natural sciences began to die down, and conditions for scientific work gradually returned to normal.

In 1929–1932 a sharp dispute also arose in biology, and particularly in genetics. It involved the problem of inheritance of acquired characters and the reality of the gene as a hereditary substance, which became the main issue of all following biological discussion. The proponents of the inheritance of acquired characters, a scanty number of Lamarckists[2] or neo-Lamarckists, grouped themselves around the Timiryazev Biological Institute. Their opponents, biologists and geneticists (Agol, Levit, Filipchenko, Serebrovsky, M. M. Zavadovsky, and others), were Marxist scientists who united around the Natural Sciences Section of the Communist Academy.

Each side tried to establish its point of view as the only one consistent with Marxism and dialectical materialism. The basic argument of the geneticists, in favor of their materialistic conceptions, rested on the facts of genetics, which at that time had for the most part been gathered abroad. In addition

to vast but factually debatable material on their side, the
Lamarckists accepted the thesis that Engels advanced in his
famous theoretical study of the role of work in the process
of transformation of ape into man—the transmissibility of characters acquired through food and exercise. It should be noted
that Engels did not reinforce his assumption by any strictly
verified facts. It must also be taken into account that Engels'
work belongs to a period before genetics as a science of heredity existed, and before Lamarckism was experimentally disproved.

In reality, attempts to use dialectical materialism for the
strictly ideological evaluation of one or another solution to
the scientific problem of the mechanisms of heredity were not
valid either in 1929–1932 or later. As history shows, the solution of the problem depended exclusively on experimental
investigations, the results of which far from confirmed the
philosophical prognoses.

The geneticists had an advantage over the Lamarckists in
this respect, and their polemic was theoretically better based
and supported by facts. However, in 1931–1932 many geneticists were considered to belong, philosophically, to the school
of so-called menshevizing idealism, a trend condemned and
christened with this absurd term by Stalin himself. Because of
this, the majority of geneticists was removed from the Communist Academy, but repressive measures were not yet in such
fashion as they became later, and only a few scientists suffered
personally. Thus Chetverikov, the creator of the Soviet school
of experimental genetics and the founder of population genetics, was exiled from Moscow. (Many of his students are
outstanding Soviet geneticists: Astaurov, Sakharov, Romashov,
Timofeev-Resovsky, Rokitsky, Dubinin, and others.) Having
been banished first to Sverdlovsk and then to Vladimir, Chetverikov was for many years unable to continue his genetic
studies. It may not be superfluous to note that Chetverikov's
work has not lost its significance even now. In 1961 a com-

plete translation of one of his fundamental works, "On certain aspects of the evolutionary process from the standpoint of modern genetics," which first appeared in 1926 in the *Zhurnal Eksperimental'noi Biologii,* was published in the United States. In an introduction to this translation, the American geneticist, I. Michael Lerner, wrote that, although Chetverikov died in obscurity, his best monument will be the vast field of population genetics developed under the influence of his studies and now attracting hundreds of scientists.

LYSENKO AND PREZENT BEFORE 1932

During this period, Lysenko did not participate in the genetics debates. As to Prezent, he was actively supporting the genetic concepts against which he later battled so vigorously. In 1930, at the All-Union Congress of Biologists, he presented a paper on the harmony between Marxism and Morganism.[3] Prezent and Lysenko enlivened the genetics debate in 1935 only after their "creative partnership" was established. They went much farther than had their Lamarckist predecessors in accusations against Soviet geneticists, and denied all the basically useful theoretical and practical concepts of classical genetics that were recognized even by Lamarckian scientists in 1929–1932.

The intensification of the genetics controversy in conjunction with the joint appearances of Prezent and Lysenko and its subsequent transformation into the struggle against "enemies of the people" were not happenstance. Even before the partnership was established in 1933–1934, each in his own sphere had been actively utilizing the resurgent political battles of 1930–1932 as a means of fighting his scientific opponents. The same can be said about the debate between Vil'yams and the more educated agronomists, some of whom (Doyarenko, Krutikhovsky, Chayanov, and others) were arrested precisely in 1931–1932.

In those years, Prezent pursued work in the field of meth-

odology for teaching the natural sciences. A lawyer by education, incapable of independent experimentation, he considered
himself a specialist theoretician on Darwinism and the teaching
of natural sciences in secondary schools. His bent for political
demagoguery was particularly strongly displayed in this period
in the discussion with Raikov, an outstanding Darwinian scientist, educational methodologist, and author of many valuable
books on the history and methodology of natural science (for
example, *Russian Predecessors of Darwin*). In 1930–1931, Prezent participated in what was first a discussion and later simply
a slanderous campaign, as a result of which Raikov and many
of his students were arrested, and the term "Raikovism" was
brought into general usage, the usual way of condemning a
scientific trend in those times.

Prezent's special address to Leningrad educators on the
harmfulness of Raikovism was published as a separate pamphlet in 1932 in an edition of 20,000. The whole pamphlet consists of unsubstantiated political slander against Raikov, who
is denounced as an agent of the world bourgeoisie, who would
arouse nothing but loathing, disgust, and hatred in every honest
comrade.[4]

Fortunately, after several years of imprisonment, Raikov was
rehabilitated and freed in 1936. He continued to work for the
welfare of Soviet science and contributed much to it. In 1955
the pedagogical and biological community solemnly marked
his seventy-fifth birthday. He was elected to the Academy of
Pedagogical Sciences, and a *Festschrift* was published in his
honor. In 1960 the eightieth birthday of this outstanding Soviet
scientist was also celebrated.

Prezent's slanderous attack on Raikov was not an exception.
In those years, Prezent had already developed his special style
of scientific-political demagoguery, which later flourished
under the conditions of the personality cult. A typical example
is provided in the pamphlet already cited, in which Prezent

attacked an innocuous poem by a Leningrad teacher (Sokolov), dedicated to the First of May as a holiday for town and village. In it, Prezent found elements of class betrayal: "That the First of May is a holiday of struggle and not of flowers and universal reconciliation is not mentioned. The Soviet pedagogue Sokolov should know this in the thirteenth year of the revolution. For such verses Sokolov will be applauded by all social-democrats, all social-fascists. No doubt Sokolov's poem about the First of May is on the yellowish side." One could cite many such examples of Prezent's "class vigilance." Indeed, two to three years later, it was these tactics that Prezent brought into the movement headed by Lysenko.

Lysenko had first received some notice in 1926–1927 in connection with experiments in Gandzha (Azerbaidzhan) on winter planting of peas to precede the cotton crop. It is difficult to judge the originality of these experiments, but from the practical standpoint they were doubtless useful: under mild winter conditions the green cover of the fields permitted their utilization as pasture even in winter. But Lysenko tried to give this first work of his a sensational character, first in the Transcaucasus but later more widely. In August, 1927, the first feature story on Lysenko was published in Pravda,[5] under the title "The fields in winter." Its author was the then well-known journalist Fedorovich. It was written in an original, attention-catching style, and gave a graphic portrait of the young Lysenko:

If one is to judge a man by first impression, Lysenko gives one the feeling of a toothache; God give him health, he has a dejected mien. Stingy of words and insignificant of face is he; all one remembers is his sullen look creeping along the earth as if, at very least, he were ready to do someone in. Only once did this barefoot scientist let a smile pass, and that was at mention of Poltava cherry dumplings with sugar and sour cream. . . . The barefoot Professor Lysenko now has followers, pupils, an experimental field. He is visited in the winter by agronomic luminaries who stand before the green fields of the experiment station, gratefully shaking his hand. . . .

And indeed, in 1927, especially after the publication of this story, many came to Lysenko in Gandzha. Among his guests, in particular, was Professor Tulaikov, then the director of the South-East U.S.S.R. Institute of Cereal Culture. Later Tulaikov described this meeting in the *Sel'skokhozyaistvennaya Gazeta.*[6]

Apparently, under the influence of this sensation, Lysenko had already started planning radical changes in science. In 1957 the journalist Y. Dolgushin published a book in which he quoted a letter, dated 1928, from his brother, Lysenko's closest collaborator, D. A. Dolgushin. The letter describes, with rapture, Lysenko and his revolutionary ideas for the reconstruction of science: "Much of what we have learned in the Institute, Lysenko considers to be harmful nonsense and asserts that success in our work depends on how soon we can forget it and liberate ourselves from the narcotic."

Lysenko acquired a really broad reputation, however, with his "discovery" of so-called vernalization (yarovization), an agronomic practice whereby winter crops are obtained from summer planting. This was the work which Lysenko attempted to sensationalize on a worldwide scientific and agronomic scale, the work which, in essence, resulted in his rapid promotion to the forefront of Soviet science. It is advisable, therefore, to examine the history of this "discovery."

While working in Gandzha in 1926–1928, studying the influence of planting dates on the length of the vegetative period of cereals, Lysenko discovered that winter forms sown in the spring instead of the autumn will produce spikes after preliminary exposure of the seed to cold. The first series of these experiments, without practical recommendations, was published by Lysenko in 1928 as a monograph (No. 3) of the Azerbaidzhan Experiment Station, "The influence of tempera-

ture on the length of the developmental period of plants."
This work, together with supplementary experiments conducted in 1928, provided the material for Lysenko's paper at
the All-Union Congress of Genetics, Selection, Plant and Animal Breeding held in Leningrad in January, 1929. Nearly 300
papers by Soviet and foreign scientists were presented at the
meeting, which was the outstanding scientific event of the day.
Its chairman was Vavilov. The paper by Lysenko and Dolgushin on the nature of winter crops went largely unnoticed.
It was, however, subjected to serious scientific criticism with
regard to both its methodology and its claim to being an
important discovery. Actually, from the scientific standpoint,
Lysenko's work presented nothing original. Only the subsequent (and incorrect) interpretation of his experiments and
the term "vernalization" were original. At the plenary session
of the Congress, Maksimov gave a paper on "Physiological
methods of regulating the length of the vegetative period," in
which the same phenomena were presented at a much higher
scientific level with a rather complete historical review of the
numerous preceding works along the same lines.

The next day the newspaper *Leningradskaya Pravda* carried
a banner headline, "It is possible to transform winter into
spring cereals: an achievement of Soviet science," but the
story was on Maksimov without any mention of Lysenko.[7]

At that time Maksimov was the head of the physiological
laboratory of the Institute of Applied Botany and New Crops
(renamed in 1930 the All-Union Institute of Plant Breeding—
AIPB). He had carried on his experiments following instructions from Vavilov to work out methods of protecting
valuable collected winter forms of cereals against the severe
winters of the northern regions of the U.S.S.R. Maksimov's
experiments were already started in 1923. In the period of
fanning up the sensationalism of the vernalization process he
repeatedly tried to recall his scientific priority. In particular,
he wrote in the *Sel'skokhozyaistvennaya Gazeta:* "In our

Institute of Applied Botany we have long used experimentally
the method of germination in the cold, which permits obtaining crops of winter forms in the first year without damaging
the very valuable seeds of new winter varieties by various
winter adversities."[8]

Maksimov also wrote a detailed critical analysis of Lysenko's
work.[9] But shortly thereafter he became a victim of the campaign against bourgeois scientists and, despite Vavilov's vigo-
rous protests, after a brief arrest was banished to Saratov.
There, in 1934, Maksimov "confessed" his "errors" in the
evaluation of Lysenko's discovery.

Yet in January, 1929, Lysenko returned from Leningrad
in an unhappy mood. Y. Dolgushin, whom he visited on the
way home, recalls, in the book already mentioned, that "the
pillars of science used the tried and tested method of fighting:
they ignored Lysenko's paper. . . . Returning from the meeting of geneticists, Lysenko understood that he addressed himself to the wrong quarters. This discovery was of no use to
the dogmatic followers of Mendel and Morgan."

In the same year, and to some degree because of his father,
Lysenko became the center of the vernalization sensation. In
the spring his father had sown seeds of the winter variety
Ukrainka, which wintered under the snow, and had obtained
a yield of 24 centners per hectare. (In the first article on this
experiment the yield was exaggerated as being over 30 centners.) Hearing of his father's experience, Lysenko immediately
organized a noisy campaign. A special evaluating committee
was formed by the Commissariat of Agriculture, and excur-
sions were organized to visit the elder Lysenko's farm.

It was in 1929 also that Lysenko started his work in the
Odessa Institute of Genetics and Breeding, where a special
department of vernalization was created by decision of the
Commissariats of Agriculture of the Ukraine and the U.S.S.R.
The sensational features of the work were abetted by the
massive losses of winter crops that had occurred in 1927–1928

in the Ukraine because of frost, so that vernalization was viewed as a possible savior from further disaster.

The then Commissar of Agriculture, Yakovlev, played a leading role in the creation of the department of vernalization and the support of its sensational aspects. In his speech at the second All-Union Congress of Shock Collective Farmers,[10] Lysenko called Yakovlev one of the founders of vernalization.

On the basis of this work, Lysenko, in 1931–1934, advanced the so-called theory of phasic development of plants. This theory, the weaker aspects of which became clear only much later, was rapidly recognized in the thirties as an outstanding achievement of Soviet science. It must be noted that the rational elements in the first publications of Lysenko were supported by many scientists, including even Sabinin, a man of exceptional principles and honesty. The then President of the Academy of Sciences, Komarov, Professor Rikhter, Academician Keller, and many other physiologists and botanists appraised this work favorably. In fact, Maksimov was about the only scientist in 1929–1931 who criticized Lysenko's work on plant development, since he was working in the same area and saw more clearly Lysenko's erroneous tendencies and methodological mistakes. Yet the widespread use of vernalization did meet some opposition among scientists and collective farmers. Taking a serious backward glance at the discussion, it may be clearly seen that the question of the advisability and efficiency of vernalization was indeed a debatable one and that the skepticism about it was justified. Vernalization, at first applied to winter wheats, was then shifted to use with spring forms, since the yields of winter varieties that had been subjected to the process were found to be decreased.

As applied to spring varieties, the method consisted in soaking the seeds of wheat and other crops in a shed for several days, and turning them over constantly, under controlled humidity and temperature conditions. The seeds were sown in the moist, swollen condition which, according to Lysenko's data, shortened the vegetative phase by several days. If the second half of the summer were dry, this could increase the yield to an insignificant extent by protecting the plants from drought.

However, treatment of tens of thousands of tons of seed on each collective or state farm was a burdensome and risky procedure, requiring special sheds and great expenditure of work forces. At the same time there was a danger that overheating and germination of the soaked seed could lead to their loss—a frequent eventuality. The direct costs of sowing were doubled since the standards of quantity of soaked seeds per hectare were ensured only by going over the field with a seeder twice. According to experimental data, in the absence of drought in late summer, vernalization lowered the yield. Some varieties of wheat failed to respond to the treatment altogether. This listing of difficulties encountered with vernalization is by no means exhaustive, but it clearly shows that agronomists had sufficient grounds for debate on an issue of such importance to the agricultural practices of our country. It should be noted that vernalization of spring cereals fell off sharply even before the war, and the device was later forgotten and not propagandized even by Lysenko himself.

At the beginning of the thirties, however, Lysenko as well as Prezent used methods of political demagoguery, which ensured them an advantage in the debate with opponents of vernalization. Very characteristic, for instance, was Lysenko's speech at the Second All-Union Congress of Shock Collective Farmers in 1935, delivered in the presence of Stalin and all members of the government. Lysenko described the vernalization debate in the following terms:

In fact, comrades, while vernalization created by Soviet reality could in a relatively short period of some four to five years become a whole branch of science, could fight off all the attacks of the class enemy (and there were more than a few), there still is much to do. Comrades, kulak-wreckers occur not only in your collective farm life. You know them very well. But they are no less dangerous, no less sworn enemies also in science. No little blood was spilled in the defense of vernalization in the various debates with some so-called scientists, in the struggle for its establishment; not a few blows had to be borne in practice. Tell me, comrades, was there not a class struggle on the vernalization front? In the collective farms there were kulaks and their abettors who kept whispering (and they were not the only ones, every class enemy did) into the peasant's ears: "Don't soak the seeds. It will ruin them." This is the way it was, such were the whispers, such were the kulak and saboteur deceptions, when, instead of helping collective farmers, they did their destructive business, both in the scientific world and out of it; a class enemy is always an enemy whether he is a scientist or not.[11]

This speech of Lysenko greatly pleased Stalin who, at its end, exclaimed: "Bravo, comrade Lysenko, bravo!"

It has now become entirely evident that the transformation of the debate on vernalization into a struggle with alleged class enemies was an attempt at intimidation and annihilation of scientific opponents that for many years blocked ascertainment of truth in this area. It may not be superfluous to note that, up to 1934, Lysenko's preparation in the theoretical problems of biology was very weak; therefore he easily fell under the strong influence of Prezent. Lysenko knew this himself. In the speech cited above, he said: "I often read Darwin, Timiryazev, Michurin. In this I was helped by my collaborator, Prezent. He showed me that the roots of the work I am doing lie in Darwin. And I, comrades, must confess here straightforwardly in the presence of Iosif Vissarionovich [Stalin] that to my shame I have not studied Darwin properly."

INITIAL ATTACKS ON VAVILOV

Nikolay Ivanovich Vavilov, who in subsequent years was the leader of the trend opposing Lysenko, was by 1929–1931 a noted scientist, the President of the Lenin All-Union Academy of Agricultural Sciences (LAAAS) and of the AIPB, as well as being a member of the government's Central Executive Committee. But, in spite of his fame, great merits, and high administrative position, he became the object of the first serious attacks.

The initial critical assault came on January 29, 1931, in the newspaper *Ekonomicheskaya Zhizn'* in which a long article by Kol', entitled "Applied botany, or Lenin's renovation of the earth," was especially devoted to Vavilov and the AIPB. It began by saying: "Under the cover of Lenin's name a thoroughly reactionary institution, having no relation to Lenin's thoughts or intents, but rather alien in class and inimical to them, has become established and is gaining a monopoly in our agricultural science. It is the Plant Breeding Institute of the Lenin Academy of Agricultural Sciences." Several months later the same newspaper published Vavilov's reply,[12] but it was accompanied by unfavorable comments and a hint that pure science served Vavilov as a cover-up for sabotage.

The second serious warning to Vavilov was the government decree on selection published on August 3, 1931.[13] It posed completely unrealistic problems for the LAAAS and the AIPB. Besides demanding that the ten to twelve years required to develop cereal varieties for different regions be reduced to four years (by using hothouses), the decree posed the problem of renewal of the composition of varieties throughout the whole country with all essential characteristics in nearly all crops. In wheat, in particular, high yield, uniformity, crystallinity, nonlodging, nonshattering, resistance to cold, drought, pests, and disease, good baking quality, and other traits were to be obtained in three to four years. (The use of hothouses of limited area in selection studies sharply narrows the possibilities of applying selection pressures, and in fact gives no opportunity to select for performance in environments different from those provided by ordinary hothouses.) The resolution was published in the name of the Central Control Commission of the party and the U.S.S.R. Commissariat of Worker-Peasant Inspectorate on the basis of a report by the similar R.S.F.S.R. Commissariat, i.e., it was a result of a governmental inspection of the work of the LAAAS and the AIPB. Along all lines the resolution was contrary to Vavilov's position and to realistic possibilities, not only of Soviet but of worldwide plant breeding. But it served as a base for subsequent criticisms of AIPB, and of Vavilov as being incapable of solving the problems. The resolution served this purpose well, although the three- to four-year program it put forth was not fulfilled even in thirty years. Vavilov viewed the accelerated goals for renewal of seed very skeptically, while Lysenko immediately published a solemn pledge to develop new varieties with preplanned characteristics in two and one-half years.

These were the points of departure for the later controversy. The years 1932, 1933, and 1934 passed relatively quietly. But Lysenko, heading the vernalization department of the Odessa Plant Breeding-Genetics Institute (then under the Ukrainian Commissariat of Agriculture, but incorporated into the LAAAS in 1935), was able to achieve the dismissal of the director of the institute, Sapegin, and himself become its leader. Lysenko's fame also continued to grow, especially under the influence of collective farm reports of the success and spread of vernalization. And after Stalin's famous "Bravo, Lysenko, bravo!" a new and special period began in Lysenko's activities and in the history of Soviet biology.

CHAPTER 2

The Struggle Begins

THE CRUCIAL QUESTION in the genetics debate was the problem of heredity and variation of living organisms, the central problem of all biology. Before 1935 the biologists of our country, as well as those in the rest of the world, held to the classical concepts—the chromosome theory of heredity and the theory of mutation—which had been elaborated on the basis of the remarkable studies of Mendel, Morgan, Johannsen, de Vries, Vavilov, Kol'tsov, Goldschmidt, Muller, and other outstanding scientists. These theories were established and recognized throughout the world as basic postulates of genetics. They were supported by enormous amounts of factual material, and in both theoretical and practical significance they ranked with Darwin's theory on the role of natural selection in the evolution of species.

In 1935–1936, however, Lysenko and Prezent announced a new concept of heredity in opposition to the generally accepted chromosome theory which they denounced as reactionary, idealist, metaphysical, and barren. This negative attitude toward the generally accepted theories of heredity and breeding methods had first been expressed by Lysenko and Prezent in a minor polemic with geneticists at the end of 1934, in the Moscow House of Scientists. Lysenko repeated his critical theses in February, 1935, in the speech cited in Chapter 1. In 1935–1936 the sharp criticism of the basic postulates of classical genetics and breeding was initiated in the journal *Yarovizatsiya (Vernalization)*, edited by Lysenko and Prezent. Toward the end of 1936 the journal *Sotsrekonstruktsiya Sel'skogo Khozyaistva* also opened a discussion of these problems, allowing much space not only to the proponents of the new ideas, but also to those opposed. The discussion gradually assumed a nationwide scale. Its first climax was reached at the special session of LAAAS on December 19–27, 1936. The proceedings of this session were widely reported in many agricultural journals and the central press. In 1937 they were published in full by the LAAAS under the title "Debatable issues of genetics and breeding." With this session, Soviet biological and agronomic sciences began their divided course, heading in two theoretically contrasting directions.

Lysenko and Prezent led one of those directions, followed by a group of young scientists from Lysenko's Odessa institute (Ol'shansky, Dolgushin, Plesetsky, Glushchenko, and others). This group was supported by some pupils of Michurin, a number of animal husbandmen (including Nurinov and Kislovsky), and by the Academicians Perov, B. M. Zavadovsky, and Vil'yams.

The opposite side in the polemic was represented in 1936 by the majority of leaders of the genetical, cytological, and breeding institutes of our country.[1] Vavilov, at that time the world's outstanding plant breeder, applied geneticist, and geographer, enjoying merited recognition and fame in many countries, was the factual head of the opposition to Lysenko's genetical ideas. It should be noted, however, that Vavilov and the other scientists took a favorable view of certain other ideas then being worked out by Lysenko and his institute (for example, phasic development of plants, and summer planting of potatoes).[2]

What, then, was the essence of the disagreements between the genetical hypotheses of Lysenko and Prezent and the classical theory of heredity? What were the divergences of opinion between the debating sides on selection and plant breeding? These questions must be discussed at least briefly if we are to understand what the fight was about. Obviously, the opposing concepts must be viewed from the standpoint of the scientific knowledge available in 1936–1937.[3]

THE NEW BIOLOGY

Lysenko and Prezent repudiated the classical theory of heredity by assuming that heredity is a general internal property
of living matter, and as such does not need a separate genetical system localized in the chromosomes, and transmissible
from generation to generation. The existence of genes—material, self-reproducing, intracellular carriers of heredity—was
rejected out of hand by Lysenko, Prezent, and their followers.
The deduction of the existence of genes had logically ensued
from purely experimental investigations based on most extensive and exact factual material. To disprove the gene theory
convincingly it would, of course, be necessary to demonstrate
that the available arsenal of facts of classical genetics does not
provide the logical premises for the theoretical deductions
made; in other words, that some other valid concept exists.
Prezent and Lysenko unfortunately did not follow such a
path of productive polemic. They rejected the gene theory
on *a priori*, abstract considerations, ignoring the factual material of genetics. They attempted to abolish genetics on the
grounds that it was an allegedly formalistic, bourgeois, and
metaphysical science, and to inaugurate their own new genetics.

What, then, were the basic principles of this new genetics
in 1936, and what arguments and facts were put forth in that
period to disprove the chromosome theory of heredity? It
may be appropriate to turn to the appearance of Lysenko
and Prezent at the 1936 LAAAS session. (Later aspects of the
new concepts will be touched on in the examination of the
subsequent phases of the controversy.)

The opening third of Lysenko's rather extensive speech contained general Darwinian propaganda. Turning then to a critique of classical genetics, Lysenko pointed to the facts which,
in his opinion, called for a review of the fundamental genetical

concepts: "What, then, is the work that compels me, Dr. I. I. Prezent, and a number of other scientists to pose the question of reviewing the basic genetical position? . . . There are two problems. One is the problem of the increased quality of seed of self-fertilizing plants by intravarietal crossing, and the other is the problem of the alteration of the nature of plants in the required direction by appropriate unbringing."[4]

Farther along, Lysenko described in detail his proposal for intravarietal crossing of self-fertilized plants which, in his opinion, could increase yield. This method, later completely forgotten because of its ineffectiveness, had absolutely no relationship to the chromosome theory of heredity. And, even had it been retained in practice, there was no basis whatsoever for contrasting it with fundamental genetic positions. (The theoretical bases and the fate of this method will be considered in greater detail later.)

The second problem alleged to be contrary to the laws of genetics—the alteration of the nature of plants in a predetermined direction by environmental means—was represented in Lysenko's works in 1936 by a single example of transformation of the winter wheat variety Kooperatorka into a spring form. Moreover, the description of this experiment, given in detail in Lysenko's address, represents an only too striking demonstration of his methodological inadequacy.

(In later years Lysenko reported other analogous experiments. The question of reversible transformation of winter and spring forms will be examined later in greater detail. Here, it is the initial "historical" experiment from which the repudiation of classical genetics started that is of interest.)

For purposes of objectivity, Lysenko is now given the floor:

Our most prolonged experiments at this time are those transforming the winter wheat Kooperatorka into a spring form. These experiments were initiated in March, 1935. In the period since, we have grown three generations and have sown the fourth in September, 1936.

The auspicious results of these experiments made us include a number of other plants in our work, but to date we have had time to grow only one generation and sow the second. Hence, with the exception of experiments with rye, we have no results as yet with these plants.

We shall recount briefly the results of the experiments on the transformation of the winter wheat Kooperatorka into a spring form.

For the experiments we took two plants each of Kooperatorka and the Saratov station variety, Lutescens 329, sown March 3, 1935, in the hothouse, in a single pot, by the Institute specialist, comrade M. K. Babak.

The purpose was not to allow the winter plants to go through the vernalization state and thus to prolong their existence as much as possible without their heading. But the pot with these plants sown on March 3 was left not in a warm hothouse but in a cool one where the temperature from March 3 to the end of April was frequently no higher than 10–15° C. Only beginning with May was the temperature higher and, most importantly, never below 15° C. Since the Lutescens 329 variety was more of a winter type than Kooperatorka, both its plants lived until late fall and perished without heading. At the beginning of August the Kooperatorka plants had a shrubby appearance with many living and dead leaves. Individual shoots of these plants developed straws in the beginning of August. Approximately in the middle of August one of the Kooperatorka plants perished because of pests gnawing at the roots. Only one plant remained, from which several paired seeds were collected on September 9. The heading period of this plant was exceedingly prolonged, lasting until January, 1936, when it perished with many green spikes.

On September 9, 1935, the first collected seeds of the Kooperatorka plant were sown. Simultaneously, ordinary seeds of Kooperatorka, taken from the storehouse, were sown for comparison and control. The sowing was done in the warm hothouse where, in November-December, the temperature usually is no lower than 15–20°C.[5]

Then follows a description of the differences between the

offspring of the experimental plant and those of the controls, in subsequent generations. We can willingly accept both the existence of such differences and the fact that, in the end, after a number of generations, spring forms were obtained. *But to discuss this experiment as a scientific one is absolutely impossible, since it was an experiment with a single plant, offspring of a single individual, a single seed. An experiment without replication is not a scientific experiment.* The single seed could have been a hybrid, a mutant, or a contaminant. One casual seed does not represent a variety.

Even if it were possible to admit the direct and reverse transformation of a winter into a spring type under the influence of the environment, such a phenomenon neither directly nor indirectly contradicts the chromosome theory of heredity. Lysenko considered that, if he could alter a winter into a spring form and then reverse the process, there are no immutable genes for winter habit, and all depends on the environment: hence there are no genes of any kind. But this analysis lacks logic.

It is possible that cereals do not have individual genes for habit, and that it is determined by many genes. It is also possible that there are single genes whose expressions are modified by the environment. In genetics there have been hundreds of instances in which what is genetically controlled by the chromosomes is not only some external trait, such as form or color, but also the adaptive reaction to the environment. The capacity of plants to change from state A to state B, and vice versa, may be genotypically determined if it becomes advantageous under changed conditions.

Thus, without giving a single theoretical argument against the classical concept of heredity based on fact, Lysenko categorically declared that he could not agree with the basic postulate that "chromosomes of cells contain a hereditary substance separate from the rest of the organism (genotype)," a postulate which, he said, was "invented by geneticists."

T. D. Lysenko

Lysenko looking over
a field of grain.

Lysenko's father,
D. N. Lysenko

O. Lysenko (T. D. L.'s son), T. D. Lysenko, and P. P. Lobanov.

Lysenko receiving medal from Deputy Minister of Agriculture G. K. Pysin, 1962 Exhibition of Achievements of U. S. S. R. National Economy.

In conclusion, Lysenko said:

The brilliant work in cytology has already contributed much to our knowledge of the morphology of the cell and especially its nucleus. All of us not only do not deny this but fully support the development of this science . . . These are all necessary branches of science adding to knowledge. But we do deny that geneticists, together with cytologists, will see the gene under the microscope. By using the microscope it is possible and necessary to see a greater number of details in the cell, the nucleus, and the individual chromosomes, but they will be bits of the cell, nucleus or chromosome, and not what geneticists understand by the term "gene." The hereditary basis does not lie in some special self-reproducing substance. The hereditary base is the cell, which develops and becomes an organism. In this cell different organelles have different significance, but there is not a single bit that is not subject to evolutionary development.[6]

In this manner Lysenko formulated his basic genetical idea (the presence of some property of heredity distributed throughout the cell) at the end of the session, without any connection with any facts whatsoever. Subsequently this idea changed and took shape, but in 1936 it was not even a hypothesis, only an unproved, abstract, and little-understood postulate which appeared independently of the developments in biology. Even less convincing was Prezent's talk at the same session. It was an empty, superficial piece of publicizing without the least hint of an attempt to discuss concrete facts.

Thus an elementary analysis of the 1936 genetics discussion clearly shows that the two trends of Soviet genetics were not equivalent as scientific doctrines. On the one hand, we see a serious branch of science, the big area of world genetics, a harmonious edifice of interconnected, theoretical concepts, logically following from a colossal amount of factual material, and represented in our country by a large group of qualified specialists in genetics. On the other hand, we meet an embryonic idea, lacking serious scientific content, not corroborated by sufficient reliable data, and supported by a small group that did not include even a single geneticist. But the representatives of this group were distinguished by close solidarity, great self-confidence, and an inclination to demagoguery and political analogies.

Promoters of such shaky and insecure trends usually seek support from any popular names, and frequently cite as authorities deceased and (obligatorily) native scientists. This was the course also taken by Lysenko and Prezent. They declared their genetics to be "Michurinist"—the teaching of Timiryazev and Michurin. Yet it is known that Timiryazev was never a geneticist, and never studied heredity experimentally. He was an authority in plant physiology, and his contribution to genetics was limited to articles in the *Granat Encyclopedia*. Timiryazev's attitude toward Mendel's laws was superficial and subjective.

As to Michurin, his skepticism toward transferring the "pea laws"[7] to fruit trees, with their complex hybrid origins, did not apply to genetics as a whole, and in many of his later works he recognized the existence of genes.

THE NATURE OF MUTATIONS[8]

Classical geneticists approached the problem of variation from the standpoint of mutations, i.e., undirected changes in the genotype. Their opponents ignored mutational variability for three reasons. First, because relating mutation to changes in the genes presupposes the existence of genes; second, because mutational theory clearly distinguishes between genetic and environmental variability; and, third, because the indeterminate, undirected nature of mutation was contradictory to Lysenko's principles of environmentally induced hereditary changes in a particular direction.

The existence of mutations in living systems is an objective reality which cannot be questioned. An important discovery in this connection was the possibility of artificial increase in mutation rates as produced in fungi in 1925 by the Soviet scientists Nadson and Filippov. In 1927 H. J. Muller, in the United States, carried out his classical observations on the production of mutations by X-rays, for which he later received a Nobel prize. (In 1933–1937 Muller, on invitation from Vavilov, worked in the U.S.S.R.) The Soviet scientists Lobashev and Sakharov first discovered the mutagenic properties of certain chemicals (iodine and ammonia). Somewhat later the Soviet scientist Rapoport and, almost simultaneously, the British geneticist, Charlotte Auerbach, discovered specific, universally mutagenic substances, thereby starting a new page in experimental genetics. From these beginnings an objective molecular theory of mutations as enduring, reproducible changes in the molecular structure of chromosomes or, rather, their constituent genes has been elaborated.

It must be emphasized again that mutation and undirected change are firmly established facts. The issue is only about their role in evolution and their practical significance. Mutation of a specific gene occurs spontaneously in one organism out of tens of thousands. If this fact is viewed from the standpoint of generation number, it seems that a given gene will mutate only once in tens of thousands of generations, i.e., in thousands and tens of thousands of years. This objective computation was used as justification for ignoring the role of mutation and for criticizing the gene theory, without taking into account the fact that an individual genotype contains tens of thousands of genes, so that, considering all of them, changes in the genotype are very common. Moreover, should the mutation of each gene occur too frequently, stabilizing natural selection would be impossible, and a species could not persist in nature any length of time. Indeed, increases in mutation rates in unstable genotypes are invoked now as the explanation for extinction of some species of animals when too serious changes occurred in the environment.

Nevertheless, the thesis that each individual gene mutates only once in tens of thousands of years *was* used by the opponents of genetics as a bugbear, as evidence of the essential immutability of genes, as something absurd and allegedly incompatible with the dialectical materialism that asserts that everything in nature changes and develops (as if dialectical materialism decides the question of the terms and rates of change).

The criticism of mutation and population theory was entirely baseless and had the aspects of unscientific ridicule by laymen. A quotation from Prezent's speech at the 1936 session will illustrate. In his speech, Prezent replied to Muller, who had given a thorough and beautifully reasoned speech at the session on the nature of constancy and variability of the genes:

Further, the geneticists consider that hereditary changes occur only once in tens or even hundreds of thousands of years. (*Voice from the audience:* "Where is this said?") If one of the geneticist comrades asks this, I shall tell him where it is said. It is said not by a second-rate but by, so to speak, a first-rate geneticist; it was said by Professor H. J. Muller . . . But this is not all there is to it. Mutation occurring independently of the environment once in tens or hundreds of thousands of years in the vast majority of cases turned out to be, according to genetics, lethal, or fatal to the organism.

So I ask, where then is the material for natural selection, which sometimes in a comparatively short time transforms the appearance of plants and animals. If hereditary changes occurred as portrayed by formalist geneticists, we should scarcely have had elephants descended from fossil forms. The whole point is that there can be metaphysical ideas about nature but there cannot be a metaphysical nature. Lysenko, with his Kooperatorka experiments, has shown that, if one approaches a plant skillfully, knowing life and not merely the external traits of a plant, if one chooses methods of influence not as the geneticists do, "the stronger, the better," but selects methods *consonant with the given stage of development of the organism,* then in a brief period it is possible to alter the hereditary nature of the plant.[9]

An analogous attitude toward the problem of mutation was also displayed by Lysenko. Without going into detail, in his closing remarks he simply brushed aside genetical mutations as some sort of absurd delusion: "The fundamental error of geneticists consists in their recognition of immutability in a prolonged series of generations of genes. True enough, they recognize gene changes after tens and hundreds of thousands of generations: many thanks for such variability."[10]

The study of mutations in germinal and somatic cells was a most important area of genetics and biology. The investigators discovered here a mechanism which, in the presence of selection, ensured the evolution of living nature. They found methods of intensifying the nondirectional action of this mechanism. This was an outstanding victory for science and for Darwinism. To ignore, to distort, and to ridicule this achievement was simply foolish. That the alteration of some strictly determined trait occurs by evolution, let us say, once in ten thousand years can surprise a literate biologist not by the slowness but by the rapidity of the process. Evolution of species is in no way based on alteration of many, not to mention all, traits. Chlorophyll has the same structure in higher flowering plants as in lower algae. In terms of evolution these species are apart not by thousands or millions of years, but by a billion. Yet chlorophyll did not change, regardless of whether or not it contradicted Prezent's understanding of dialectics. If chlorophyll did not change, neither, consequently, did the cycle of its synthesis, in which dozens of systems participate. Nor did the main path of photosynthesis, the fundamental biochemical process of the plant world, change.

Accordingly, the genes determining these characteristics did not change. Thousands of examples can be given. The pigment of mammalian hemoglobin is found in some bacteria;

reactions of glycolysis, oxidation, and phosphorylation are all the same in the whole living world. All of these facts were well known in 1936. The wonder was not that elephants descended from mammoths, but how small was the complex of genetic changes required for this, and how many biochemical, physiological, and morphological traits remained essentially identical in the elephant and the mammoth, in spite of the thousands of years separating them. Only the genetical concepts of gene stability and a genetical treatment of the role of selection can bring about an understanding of this phenomenon. Nonetheless, all this area of biology, of utmost theoretical and practical importance, was ignored by Lysenko and his partisans. But to ignore entirely the whole problem of variability was impossible. Denying any significance to mutation, they still had to explain variability in some other way and to create a new doctrine of variation and evolution.

MULLER'S ADDRESS IN 1936

In considering the problem of mutations, it is necessary to say a few words about Muller's active participation in the genetical discussion. Muller, an American scientist and friend of Vavilov, came to work in the U.S.S.R. as a socialist sympathizer. In subsequent years, men of Prezent's type included Muller among the enemies of our country and the reactionaries. This was wrong. Concluding his 1936 LAAAS address, Muller said with enthusiasm:

The Soviet Union has every reason to be proud that, despite the numerous urgent material needs it is overcoming in the process of building a great new society, it has been able to raise a number of branches of theoretical science, including genetics, to a level recognized by all to be equal to or higher than the level of those sciences in other countries. Foreign friends of the Soviet Union (and among geneticists there is an especially large number of sincere friends of the U.S.S.R.) are proud of this proof of the triumphal march of the civilization which is advancing here. It is possible to observe with satisfaction that much attention is paid in the U.S.S.R. to the connection between genetics and practical plant and animal breeding. Not a single scientific worker with any degree of progressive social outlook but can experience the greatest satisfaction at seeing his science serving the interest of the working masses. In this regard we must serve as an example to all others. We must therefore be doubly vigilant not only to hold high the banner in the more theoretical branches of our field, but also to hold it even higher in the linking of theory and practice.[11]

Even earlier, at the jubilee session of the AS devoted to the tenth anniversary of Lenin's death, Muller had given an excellent speech on "Lenin's teachings in his attitude toward genetics." It contained a very deep and serious dialectic-philosophic treatment of genetic problems.[12]

At the beginning of 1937, Muller went to Spain, as he assumed, temporarily. We quote here an excerpt from a letter preserved in Vavilov's personal archives, and addressed to Professor Otto Mohr, April 8, 1937: "Professor Muller is currently in Madrid to aid in the organization of medical services for the republicans. He is full of enthusiasm, wanting to help Spanish republicans, and has gone there for four months. He should return to Moscow in about three months." But Muller's trip to Spain was prolonged, and he remained there virtually to the end of the Civil War. His attitude toward our country changed only after he learned of the destruction of many of his Soviet friends.

At the end of 1948, Muller, having previously been elected a foreign member of the AS, announced his resignation from the Academy as a protest against the persecution of Soviet geneticists which followed the LAAAS session in August of the same year. In this connection the praesidium of the AS issued a special announcement. Its nature can be judged by its final words: "The U.S.S.R. Academy of Sciences parts without regret from its former member who betrayed the interests of authentic science and openly joined the camp of the enemies of progress and science, of peace and democracy."[13]

LYSENKO ON VARIATION

By 1936 the new trend had acquired no serious facts of its own on the problem of variability, if one excepts the transformation of a single plant from a winter to a spring form. Hence it countered genetic theory with the old and repeatedly disproved principle of inheritance of acquired characters already formulated by Lamarck and augmented by the idea of the straightforward direction of effect of environment on genetic change. On the whole this concept held that not all acquired characters are heritable (the example of the possibility of inducing hereditary taillessness by amputating tails was not revived), but only some that arise under the influence of environmental conditions.

That environment has an effect on heredity was not denied by genetics. Geneticists recognized that, in the long run, mutations arise not only from internal but also from external conditions.[14] The difference in the two points of view was concerned with the nature of these changes. Mutations have an undirected, chaotic nature; selection determines the direction of change. According to Lysenko, variation has a direction from the start, and the changes that arise correspond to the changes in the environment. Cold, for instance, would lead not to the selection of cold-resistant mutants, but to a direct change of heredity toward greater cold-resistance.

To explain this type of hereditary variability by some logically convincing method was rather difficult. Hence, in the subsequent period, the view was expanded by the introduction of a number of purely philosophical concepts stating that the organism and its environment are a single entity, and that heredity is a concentrate of environmental conditions and represents the need for certain conditions. It became necessary to change radically the concept of heredity itself. It became necessary to sacrifice the interpretation of heredity generally accepted and understood on the basis of the actual phenomenon of like begetting like. But this was all much later—basically in the forties. In 1936, directed hereditary variability was presented in an unconvincing form with no basis in fact. It should be emphasized that it was directed hereditary variation that was under discussion; adaptive, nonhereditary variability had long been known.

The capacity for noninherited, adaptive variation is an absolute necessity for any organism since, in the course of its life, environmental conditions change hundreds and thousands of times. For such variation to become stably inherited would serve no purpose. In order to demarcate the ordinary noninherited changes in the organism, which adapts to the numerous rapid and, even more important, periodic changes in the environment, Lysenko made the abstract assumption that there are some periods in the life history of a plant in which environment, by being "assimilated" into the plant, changes its heredity. At other times, he alleged, the heredity is conservative and unchangeable.

These theses were expounded in 1936 as a hypothesis, as a scheme for the future, promising great prospects. Lysenko clearly pointed out that "in a general way, it is clear to all that external conditions play a colossal role in the endless process of formation of vegetable organisms. But, as far as I know, nobody yet has been able to prove experimentally what conditions in what developmental periods of plants are required to change the nature of subsequent generations in the desired directions."[15]

The only evidence of the prospects offered by the new idea at this time was still based on the same unconvincing example of transformation of a single plant.

Thus examination of the opposing viewpoints in the study

of variation prevailing in 1936 clearly reveals the differences between them, just as it shows the differences concerning the problem of heredity. On the one hand, genetics was concerned with the hereditary, mutational, undirected variability of living things. This variability, arising from the effects of internal and external factors, explains the renewed diversity of populations within species, which serves as a basis for natural selection and ensures the selection-directed evolution of living things in nature and in agricultural practices. On the other hand, we find the new current which, ignoring all of the material on variability collected by geneticists, promised to find an easy and rapid way to create new forms on the basis of the abstract hypothesis of straightforward-directed variation under the influence of the environment—a hypothesis which, in the opinion of its creators, required no proofs.

TWO TRENDS IN 1936

Genetics in 1935–1936 was no longer a purely academic science. It also served as a theoretical basis of plant and animal selection, seed growing and plant breeding, being closely tied to agricultural practices. It was only natural and logical that questioning of the basic postulates of genetics should lead to the assumption that the science was barren and even harmful. It followed that most practical agronomic methods and rules linked to genetics were trumped up and useless. (The creators of the new genetics did not bother to seek experimental proof for these conclusions. They were arrived at in a purely theoretical way.)

VAVILOV AND HIS SCHOOL

The development of the scientific bases of selection and plant breeding in our land, and of their practical application, was closely connected with the activities of Nikolay Ivanovich

Vavilov. He was the founder and long-term president (to 1955) of LAAAS, director of the Institute of Genetics of the AS, and of AIPB, a unique scientific institution which had acquired worldwide fame.

In looking back now on the sum of Vavilov's scientific and practical activity, many years after this outstanding scientist perished tragically, we are first amazed by his singular productivity and by the unprecedented, gigantic range and depth of his work. Vavilov had developed as a scientist before the revolution. He took his first steps in science in the Moscow Agricultural Institute (now the Timiryazev Agricultural Academy) under the direction of Pryanishnikov, who occupied the chair of plant breeding.

Vavilov chose to specialize in plant pathology, but because of his broad scientific horizons he embraced the problem in a comprehensive way, setting himself the basic task of developing, for agriculture, disease-resistant varieties of cultivated plants. This problem could not be solved without elucidation of the genetics of plant immunity, and Vavilov was the first in our country to initiate a broad investigation in the field of applied plant genetics. Before the revolution, however, the work had been based only on his personal enthusiasm and that of several voluntary collaborators. Only in Soviet times was Vavilov able to carry out his studies on a broad scale.

Russia was an agrarian country with an exceptionally backward agriculture. Not only did the peasant economy in the first years of Soviet rule stand much below the agriculture of most European countries, with respect to technology and organization, but the very kinds of cultivated plants, the methods of selection, and seed production were also at a very low level. This was true despite the fact that many local ancient Russian and Ukrainian varieties of winter and hard wheats, flax, and other crops had acquired world fame, and covered millions of hectares in Canada, the United States, and elsewhere.

Scientific selection and seed production had not reached their required development under the conditions of old Russia, however, and in that period elite seed was used only on the most advanced farms. The prolonged war and devastation almost completely liquidated our few plant-breeding successes that had been achieved in the previous years. It was in this difficult period—at the beginning of the twenties—that Vavilov proposed a bold and deeply thought-out plan for radical reorganization of the plant resources of our country. It included raising the level of selection and seed production, and enlisting all the achievements of world science and practice in the plant-breeding work in the land of the Soviets. The tenets of Vavilov on foundation material in plant breeding formed the basis of this plan.

In the creation of new varieties, plant breeders pursue many diverse goals. A new variety of wheat, for example, must not only give higher yields than local ones, insofar as possible, but must also possess other positive traits: resistance to drought, nonlodging, nonshattering, uniform maturity, adaptiveness to local conditions, resistance to pests and diseases, high protein content, good baking quality, and the like. The road to the attainment of these properties is a long one. A more rapid and effective route lies in the hybridization of varieties and types which have individual desirable traits, and the subsequent selection of the required combinations from the hybrid offspring. By hybridization and careful analysis of segregating forms, it is possible to incorporate into the improved variety being developed the exact characters needed.

The necessity for a wide choice of foundation material is clear from these considerations. The wealth of properties of the initial kinds of material provides the plant breeder the same opportunities for creative selection that the painter derives from the richness of his palette.

Vavilov, with a group of collaborators, undertook to fulfill the plans for assembling, in the U.S.S.R., a mass of foundation material for selection and introduction which would reflect the worldwide diversity of plants. He aimed not merely to collect this material but to systematize it, to investigate it comprehensively from the standpoints of physiology, biochemistry, botany, genetics, and agronomy, and to make it available to all plant-breeding stations and plant breeders of our land.

At the same time the intention was to apportion suitable varieties of forage, vegetables, and fruits from among these extensive stocks for immediate introduction and testing, with the promise of rapid and direct economic benefits. To realize this objective, an institute, later named AIPB, was created, on Vavilov's initiative, with a wide geographic network of experiment stations.

It was to further this work that Vavilov, in the middle twenties, initiated his famous expeditions to all corners of the Soviet Union and later to all principal centers of world agriculture. Over a short period of time about 200 expeditions were organized. Their members investigated the agriculture and plant resources of 65 countries and brought to the Soviet Union over 150,000 plant varieties, forms and species—all of the plant-breeding wealth created by mankind in its centuries-old history. Thus the collection of the world's domesticated plants was established. In the course of this work, Vavilov discovered the existence of geographical centers of variability of crop plants and the parallelism of variation in related species and genera (the law of homologous series).

It is important to note that the large-scale work of the expeditions and of plant introductions in our country was due to the initiative of Lenin. The All-Union Institute of Applied Botany and New Cultures was founded on his direct instructions. Having read, while ill, Harwood's[16] fascinating book, *The Renewed Earth* (translated by Timiryazev), in which the significance of plant introduction in American agriculture was described, Lenin pointed out the necessity for giving consideration to plant introduction in our land also.

The new trends in Soviet plant breeding coincided precisely with the drought and crop failures of 1921 and led to a radical change in the method of crop distribution.

Vavilov and like-minded persons held the view that the genetic system of an organism provides the mechanism for transmission of traits from generation to generation by means of the genes. They proposed a safe way to use, in plant breeding, the wide variety of traits and characters of the world's domesticated plants and their ancestors—the one the result of work by countless generations of humans, the other, a gift of nature. It was a realistic and substantiated approach. Furthermore, this work had tremendous practical effects which are still felt in Soviet agriculture. Creation of a system of productive Soviet plant breeding *would have been impossible without this work*. In his address to the 1936 session of the LAAAS, Vavilov described vividly and convincingly the theoretical and practical significance of this trend in the field of Soviet selection and plant breeding founded by him. His remarkable report reflects the results and achievements of the most important and original stage in the development of Soviet agricultural science and practice. The work described created an epoch, not only in Soviet plant breeding but also throughout the world.[17]

The report describes only a small part of the theoretical and practical work connected with the activities of Vavilov, his pupils, and his followers. The scale of the work was indeed worthy of the first socialist state. It was based on Lenin's revolutionary and profoundly scientific approach to the reconstruction of Soviet science and practice and to mastery over all the riches created by mankind. To deny these achievements was impossible. One could only be proud of them. They placed our country first in the world in the field of plant breeding; they were organically linked with socialism; they were its bright torch in world science. This, indeed, was the real Soviet, progressive science, vanguard of the united world front in biology and agronomy. The mighty torrent was swelled by many tributaries and brooks of Soviet genetics and breeding sciences, and in turn gave rise to many, at that time still embryonic, trends.

OTHER ATTAINMENTS OF GENETICS

By 1937 the best varieties of cereal crops had been produced by the standard genetical methods of mass selection and development of pure lines. At that time over 60 per cent of the land under cereal crops in our country was planted to those varieties. The inbreeding of cross-fertilizers—rejected and later prohibited by Lysenkoites—led to a revolution in the production of corn, and increased yields through use of hybrids by 20 to 30 per cent. The same inbreeding methods permitted the Soviet geneticist Grishko to develop simultaneously maturing (male and female plants) lines of hemp, which increased fiber yield per hectare by 30 to 50 per cent. In animal husbandry, genetics elaborated progeny testing, which found widespread use in many countries, for cattle breed improvement. On the initiative of geneticists, experiments on artificial insemination were started in the U.S.S.R. Crossing, followed by selection of new forms produced as a result of Mendelian segregation of hereditary traits, was the basic method of breeding in all countries. It led to the creation of a tremendous diversity of valuable varieties and breeds. In livestock breeding the appearance of undesirable traits in many valuable breeds was traced to the homozygosity of some genes. The use of a number of genetically based methods eliminated some causes of stock losses. According to Serebrovsky's computation, in one fine-wool breed of sheep alone, economies of millions of rubles were thus attained. The great achievements of genetics included the creation of disease-resistant varieties of plants and the development of enlarged forms of plants and fruits from distant hybrids by means of polyploidy or chromosome doubling.

In 1936–1937, Kol'tsov and Astaurov had already worked out the method of controlling sex determination in the silkworm, foreshadowing the tremendous potential for controlling sex in other animals. Mutations, in particular those induced by X-ray, were widely studied and used. At the same time the struggle was begun against lethal and harmful mutations and hereditary diseases, which could be revealed and anticipated only by genetical methods. This enumeration could be continued at length.

LYSENKO'S ACHIEVEMENTS

What, then, was the alternative offered by Lysenko, Prezent, and their colleagues to this practical front of Soviet genetics? The practical archives of Lysenko and his group at that period showed only two sensational achievements: vernalization and summer planting of potatoes. As will be shown later, the actual effectiveness of these techniques was greatly exaggerated, and neither had any direct relation to the genetical discussion. Nor did they controvert any of the fundamentals of genetics.

The only practical proposal that was actually contrary to the tenets of genetics in that period was the suggestion that pure-line varieties of self-fertilizers be renewed by intravarietal crossing. Such crosses within pure lines for the purpose of increasing yield were, from the standpoint of genetics, absurd. This was analogous to hopes of obtaining heterosis or hybrid vigor between crosses of genetically identical individuals. Genetics recognized the possibility of heterosis only in intervarietal, interspecific, and, especially, interline hybrids. Heterosis from crosses within a pure line would be as unlikely as an increase in the amount of water in a corked bottle from shaking it. Lysenko, however, asserted that the theory denying the effectiveness of intravarietal crossing was wrong, that heterosis in crosses of inbred lines was a fiction, and that intravarietal crossing was, in fact, the reliable method for reconstruction of Soviet plant breeding and seed production. In

1936, however, no serious experimental data were available to show that this was a reliable way, nor did any appear later. As for the prospects of creating new plant forms, the proposals of Lysenko and Prezent in that area were also at variance with the fundamental recommendations of genetics. Inasmuch as they considered that useful traits of plants are not hereditarily transmitted but arise anew in every generation under the influence of the environment, new characteristics, according to their hypothesis, could be produced by environmental influences and not from imported genetical material. But what constituted the concrete environmental conditions under which concrete traits are produced was not explained by the authors of this hypothesis, either in 1936 or later. Their thesis was illustrated only by the possibility of controlling winter or spring habits in cereal species in which both habits exist. It was natural, however, that since plant breeding faces the task of creating and improving many other traits, Lysenko's general thesis on the effect of environment did not produce much enthusiasm among the majority of experienced breeders, nor a readiness to abandon methods proved in worldwide practice.

Such were the practical aspects of the two trends in 1936. It is hoped that the reader can objectively compare their relative significance and evaluate properly both the myth of a barren genetics and the assertion that the Soviet scientists who appeared in 1936 against Lysenko and Prezent contributed nothing to the development of our science and agriculture.

This was the state of the controversy in biology in 1936, and the condition in which it moved on to 1937, a tragic year for our country. In precisely that year the genetics debate emerged from the framework of scientific discussion and turned into a political discussion, a struggle against imaginary "enemies of the people."

CHAPTER 3

The First Phase Climax

THE INTERNATIONAL CONGRESS OF GENETICS

IN ACCORDANCE with the proposal of the Soviet government, already announced by Vavilov at the Sixth International Congress, held in the United States in 1932, the Seventh Congress was to be held in Moscow in August, 1937. All international genetics organizations, institutes, and interested persons were notified by special publications, and the deadline for applications to present papers was set for February, 1937. The organizing committee of the Congress was located in the AS Institute headed by Vavilov. Its chairman was Academician Muralov, at that time head of the LAAAS. Vavilov and Komarov were the vice-chairmen, and Levit, the Secretary. The membership of the committee included Gorbunov, Karpechenko, Keller, Kol'tsov, Lysenko, Meister, Muller, Navashin, and Serebrovsky.

An international genetics congress, at which 800 to 1000 scientists were expected from all leading countries of the world, held in Moscow, would represent international recognition of the achievements of Soviet genetics, and a show of its practical and theoretical successes against the background of world science. This congress undoubtedly would draw the attention of the Soviet government and Soviet public to the perspectives and significance of this science and to the great respect earned by Soviet scientists abroad. The representatives of the two trends awaited the event with different feelings—the one side with hope and confidence, the other with anxiety, since the scientific results which the new trend could demonstrate at the congress could not receive serious approval of the foreign scientists. But the course of events in Soviet biological sciences took such a turn in 1937 that the Seventh International Genetics Congress did not take place until 1939, and then not in Moscow, but in Edinburgh, Scotland. Soviet scientists were not present at that congress.

THE "ENEMIES OF THE PEOPLE"

In the spring of 1937, after Stalin's famous address at the March plenary session of the CC, "On the deficiencies in party work and the measures for liquidating Trotskyites and other double-dealers," the scientific discussion on genetics was transformed into a debate against the "enemies of the people" in the pages of the journal *Yarovizatsya*, the founder and chief editor of which was Lysenko. In reproducing Stalin's address, the editorial board placed immediately after it an article by the deputy editor and Lysenko's closest aide, Prezent, in which he identified the so-called Trotsky-Bukharin opposition with that shown to the school headed by Lysenko. In this article Prezent wrote:

The Soviet scientists who want to build a Soviet school of agrobiology, but are not fully aware of the role which creatively developed Darwinism plays in the critical reconstruction of agrobiology, should give thought to the fact that, while our Soviet scientific public has expanded the front of the struggle against metaphysics in questions of life and development, in the persons of Michurin, Lysenko, and all marching with them under the banner of reconstruction of biological science on the basis of Darwinism raised to the level of Marxism, the powers of darkness turned out to be opposing this exceptionally creative direction of Soviet biology. The enemy of the people, the Trotskyite Uranovsky, who appeared in the role of "methodologist" of the Academy of Sciences, selling out wholesale and retail our scientific interests, following the wrecking line in the field of scientific politics, defending "pure science for the sake of science," in every way defamed those who fought for the turn of science in our country toward the needs of socialist construction. It is exactly at the hands of these bandits, Uranovsky, Busygin, and company, with "benevolent participation" of the leadership of the University, that instruction of students in Darwinism and the Darwinian bases of the biology of development, in the Leningrad State University, was annihilated.[1] The annihilation took place in a literal and not in a figurative sense. Uranovsky, crawling on bent knees after the latest reactionary word of "scientists" abroad, was able, as his last malicious spit at our Soviet science and, so to speak, in the manner of servile groveling on a world scale, to publish in the Academy journal *Priroda*, where he was then deputy editor, "an appeal to U.S.S.R. scientists" by a certain Emery Wood, slandering our young scientists, and threatening that publication in Russian by Soviet scientists would lead to "chaos."[2]

Another Trotskyite bandit, the geneticist Agol,[3] having labored not a little in littering the minds of our readers with the metaphysics of Weismannism, as is becoming a menshevizing idealist, in every way tried to separate theory from our socialist practice. It is very significant that Agol's geneticist friends abroad took up arms against the "geneticists-vernalizers."

Just as "honestly," the anthropogeneticist Levit,[4] who provided man-haters with "material" on the alleged "hereditary foredoom" of man, earned a kiss from the hardened opponents of Marxism in science.

It is significant that the friend of the Trotskyites, the enemy of the people, Bukharin, true to his "theory" of peaceful infiltration, in speaking "of Darwinism and contemporaneity" in his article on "Darwinism and Marxism" makes no mention whatsoever of that wave of anti-Darwinist metaphysics which comes from the side of bourgeois genetics. Bukharin fully accepts the metaphysical aspects of genetics and directly announces that "the doctrine of combinational variability on the basis of Mendel's laws, that of Johannsen's 'pure lines' and the 'generalization of the American school headed by Morgan' are 'the further development of Darwinism.'" For Bukharin, Timiryazev and Michurin do not exist. But Bukharin likes very much Vavilov's "law of homologous series." The point here, in substance, is not in these erroneous and anti-Darwinian theories but in the fact that Bukharin, having sold out socialism also sold out the interests of Soviet science and, clinging to the incorrect positions of bourgeois science, consciously falsified them as "the further development of Darwinism."[5]

Immediately following the Prezent article was one by Kol', accusing Vavilov of being a reactionary, of sabotage and other sins. In part it said: "Vavilov and his collaborators, in visiting Abyssinia, Palestine, North Africa, Turkey, Mongolia, Japan, and other countries, were interested less in selecting ecotypes superior for the Union, as did the Americans for their country, and more in collecting morphological wonders to fill empty spaces in his homologous tables." According to Kol', the role of Vavilov in "the destinies of our genetics and plant breeding" was "unhappy enough and had many harmful consequences." His "erroneous" methods, it was said, "postponed for many years the utilization even of the inadequately collected ecotypes." "Vavilov," Kol' continued, "attempted by various contrivances and distortions of facts to preserve further the hegemony, in science, of his theories (now shattered by reality), which have already done no little harm to our reconstruction." Finally, "It is typical of AIPB that, in many achievements now self-attributed to it, the tactical role of the institution was exclusively reactionary, and only a hindrance."[6]

These and analogous statements by Kol' are absolute fabrications. The editorial board of *Yarovizatsiya* gave space to Kol', who had been dismissed from the AIPB for disrupting the work on plant introduction, solely to discredit the classical and most valuable work of Vavilov in assembling a collection of the world's domesticated plants as a basis for plant-breeding work on a nationwide scale.

A sharp campaign against Vavilov, Kol'tsov, and other geneticists was also started in 1937 by the newspaper *Sotszemledelie*. In an article by Prezent and Nurinov[7] in connection with criticism of Kol'stov, it was hinted that Trotskyite agents of international fascism "are searching for any entry by which to thread their way into our science." Two months later the newspaper published an article by Dunin, "Darwinism and science," which said, in part:

The Soviet public now well knows just who are the anti-Michurinists, such "scientists" as Academicians Kol'tsov and Serebrovsky, and the various "knights of the gene," jealously guarding the special and monopolistic role of the genes. Yet the fact that the enemy of the people, Bukharin, fought Darwinism together with these "knights" is passed over in silence. Indeed, this looks like a fox, but smells of a wolf!

As becomes a double-dealer, Bukharin "shed tears" on the death of Michurin. At the same time he wrote, not for the wide masses but apparently for a more "selected" circle, about genetics being a further development of Darwinism.[8] Of course, Bukharin is an enemy of the people for sure, and well knew where such further development leads. It places outside of scientific law the revolutionary work of Michurin and Michurinists, condemning it as antiscientific and harmful amateurism, and tinkering. Every Soviet citizen and, in particular, scientific workers must give serious thought to the motives behind the Bukharin strategy and tactics in approaching the problem of Darwinism and Michurinist methods.[9]

Even more concrete support for this position came from Yakovlev, then in charge of the agricultural department of the CC. In a speech at a meeting of collaborators and authors of the publishing house of agricultural literature, he subjected to sharp, incompetent, and unfounded criticism Vavilov's theory of plant variation, the work of Vavilov's pupil, Pangalo, and the chromosome theory of heredity. All were pronounced reactionary and anti-Darwinian. Beyond that, Yakovlev, as noted, being then in a highly responsible position, declared:

The point is to secure the further elaboration of genetics as a science from the standpoint of the theory of development, instead of converting it into a maidservant of Goebbels' department.

Only this will provide the possibility of lifting this science, now in its very first stages, to a high level. Only this will give the opportunity for our geneticists to earn the respect of the progressive scientists of the world . . . I repeat for clarity: Darwinists are for and not against genetics; Darwinists are not against genetics, but they are against the fascist distortion of genetics and fascist utilization of genetics for political aims, inimical to the progress of mankind.[10]

And this accusation was advanced against Soviet geneticists named in the article and by no means against German geneticists and anthropologists. It should be noted that the identification of Soviet genetics with the concoctions of fascist racists was a conscious and deliberate lie. The racist theories of fascism were in fact subjected to convincing and competent criticism in the work of the Soviet genetical school. In reality, fascism was afraid of the real scientific genetics: in Hitler's Germany a number of genetics institutes were closed, and outstanding German geneticists were forced to leave their native land.

Several weeks later Yakovlev repeated his absurd thesis about the transformation of Soviet genetics into the handmaiden of Goebbels' department, and the fascist distortion of Soviet genetics in an article "On Darwinism and some anti-Darwinists," published in the central press.[11] Again the fundamental thrust of the article was against Vavilov and his pupils.

Accusations against many Soviet geneticists as being reactionaries, idealists, and wreckers were advanced in 1937 in many articles in the Lysenko-edited *Yarovizatsya*, as well as elsewhere, including the mass press. *This was a conscious, organized, and purposeful baiting, in a premeditated way, to expose scientific opponents to the blows of the punitive organs of our country.*

In the same period, AIPB, which had created the first geographic network (of some 130 variety-testing stations) in the U.S.S.R., was also accused of organizing the wrecking of variety testing and seed production. The stations were reorganized into a system independent of the AIPB, and their number increased to a thousand. This reorganization was carried out not merely as a timely measure, however, but under the banner of struggle against saboteurs allegedly operating in the network under the leadership of the AIPB and the U.S.S.R. Commissariat of Agriculture. In a special report, Yakovlev expanded intensively the accusation of wrecking in land-adminstering organs and in the testing network. A large wave of repression spread over these organizations.[12]

THE CANCELLATION OF THE CONGRESS
AND THE FIRST ARRESTS

The transformation of the genetics debate into a one-sided political battle could not pass unnoticed by international genetics organizations, which naturally expressed concern about the fate of the Moscow Congress due to convene in only a few months. The concern was not unfounded. About three months before the scheduled opening the President of the Permanent Committee on International Genetics Congresses, Professor Otto L. Mohr of the University of Oslo, received a letter from the Soviet organizing committee announcing postponement of the Congress to August, 1938. This was in fact equivalent to a cancellation, since all of the papers and contributions to the Congress would then be out-of-date, and a fresh start would have to be made on everything.

At the end of June, 1937, Mohr received still another letter signed by twelve leading Soviet geneticists. [*Translator's Note:* A Russian translation of the letter—originally written in English—a copy of which is in the personal archives of Vavilov, is omitted here. Its main points included: (1) a denunciation of false rumors about the arrests of Kol'tsov, Serebrovsky, and Vavilov as the work of provocateurs attempting to prevent the holding of the Congress in Moscow; (2) a statement on the state of development of Soviet genetics; (3) assurances that conditions for a successful Congress in 1938 would be met. The thirteen signatories, including some members of the organizing committee, were Meister, Vavilov, Navashin, Kol'tsov, Serebrovsky, Kostov, Levit, Dubinin, Sapegin, Kislovsky, Gershenson, Levitsky, and Karpechenko.]

The letter's prognosis of a successful Congress in 1938 was not fulfilled, for by then Meister, Levit, and Gorbunov, all members of the organizing committee, as well as its president, Muralov, had been arrested. Lysenko became president of the LAAAS.[13]

Muralov's arrest had been preceded by an intensive campaign of exposure of "enemies of the people," supposedly active in the leadership of the LAAAS. Those in other agricultural institutes (cotton breeding, animal husbandry, agricultural chemistry, plant protection, etc.) were routed out as wreckers. The "creators" of the new genetics joined this campaign. At the meeting of the party organization of the LAAAS devoted to a discussion of Muralov's report, Lysenko and Prezent appeared with "exposures" of Muralov's large-scale errors.[14] Even at that, all the accusations amounted to was Muralov's failure to support without qualification intravarietal crossing and the concept represented by Lysenko and Prezent.

THE CAMPAIGN AGAINST VAVILOV

In the same period very sharp attacks were renewed against Vavilov and the AIPB. An article entitled "On old positions," authored by Vladimirov, Itskov, and Kudryavtsev (the latter two were department heads and board members of the Commissariat of Agriculture), said in particular:

The unmasked enemies of the people who occupied a leading position in the Agricultural Academy and Grain Administration of the U.S.S.R. Commissariat of Agriculture labored not a little to confuse the variety situation. The country was spending gold to import from abroad new varieties which turned out to be our own, previously exported from the U.S.S.R. . . . . It would be unforgivable complacency to consider that, after the unmasking of the group of enemies of the people, all is well on the plant-breeding front. The roots of sabotage no doubt remain. It is enough to have a look at the very methods of the AIPB to be convinced of this. The single fact that the variety-testing network was within this institute tells much . . . .

The expeditions of AIPB consumed tremendous amounts of public funds. We do not deny the considerable effect of the expeditions on the development of Soviet breeding. But it is necessary to say that, on the whole, the world collection does not justify the expenditures on it. In working on the collection the institute gave the country hundreds of literary monographs and systematic botanical descriptions instead of new varieties for widespread production. Not one breeder of the Union, no matter how long-lived, would have time to read them all . . . .

The reproduction of rye and wheat from elite seed, in 126 collective farms of the Leningrad region, was clearly organized with destructive aims. The leadership of the institute (its director Vavilov) and the party organization (the secretary of the party committee, Comrade El'nitsky) do not fight this. More than that, they give refuge at the institute's experimental stations to men who cannot be politically trusted. The scientific leader of the Voroshilovgrad station for rust control is a certain Sobolev, a former nobleman, banished from Leningrad. His assistant Gil'denbrandt is a former landowner, also banished from Leningrad.[15]

After the arrests of a series of LAAAS workers, the newspaper *Sotszemledelie* published an article: "To sanitize the Academy of Agricultural Science. To root out mercilessly enemies and their yes-men from scientific establishments."[16] Among the accomplices of the enemies of the people named in this article were such scientists as the academicians Vavilov, M. M. Zavadovsky, and Konstantinov, who were charged with an inimical attitude toward Lysenko's work. Serebrovsky's position at this time also became very precarious. At a

March 14, 1938, conference at the LAAAS, he cited excerpts from a number of provincial newspapers in which arrests of zootechnicians using "Serebrovsky's fascist anti-Darwinian method" were reported.[17]

After becoming the Academy's president, Lysenko once more proclaimed that "enemies of the people operated in the old leadership."[18] At the same time the newspaper *Sotszemledelie* assigned the following task to the LAAAS: "It is necessary to expel from the institutes and stations the methods of bourgeois science, which were cultivated in every possible way by the enemies of the people, the Trotskyite-Bukharinist diversionists who operated in the All-Union Academy of Agricultural Sciences."[19] And once more the spearhead of the attack was directed at the geneticists who had not yet been "finished off."

At the beginning of 1939 the Lysenko-edited journal *Yarovizatsiya* published Prezent's article "On pseudoscientific theories in genetics," in which he attempted to draw a far-fetched, slanderous parallel between the work of Vavilov and the absurd ideas of the reactionary and anti-Marxist philosopher, Dühring:

Comparing what Dühring had written with what Vavilov says of homologous rows of variation, which supposedly proceed in a parallel way independent of the degree of relationship or conditions of life, the only apparent difference is that Dühring talks of "row-positions" as the basis of similarity in the development of organisms, whereas Vavilov talks of parallel rows. Dühring openly calls Darwinism a "livestock philosophy," an "absurdity," and so forth, while Vavilov, who at one time openly came out against Darwinism (see his 1920 work on "The law of homologous rows"[20]) now is verbally trying to reconcile his anti-Darwinian theory with Darwinism. But the "theory of parallel rows" and that of "row positions" are essentially the same.

Our native geneticists, those attempting to defend the "truths" of Mendelism-Morganism, should take pause over the significant fact that the philosophical foundations of the theory they defend had already found a place in the history of pseudoscience, in Düh-ring's pseudophilosophy, exposed by Engels. Our native Morganists should give serious thought also to the theoretical pathways and class roots, which led Kol'tsov, Serebrovsky, and a number of others to the construction of the science of "human breeding" directly connected with brutal fascism.

Scientific workers who carry the metaphysics of Mendelism-Morganism onto the soil of Soviet science try to give the appearance of fighting for the last word in science. We fail to see anything "new" in the philosophy of contemporary Morganism. These "latest tidings of science," in their general philosophical forms, were expressed by the ardent anti-Darwinist and racist, Dühring, whose theories were demolished by Engels in his famous "Anti-Dühring." Is it not worthwhile to compare Dühring's views with those of the Morganists? The struggle against the remnants of bourgeois opinions in science, the implacable struggle against pseudoscience and the idealistic and metaphysical distortions, is the business of every scientist and every scientific institution of our land.[21]

This intensive campaign against Vavilov could not fail to reflect on his position at the institute, on which Prezent now began to call frequently as an emissary. An anti-Vavilov group formed within the organization.[22] Most active against Vavilov was the head of the subtropical department, Shlykov, who began a slanderous campaign, running down all of Vavilov's achievements and advertising his own "merits." In an article entitled "In the chains of pseudoscience," Shlykov wrote:

Who of us does not know that, in building the most advanced agriculture in the world, we must fully utilize the achievements of world science and practice in producing varieties and cultivating plants which we now lack? This was the government assignment to our institute. But it so happened that, together with foreign plants, bourgeois theories and pseudoscientific trends infiltrated the institute. For some reason they found in it a favorable soil and in Vavilov a zealous expositor, propagandizer, and follower.

Here belong the theories of formal genetics, Batesonian Mendelism, "the law of homologous rows," "centers of origin," and many other theories of bourgeois thought and practice. Instead of demonstrating the soundness of his theoretical position, Vavilov attempts to hide behind the approval of it expressed in the world (i.e., bourgeois) literature. But who does not know that the literature denies the scientific significance of Marxist-Leninist materialistic dialectics and the materialistic theory of development?[23]

The schism in the institute deepened, particularly after Lysenko appointed a young specialist, Shundenko, as deputy to Vavilov, over the sharp protests of the latter, who thought Shundenko to be of indifferent ability and who despised him for his servility toward Lysenko. Upon his appointment, Shundenko, who was directly responsible only to Lysenko, ignored Vavilov's orders and tried in every way to force his resignation from the institute.[24] The Shundenko-Shlykov group also tried to press upon the AIPB party organization a resolution for Vavilov's dismissal from the directorship. The protocol of the January 11, 1939, meeting of a commission of the party organization (consisting of Shundenko, Shulyndin, Khachaturov, Shlykov, and Sizov)[25] to work out a resolution regarding the general situation in the institute is available. The draft of the commission's decision adopted on January 21, 1939, and signed by Shlykov, includes the following point: ". . . the party organization considers essential for the purposes of reconstruction of the institute the dismissal of Vavilov as director, since, as the ideologist of formal genetics in the U.S.S.R., by remaining at his post he aids the activization and consolidation of anti-Darwinians throughout the Soviet Union, thereby interfering with the rapid rebuilding of the experimental and plant-breeding network of the Union along Darwinist lines." We do not know whether the commission's resolution was adopted by the party meeting, but the draft itself eloquently testifies to the methods employed against Vavilov at that time.

VAVILOV AND HIS FIGHT FOR
SCIENTIFIC TRUTH

Vavilov and his friends did not shun the polemic during that period. They bore the thrusts with dignity and, in various appearances, articles, and books, explained with vigor their scientific positions. They continued to work intensively and to follow the achievements of world science, thereby actively aiding the development of socialist agriculture. In their polemics with Lysenko and Prezent, not one of the geneticists stooped to political accusations. Despite the intensity of the conflict, they depended only on scientific arguments.

Two little-known discussions took place in 1939 which are recorded in stenographic reports to be found in Vavilov's personal archives. Analogous reports are also contained in the AIPB archives.

In March, 1939, a session of the regional bureau of the section of scientific workers was held at the AIPB. There was a frank exchange of opinions which clearly revealed the contradictions then rending agricultural and biological science in connection with the methods of discussion used by the Lysenko group. Although it cannot be given here in detail, the stenographic account is of great historic-scientific interest. We have seen, above, the style of the criticism to which Vavilov and other geneticists were subjected. For contrast, an excerpt from Vavilov's speech is given to show how calmly and courageously this criticism was borne, and what deep patriotic concern Vavilov and his followers displayed, understanding the dangers of the road toward which Prezent, Lysenko, Ol'shansky, and others were turning our biological science.

Reflecting in his address the remarkably significant results of the work of the institute and recounting the introduction of dozens of new varieties into the country's agriculture (for example, half the area in barley in the U.S.S.R. was then planted to AIPB-produced varieties), Vavilov concisely but strikingly elucidated the essence of the difficulties facing our science:

A grave specific defect in our circumstances is the current discord in science. This is a complex question. We are a large institution embracing the immensity of science, the problem of crops, their distribution, their introduction to practice, the assimilation of territory into agronomic production, etc. The question does not concern all this immensity; it concerns genetics, but this is now a topical subject, since our concepts have greatly expanded. Of course, as always in science, the solution will come from direct experimentation, from facts, but this is a long-term operation, especially in our field of plant breeding. . . . It must be said that the discord is very serious. I cannot go into the details here, but shall simply say that there are two positions, that of the Odessa institute and that of AIPB. It should be noted that the AIPB position is also that of contemporary world science, and was without doubt developed not by fascists, but by ordinary progressive toilers. . . . And, if we had here an audience of the most outstanding breeders, practical and theoretical, I am sure they would have voted with your obedient servant and not with the Odessa institute. This is a complex matter. It is not to be solved by decree of even the Commissariat of Agriculture. We shall go to the pyre, we shall burn, but we shall not retreat from our convictions. I tell you, in all frankness, that I believed and still believe and insist on what I think is right, and not only believe—because taking things on faith in science is nonsense—but also say what I know on the basis of wide experience. This is a fact, and to retreat from it simply because some occupying high posts desire it, is impossible. . . . The situation is such that, whatever foreign book you pick up, it goes contrary to the teachings of the Odessa institute. Would you order that these books be burned? We shall not stand for this. To our utmost strength we shall follow what is happening in progressive world science. We consider ourselves true Darwinians, because the problem of mastery of the world's riches, the world's plant resources created by mankind, can be solved only by this approach, and there should be no irresponsible name-calling.

A voice from the audience of Lysenkoites was heard: "But you proceed from immutability of genes and of the nature of plants." Vavilov lucidly replied:

Here we are made out to be something different from what we are; in polemics all is possible. We know that Engels, in his *Dialectics of Nature*, once called Newton nothing less than an "inductive ass." Here the book was translated from a manuscript draft and so this statement stayed in the book, but Engels himself very likely would have crossed out that sentence. Newton remained Newton, a man of whom it is said, on the monument in Cambridge, that he surpassed the human mind; yet in the heat of argument Engels called him an "inductive ass." And in the course of argument, not only Newton was made into an ass. We caught it also. Genetics is first of all a physiological science, and its basic problem is that of transforming organisms. That is what genetics is for. But in the course of investigations it becomes clear that to alter hereditary nature is not that simple. They have tried to shatter it and did not succeed. Things turned out to be more complex. . . . Unfortunately, in our debate, we do not know history well. There are no conservatives who believe that genes are unalterable; the problem is entirely one of variability.

One of Lysenko's followers, Khoroshailov, making his appearance directly after Vavilov, announced that Engels was right about Newton. "For all that," he exclaimed, "Newton was an inductive ass and remained one, no matter what it says on his monument."

THE LAAAS PRAESIDIUM MEETING

On May 25, 1939, the LAAAS praesidium, chaired by Lysenko, examined the report of the AIPB, submitted by Vavilov. On Lysenko's motion the report was rejected, although it vividly reflected the tremendous work carried out by the institute. A detailed excerpt from the stenographic account is given below.[26] It refers to Vavilov's closing words, in which he explained the theoretical basis of his work then under attack. The nature of the remarks of Lysenko and of L.,[27] who sat next to him as a delegate, should be noted.

VAVILOV: The plant-breeding institute carried out a tremendous task, and I say this deliberately as I understand it. The institute issued a theory on the basis of breeding, and lately the leading Western European countries are participating in this work. You shall see what wonderful specialists we have, and we ourselves feel that we are theoretically more well-founded than they are abroad. What is this based on? . . . The foundation material, this is the holy of holies, from which breeding work starts. We know well what the local varieties are, what the foreign ones are, where are the polyploids, where is the yielding capacity. All of this was in a state of chaos before. What did we do at that time? This is what we did: we would order, from a catalogue, seed from some German or American firm, without any biographical information about it. We used, in fact, all kinds of bastard knowledge. Now the institute bases its selection work wholly on Darwin's evolutionary teaching. I definitely state that we started the study of plant culture precisely by taking into account Darwin's work.

L: You consider that the center of the origin of man was some place else, and we are on the periphery?

VAVILOV: You misunderstood me. I do not consider it so. What is doubtless the case is that mankind originated in the Old World when there were no men in the New. All available data show that man came to America but recently. Mankind originated in the Tertiary period and was localized in South Asia and Africa. One can speak of man objectively.

L: Why do you speak of Darwin, and why do you not choose examples from Marx and Engels?

VAVILOV: Darwin worked on evolution of species earlier. Engels and Marx held Darwin in high regard. Darwin is not all, but he is the greatest biologist, who proved the evolution of organisms.

L: It turns out that man originated in one place. I don't believe that he originated in one place.

VAVILOV: I have already told you, not in one place but in the

Old World, and contemporary biological science, Darwinian science, says that man appeared in the Old World, and that only 20 to 25 thousand years ago did man appear in the New World. Before then there was no man in America, and though this may be curious, it nevertheless is well known.

L: This is connected with your views on domesticated plants?

VAVILOV: . . . my basic idea . . . is that . . . one and the same species of plant does not arise independently in different places, but spreads through the continents from some one region.

L: Everybody says that the potato came from America. I don't believe this. Do you know what Lenin said?

VAVILOV: . . . we know well that potatoes appeared in our country under Peter the First.

L: How do we know it was under Peter the First?

VAVILOV: There are precise historical documents. I could with great pleasure tell you about it in greater detail.

L: I asked you a fundamental question, and it turns out that, if potatoes appeared in one place, we must acknowledge that . . . .

LYSENKO [interrupting]: Potatoes were brought into the old Russia. This is a fact. One cannot go against facts. But that's not the point. . . . The question is whether, if the potato originated in America, it means that in Moscow, Kiev, Kharkov, it could not arise from an ancestral species until the Second Coming? Can new varieties arise in Moscow, Leningrad, any place? I think they can. And, then, how does one view your theory of the centers of origin, that's the point.

VAVILOV: . . . unfortunately our language has become clumsy, and specialized . . . difficult to understand, not only for other specialists but even for botanists. . . . We do not understand each other, yet we discourse of great things. We have worked out methods of studying plant life, but to understand each other we must first learn the vocabulary.

We Soviet geneticists . . . are doing much, but dumplings don't fall into one's mouth that easily. Perennial wheat is a fine thing, yet it was destroyed by frost this severe winter. Here Derzhavin produced a variety. It was a deuce of a variety: large-grained, tall, but the straw is brittle, and it would take ten years of hard work to obtain what is needed. . . .

The one-sidedness of which you talk is a deep untruth. An

anomaly unacceptable in the Soviet Union is created when, by means of theoretical discussions, subtle games are played.

You can imagine how difficult and complex it is to guide graduate students, when all the time one is told that one does not share Lysenko's views. History will indicate which one of us is right. . . . I am an overburdened man; not only do I work as the academic secretary, the deputy, but even as a financial administrative assistant. I should have explained this in greater detail. Of course, species can originate on the periphery. If Trofim Denisovich (Lysenko) would only listen calmly instead of shuffling pages— life goes on. . . .

LYSENKO: You and I have talked calmly together in private; here it is different. This is the first time I have heard you say that species do originate. Apparently, I misunderstood. But here [apparently pointing to a manuscript] it does say that evolution is oversimplification.

VAVILOV: Evolution is oversimplification of specific events. This is a fact you could verify.

LYSENKO: I don't question that evolution is a fact. But is it true that evolution is an oversimplification, an unwinding? Is it true or not?

VAVILOV: It's an undisputable fact. Take the 100 per cent Darwinist, Severtsov. (I myself am under suspicion by you.) There is a law of reduction; often many animal groups had a history of the reduction of many organs toward a vestigial state. There is also a law of increase in complexity. . . .

LYSENKO: I understood from what you wrote that you came to agree with your teacher, Bateson, that evolution must be viewed as a process of simplification. Yet in Chapter 4 of the history of the party it says evolution is increase in complexity. . . .

VAVILOV: . . . in short, there is also reduction. When I studied with Bateson. . . .

L: An anti-Darwinist.

VAVILOV: No. Some day I'll tell you about Bateson, a most fascinating, most interesting man.

L: Couldn't you learn from Marx?

VAVILOV: Recently a book of Haldane's came out. He is an interesting figure, a member of the British communist party, an outstanding geneticist, biochemist, and philosopher. He wrote an interesting book entitled *Marxism and Science*, in which he tried . . .

L (interrupting): And got a dressing down.

VAVILOV: Of course he got a dressing down in the bourgeois press, but he is so talented that he was admired even while being scolded. . . . He said that Marxism is more applicable to evolution, to history . . . that it can foresee much, just as Engels foresaw, fifty years ahead, many contemporary discoveries. I must say that I am a great lover of Marxist literature, not only of ours but of the foreign, too. There, too, many attempts at Marxist validation are made.

L: Marxism is the only science. Darwinism is only a part; the real theory of knowledge of the world was given by Marx, Engels, and Lenin. And when I hear discussion about Darwinism without mention of Marxism, it may seem, on the one side, that all is right, but on the other, it's a horse of a different color.

VAVILOV: I studied Marx four or five times and am prepared to go on. . . .

LYSENKO (from his concluding remarks): I agree with you, Nikolay Ivanovich [Vavilov], it is somewhat difficult for you to carry on your work. We talked of this many times and I was sincerely sorry for you. But, you see, your being insubordinate toward me—and this means AIPB is being insubordinate to me. . . . I say now that some kind of measures must be taken. We cannot go on in this way. You state openly this is dishonest. This is what you say, but you think differently. . . . We shall have to depend on others, take another line, a line of administrative subordination.[28]

UNDER THE BANNER OF MARXISM

Deliberately slanderous fabrications were also presented by Lysenko supporters at the discussion organized by the journal, *Under the Banner of Marxism*, in 1939. Its organizer, the philosopher Mitin, in his concluding speech, subjected Vavilov and his adherents to a sharp but inept critique. He drew a vulgar analogy between the genetics debate and the discussions against "menshevizing idealism, the juridical theories of the Trotsky-Bukharin-Pashukanis gang" and "wrecker-menshevik concepts" of others.[29]

Vavilov's deep and pithy speech at this discussion, imbued with concern for the fate of Soviet science and agriculture, deserves serious attention.[30] Even then he forewarned of the many difficulties which were later to beset our science. Even then Vavilov proposed, in spite of Lysenko's criticism, a number of agronomic practices which were introduced only fifteen to sixteen years later (e.g., use of hybrid corn). Even then Vavilov spoke of the intolerability of isolation of Soviet biology from world science. It is a pity that the men then responsible for the destinies of our country were deaf to the voice of this great scientist.

Possessing great erudition and scientific experiences, and understanding that the fate of Soviet biology was of greater consequence than his personal fate, Vavilov firmly defended his positions. He clearly exposed the pseudo-innovative nature of the "new genetics": "The specificity of our differences lies in the fact that under the guise of progressive science it is proposed that we return essentially to viewpoints of the first half or middle of the nineteenth century, outlived by science."[31]

The proposals for introduction of hybrid corn in the U.S.S.R. were based on its success in the United States where its use had increased yields by 20 to 30 per cent on millions of acres. The hybridization program was organized by Vavilov and his collaborators, and AIPB already had a number of usable inbred lines. But this progressive practice met the sharp resistance of Lysenko, Prezent, Ol'shansky, and others, who continuously kept discrediting it in the pages of the agricultural press after 1936, without any substantiation whatsoever.

THE LAST STAGES

Vavilov's courage and steadfastness in the defense of his principles and scientific conviction became, in 1939, the main stumbling block in the way of complete victory for Lysenko-ism, and a decisive offensive was mounted against him. Mitin's speech, already noted, which contained a number of vulgar and unfounded accusations against genetics and was directed basically against Vavilov (who was proclaimed a scientific reactionary), was reprinted in December, 1939, in the central press. Several weeks later (February 20, 1940), for no apparent reason, it was reproduced in the newspaper *Sotszemledelie.*

What also irritated Vavilov's opponents was the growing recognition of his work abroad, particularly marked in that period. Even though the International Congress of Genetics met in 1939 in Edinburgh, Vavilov was elected its president. His presidential address was to have inaugurated the Congress. But he was denied permission to go to Scotland.

The AIPB, headed by Vavilov, became an object of gross administrative interference by Lysenko, president of the LAAAS. The following excerpts, which illustrate the situation, are from one of several letters written by Vavilov in mid-1940, two to three months before his arrest. They were addressed to the higher administration, and in particular to the U.S.S.R. Commissar of Agriculture, Benediktov.[32]

The abnormal situation in the direction, by the LAAAS, of the AIPB compels me to draw your attention to several matters and to request your intervention . . . To understand the peculiarity of the situation, suffice it to say that there is no leadership in practical and theoretical plant breeding, which shares other opinions [than those held by the scientific collective directorate of the AIPB], but that is not the point. Lysenko's high administrative position, his intolerance, and his low level of culture lead to a peculiar introduction of ideas that are close to outmoded scientific views (Lamarckism), and which are regarded as exceedingly dubious by the majority of those acquainted with the field. Using his position, Lysenko has actually begun reprisals against his ideological opponents. I shall cite the basic facts in the area of plant breeding.

1. In September during the director's month-long absence on an expedition, fourteen doctors, outstanding specialists, and a number of candidates[33] were dismissed from the institute in accordance with a policy of removal of those of a different mind from that of the president. Only by calling for the intervention of the Deputy Chairman of the Council of Commissars, comrade Vyshinsky, was it possible to counteract in part this gross interference, unprecedented in the scientific life of our country. . . .

3. Without consultation with the director, persons are assigned to be his deputies and his scientific secretary who are obsequious toward the president. They actually disrupt the discipline in the institute, since all their actions serve to paralyze the director's activity and curry maximum favor with the president. . . .

6. On his visits to AIPB in Leningrad, the president deliberately emphasizes, before meetings of the scientific workers, his categorical disagreements with the director, and the special significance of certain findings that confirm the president's ideas, although they are far from convincing to the majority. The completely unmerited discrediting of the director is the president's usual practice.

7. A completely intolerable situation has been created, including various material indulgences and assignments for travel to persons obsequious toward the president, of which there are a certain number. . . .

As the director of the AIPB I submit my request for the creation of a normal environment for the leadership of the institute and the elimination of intolerable subjectivity and prejudice manifested by the president.

It was not possible to count on Benediktov's actual support, since he fully backed all of Lysenko's measures. Shortly before this, at an LAAAS session, Benediktov said: "We officially condemn the tendencies issuing from Mendelism and formal genetics, and will give no support whatsoever to this current."

Sensing the coming denouement, Vavilov visited Andreev, the CC secretary, in the summer of 1940, hoping to have his support in resolving the abnormal situation in agricultural science. But, shortly after the visit, Vavilov said to his friends: "Our affairs are in a bad way, even Andreev fears Lysenko." This was justified: Lysenko had become Stalin's favorite.[34]

VAVILOV'S ARREST

The end of the story is known. In August, 1940, Vavilov was arrested. He was picked up by the members of the NKVD, hurriedly, openly, on a Western Ukraine field under the eyes of his companions, members of the last of his numerous expeditions. The expedition headed by Vavilov had been undertaken on the instruction of the Commissariat of Agriculture. Benediktov, the Commissar, charged Vavilov with the task over Lysenko's categorical objections. This time, contrary to the usual state of affairs, Benediktov had disagreed with Lysenko's opinion. One of Vavilov's friends, Bakhteev, a member of the expedition, told this writer of the last free days of Vavilov.

Vavilov and his companions first went to Kiev. From there they went by car to L'vov and on to Chernovitsy. From there, in three overcrowded cars, Vavilov and a large group of local specialists proceeded toward the foothills to collect and study plants. One of the cars could not negotiate the difficult road and turned back. On the way the occupants met a light car containing men in civilian clothes: "Where did Vavilov's cars go?" asked one of them, "We need him urgently." "The road farther on is not good, return with us to Chernovitsy. Vavilov should be back by 6 or 7 p.m., and that would be

P. M. Zhukovsky with graduate students (l. to r.) T. Lebedeva, Zh. A. Medvedev, V. Egorov.

Monument to I.V. Michurin, in city of Michurinsk.

H. J. Muller (dark suit) in Moscow, 1922.

N. I. Vavilov

Left to right: Th. and N. Dobzhansky, N. I. Vavilov, G. D. Karpechenko, Pasadena, California, autumn of 1930.

P. M. Zhukovsky

D. A. Sabinin

the fastest way to find him." "No, we must find him right away, a telegram came from Moscow; he is being recalled immediately."

In the evening the other members of the expedition returned without Vavilov. He was taken so fast that his things were left in one of the cars. But late at night three men in civilian clothes came to fetch them. One of the members of the expedition started sorting out the bags piled up in the corner of the room, looking for Vavilov's. When it was located, it was found to contain a big sheaf of spelt, a half-wild local type of wheat collected by Vavilov.[35] It was later discovered to be a brand new species. Thus, on his last day of service to his country, August 6, 1940, Vavilov made his last botanical-geographic discovery. And, although it was modest, it still cannot be dropped from the history of science. And few scientists reading of it in a Vavilov memorial volume published in 1960 could have guessed that the date of this find is a date that scientists throughout the world will always recall with bitterness and pain.

OTHER ARRESTS

After Vavilov, his closest collaborators and friends were also arrested and later perished in prison: Karpechenko,[36] in charge of the AIPB Laboratory of Genetics, a geneticist of world fame, head of a large scientific school which solved the problem of infertility of distant hybrids; Levitsky, in charge of the AIPB Laboratory of Cytology, the most authoritative Soviet cytologist, who created many new techniques and methods still in use; Govorov, in charge of leguminous seed plants, founder of a worldwide collection of these plants and creator of many highly valuable varieties. A number of other scientists were also arrested, including Kovalev, a past deputy director of the AIPB and a leading fruit breeder, as well as

Flyaksberger, a noted wheat specialist. All were subsequently rehabilitated.

VAVILOV'S TRIAL

During the review of the Vavilov case initiated by his family (1954–1955) for the purposes of rehabilitation, a number of his former collaborators and colleagues were summoned to the U.S.S.R. Procurator's Office to refute the absurd accusations advanced against him in the course of the original judicial investigations. It was in this connection that the names of the persons who in 1940 participated most closely, albeit purely technically, in this dirty affair, became known.

For the NKVD it was the already mentioned Shundenko who was engaged in the case. During his short time at the AIPB (as deputy director, appointed by Lysenko against Vavilov's strenuous protest) he created a veritable anti-Vavilov organization, continuously slandered and wrote denunciations of the AIPB and its leading workers, and in every way toadied to Lysenko. These activities were so obvious that at the meeting of the regional bureau section of scientific workers (previously noted) many speakers had already sharply condemned the undermining tactics and provocative style of this Lysenko appointee. Vavilov himself noted Shundenko's illiteracy and disruptive role. It was shortly before Vavilov's arrest that Shundenko transferred (or rather returned) to a leading post in the organs of the NKVD.[37]

The names of a number of "experts" called on to testify in 1940–1941 to provide a scientific basis for the evidence against Vavilov have also become known. They were called in for proof of Vavilov's "wrecking activities," which he denied in the course of the investigation. One of the experts, the now late Professor and member of the LAAAS, Yakushkin, was notorious in his obsequiousness toward Lysenko. In a textbook written by him, Lysenko is mentioned over one hundred times.

It is only fair to say that after 1954, when the mass rehabilitation of the victims of arbitrary rule began, Yakushkin was often summoned by investigators to verify his signature on denunciations and documents attributing sabotage to innocent, falsely condemned people. Unable to stand this ordeal, Yakushkin took to his bed for a protracted period and eventually died.[38]

Still another expert, Vodkov, distinguished himself by similar obsequiousness. In the August, 1948, session of the LAAAS, he said in part: "The new agronomic theory was created by the Soviet scientists, Lysenko and Vil'yams. Their work is the highest achievement of agronomic thought and the greatest contribution to world science. We cannot undervalue this fact, comrades. There is no need for false modesty in science: we work under Soviet conditions, under the leadership of comrade Stalin, with such scientific innovators as Michurin, Vil'yams, Lysenko."

On July 9, 1941, the military collegium of the Supreme Court, consisting of three persons, after a meeting lasting a few minutes, passed sentence on Vavilov. He was found guilty on a number of points of Article 58: Belonging to a rightist conspiracy; spying for England; leadership of the Labor Peasant Party; sabotage in agriculture; links with white émigrés; etc. At the "trial" Vavilov denied all accusations. The sentence was the supreme penalty, death. Both the first and the second appeal were denied. But the sentence was not executed immediately, contrary to the custom of the times. Apparently higher approval was necessary.[39]

Only after several months, when Vavilov was in the Saratov prison, was the death sentence commuted to a ten-year imprisonment. He survived the prison conditions only a little more than a year, and died on January 26, 1943. On September 2, 1955, the U.S.S.R. Supreme Court rehabilitated Vavilov for lack of the *corpus delicti*. On September 9, 1955, the AS praesidium restored Vavilov's name in the roster of deceased members.

VAVILOV'S DEATH

In October, 1941, in connection with the German advance, Moscow prisoners were being evacuated to the interior. Together with others, Vavilov was moved to the Saratov prison. There he was placed in the windowless, underground death cell. The condemned were even denied outdoor exercise. Vavilov spent several months in the death cell, and only in the summer of 1942, after commutation of the sentence, was he moved, by then in a serious physical condition, to a general cell block. According to Popovsky, Vavilov's file contains a letter from him to Beria, written in the death cell. Judging by this letter, Beria did not approve the sentence of execution. Moreover, after sentencing, Vavilov had been moved to the inner prison of the NKVD and given improved conditions. He was even informed of the possibility of being permitted to do creative work, although officially the sentence was still in force. But the rapid evacuation of prisoners under the October, 1941, German advance halted this process. It is not unlikely that improvement in Vavilov's conditions in August–September, 1941, was connected with the energetic interference of Pryanishnikov. Beria's wife was his student and worked in Pryanishnikov's department up to the time of Beria's arrest in 1953. It was through her that Pryanishnikov influenced Beria to save Vavilov and improve his prison conditions.[40]

Little is known so far of Vavilov's last period of life, spent in the Saratov prison. I have heard at second hand the evidence of a now-deceased eyewitness who was one of Vavilov's cell mates. According to him, Vavilov was moved to the general ward in a grave condition with symptoms of malnutrition. As he entered, he introduced himself: "You see before you, talking of the past, the Academician Vavilov, but now according to the opinion of the investigators, nothing but dung." The prisoners treated Vavilov with great respect and later when, because of malnutrition, he no longer could walk, they would carry him outside, hoping that fresh air would give him some relief.

Vavilov's wife and son were evacuated from Leningrad in 1942 and lived in Saratov, 2 to 3 kilometers distant from the prison where he was dying. Yet the members of the NKVD concealed from her Vavilov's real place of confinement, informing her that he was in Moscow.[41]

At the end of 1942, Vavilov, who had mysteriously "disappeared" from the world science scene, was elected a foreign member of the Royal Society of London. When this information reached the NKVD, the Vavilov file was urgently recalled for study. But it was too late. Life was slowly ebbing from a body exhausted by malnutrition, and it was impossible by then to save him. Vavilov died, according to the death certificate, from pneumonia. This was the heaviest loss to Soviet science in the period of the personality cult.

A local scientist, the entomologist Megalov, who had known Vavilov when he worked in Saratov in 1920, learned of Vavilov's presence in the prison. He decided to help at least by sending food parcels. At first, they were received, and a short note, "Thank you, N. Vavilov," is still preserved as a relic. After the third time, however, Megalov was told that Vavilov was no longer in the Saratov prison.

The arrest and subsequent death of Vavilov, a famed scientist whose name and work were known throughout the world, had serious international repercussions. In the years following, hundreds of articles containing justified reproofs to Soviet science were published. Most of them were cut out of the foreign journals on their arrival, so that the Soviet public has little idea of the long-term and very unflattering analysis by foreign scientists of the arrest and "disappearance" of Vavilov and others. And it was no secret to anybody abroad that the disappearance of Vavilov and the others was connected with the genetics controversy.

VAVILOV, SCIENTIST AND MAN

In spite of the length of time separating us from the death of Vavilov—that courageous and great scientist, encyclopedist, selectionist, geneticist, plant breeder, agronomist, botanist, geographer-traveler, statesman, creator of the world-famed Plant Breeding Institute, founder and first president of the Lenin All-Union Academy of Agricultural Sciences—his fame and popularity continue to grow. Multivolumed collections of his works have been published in the U.S.S.R. and the United States. Only recently, many articles and reminiscences about his life, activity, scientific discoveries, and unprecedented voyages have been published.[42]

These just and universally accepted evaluations of Vavilov's image and his theoretical discoveries are sharply different from the shameless, unintelligent, demagogic, tendentious, and slanderous critiques of Vavilov, examples of which we have given in the previous citations from the "scientific" pens of representatives of the trend headed by Lysenko.

One ought to emphasize Vavilov's patriotism, his fervent love of his fatherland, his devotion to the aims of socialism, his enthusiasm. His patriotism can be felt. Throughout his activity as scientist and leader of Soviet science, it permeated all of his polemics, and is especially brilliantly evident in his correspondence, his private letters, in which a man as a rule reveals his deepest feelings. His personal archives contain numerous highly interesting letters.[43]

Vavilov's collaborators were always astounded by his unusual enthusiasm, his capacity for work, his colossal energy. He slept no more than four to five hours a day, devoting the rest of his time to work. Every year he visited the numerous experiment stations of the AIPB and was abreast of the most minute details of the work of that enormous institution. Vavilov had published over three hundred scientific works since the revolution alone, and most of them still retain their significance. Shortly before his arrest, he started dictating to a stenographer, in the evenings, an account of his expeditions, a popular book about his travels in search of plants, and the agriculture of the world. He planned a three-volume work, but it was not completed. In 1961 his son, Yuri, found the manuscript of his father's dictation (which was thought to be lost), and the Soviet reader was able to become acquainted with it upon publication by the Geografizdat, in 1962, under the title, *Five Continents*.

Vavilov's capacity for work was simply phenomenal. Hampered by the limitations of longhand writing, in his later years he undertook to dictate. Among his personal papers, a draft of his work plans for 1940–1941 has been preserved. It included twelve books and six articles, a plan unfulfilled because of his arrest. In 1938 he began a book on *Studies in the History of Genetics*, which remained uncompleted, although the preserved chapters indicate that he proposed a broad comparison of genetics with the pseudoscientific speculations of Lysenko.

The location of Vavilov's grave is not known as yet, and collective efforts to find it have so far been fruitless.[44] But his memory will be eternal. Pryanishnikov once said of Vavilov: "We do not call him a genius only because he is our contemporary." Now, he no longer is; his activity and fate are a part of history, and we can boldly place him with the greats of world science—Darwin, Pasteur, Mendel, Mechnikov —whose discoveries contributed to the golden fund of natural science.

Among the great scientists of our time, Vavilov is distinguished by many traits characteristic of the epoch and conditions under which his gigantic talent developed. He was not merely a seeker of scientific truth, but the first discoverer of new facts, laws, and ideas; he was a foremost statesman, striving for the reorganization and uplift of the agriculture of his country; he was a scientist-fighter, a scientist-patriot, a *chevalier sans peur et sans reproche*, a man who unwittingly united around himself the progressive forces of Soviet biology; a citizen who, to affirm his scientific ideas, had to be possessed not only of the talents of a scientist, but also of courage, will, iron endurance, high principles, and an extraordinary capacity for work. Nikolay Ivanovich Vavilov was not only a scientist and public figure: he was also a hero who gave his life for his scientific convictions. His life will always be a model for the new generations of Soviet scientists.

CHAPTER 4

Medical Genetics in 1937-1940

THE PRECEDING CHAPTERS have dealt primarily with the fate of theoretical and agricultural genetics under the intensifying aggravation of the controversy in biology. The same debate also had serious effects on medical genetics which, at that time, the vulgarizers confused with racism. In 1936–1937 the problems of hereditarily determined diseases were only at the stage of preliminary investigation and elucidation of hereditary pathology: attempts at control were only beginning. *By that time, however, hundreds of diseases of genetic origin had been found and studied; and, inasmuch as their existence, sad as it might be, was a reality, human genetics had become an essential branch of medicine.* This field was no less necessary than, for example, oncology, parasitology, psychiatry, and other branches of the medico-biological sciences.

Up to 1936, i.e., up to the beginning of the genetics debates, the Soviet Union had, in fact, been the leader of this important area of applied genetics. Particularly well known were the work of the Medico-Genetical Institute, headed by Levit, and that of the Institute of Experimental Biology, directed by Kol'tsov.

ACCUSATIONS OF RACISM

Human genetics had already been subjected to sharp attacks by Prezent and the botanist Bosse during the 1936 discussion, when they had erroneously identified this field with racism and fascism. Later on, as we have seen, Prezent intensified the criticism in the same direction, making particularly sharp attacks on Kol'tsov, the foremost specialist in this area.

Kol'tsov was an outstanding scientist who had made a considerable contribution to the development of genetics and cytology. His book, *The Organization of the Cell*,[1] was a classic—the best in its time. Between 1927 and 1937 he had been the first scientist in the world to work out a number of classical concepts of self-reproducing genetical material of chromosomes and of protein synthesis, based on templates. Ten to fifteen years after his death, those concepts were proved correct by the Americans, and became the foundation of contemporary views on the biosynthesis of cell polymers, proteins and nucleic acids.[2] Kol'tsov's work on "Hereditary molecules," published in 1935 in the journal *Nauka i Zhizn'*, anticipated many current discoveries. The first studies on chemical mutagenesis (Sakharov) and on sex-determination control in animals (Astaurov) were carried out under the direction and with the participation of Kol'tsov. He was without doubt a classical pioneer in genetics and cytology, and he accomplished for science much that we can be proud of. But in 1922–1928 Kol'tsov was a contributor to the *Russky Evgenichesky Zhurnal*, and in 1922–1923 he had published articles based on mistaken eugenical theses. It must be remembered that in the first years after the revolution there was a degree of aimlessness among the old scientific intelligentsia. It would be ridiculous to judge Kol'tsov as a scientist on the basis of these long-forgotten articles, exhumed by Prezent solely for the purpose of baiting, and recalled repeatedly since then, right up to recent times.

Commenting on Kol'tsov's forgotten articles in a highly arbitrary way in 1939, Prezent did all he could to identify Kol'tsov's 1921–1922 position with his work in 1936–1939. In a completely slanderous manner he wrote: "In the institute directed by Kol'tsov and in the journal edited by him, his collaborators dragged in all sorts of pseudoscientific trash, and at times open fascist homilies, in the guise of genetics."[3] This was purest slander, because the *Biologichesky Zhurnal* referred to was then the most authoritative and serious of its kind. Yet it was closed down. At the same time, *Pravda* published a harsh article directed against Kol'tsov and Berg, and signed by a group of scientists (Bakh, Keller, Nuzhdin, and others).[4] Without citing publication dates, the authors criticized the same passages from a 1922 article of Kol'tsov that Prezent had quoted in 1937 and 1939. Comparing those passages with citations from the German scientist Lenz, the *Pravda* article implied "resemblances" between the scientific work of Kol'tsov and that of the "fascist thug Lenz." Berg was similarly attacked on the basis of his long-forgotten book, *Nomogenesis,* published in 1922.[5]

It is only natural to ask why, in 1939, it was necessary to abuse two reputable scientists for seventeen-year-old statements, long forgotten. The answer is readily found in the same article. It was published just before the elections to the AS to fill a vacancy in genetics, and the candidates for that vacancy were Lysenko (then a member of the LAAAS), Kol'tsov and Berg (corresponding members of the AS). The way to Lysenko's election had to be cleared by discrediting his competitors. Shortly before, in the same connection, an article about Lysenko as the champion battling against reactionary Morganism had appeared in *Pravda.*[6]

In another article,[7] Prezent accused not only Kol'tsov but all Soviet geneticists who disagreed with the ideas developed by Prezent and Lysenko about fascist and man-hating distortions:

It is incumbent on Kol'tsov and his companions-in-arms to account to themselves and to the Soviet public for the pseudoscientific and deeply reactionary concept which carried them into the arms of fascist ideology. They must disclose the link between the metaphysical doctrine of the immutability of the gene in the course of hundreds and thousands of years—followed by contemporary bourgeois genetics—and the independence of nature from the conditions of life, on the one hand, and the delirious attempts at controlled human breeding, on the other.

Kol'tsov's significant contribution to the development of cytology and genetics makes it necessary to evaluate more fairly his early eugenical works published in the *Russky Evgenichesky Zhurnal* in 1922–1923, which became known to the wider public in 1937, thanks to Prezent. In subsequent years and until recently, quotations from these articles have been reproduced by various authors dozens of times, but in versions advanced by Prezent. The quotations were cited to instill fear in the readers, for purposes of demagoguery, and to illustrate "racist," "man-hating," "arch-reactionary," "delirious," and "fascistic" views of Kol'tsov. This was needlessly done so often that Kol'tsov's concepts and "man-hating" became practically synonymous. Even nineteen years after his death, Kol'tsov's name continued to be defamed. Thus the famous article, "On agrobiological science and false positions of the *Botanichesky Zhurnal*," published on December 14, 1958, in the central press, said: "Every Soviet man who knows of the achievements of Michurin agrobiology must be indignant because the *Botanichesky Zhurnal* includes in the glorious ranks of outstanding Soviet scientists who have made great contributions to materialistic biology men who gave little to our science. Among them, for instance, is Kol'tsov. It is pertinent to ask what contribution was made by this shameless reactionary, known for his delirious theory advocating 'improvement of mankind.' "[8]

Meanwhile a study of the cited works of Kol'tsov in the original (not an easy task since the *Russky Evgenichesky Zhurnal* has been removed from libraries) clearly shows that Prezent and the other writers mentioned had deliberately distorted and falsified the sense of Kol'tsov's eugenical writings. Thus Prezent draws attention to Kol'tsov's statement regarding the possibility of breeding human races according to Mendelian laws.[9] Yet he conceals the fact that Kol'tsov said this in a science-fiction reference, as a theoretical possibility that Martians might use if they conquered the earth, and proved to be creatures of a higher order than man, who viewed earthmen as domestic animals (in the spirit of Wells' *War of the Worlds*). Kol'tsov referred to these purely fantastic considerations merely to illustrate the obvious fact that, from the standpoint of heredity, man as a living being is subject to the same laws as the rest of the animal kingdom.

Prezent's designation of Kol'tsov as a racist stems from a statement by the latter that it is possible there will be parties or groups propagandizing genetic differentiation of mankind into intellectuals, laborers, artists, etc. "Yes," exclaims Prezent, "there are such parties in the shape of German fascism." Yet Kol'tsov in the next sentences said that such a way is contrary to the socialist ideal, which demands a harmonious combination of capacities.

In these and other eugenical writings of Kol'tsov there are many erroneous and outdated statements. But there is nothing of man-hating in them. Beyond that, Kol'tsov, as a eugenicist, was the first in the U.S.S.R. to begin very important investigations in medical genetics and to make a number of remarkable discoveries on the inheritance of blood diseases. These studies are an important contribution to medicine and biology. It should also be noted that the *Russky Evgenichesky Zhurnal*, despite some articles of an unhappy nature, had a very progressive tendency. It was one of the first journals on human genetics in the world, and in it were first described dozens of previously unknown hereditary diseases. Medical genetics has since investigated hundreds of genetically transmitted pathological conditions, yet in the U.S.S.R. studies on human genetics were virtually completely stopped. (The first book in Russian on human genetics was not published until 1964.)

In connection with the arrest of the foremost medical geneticist, Levit, and of his co-workers, the Medico-Genetical Institute was shut down. The virtual ban on investigations in human genetics had very harmful consequences, not yet fully understood nor assessed. The direct responsibility for this lies with those "critics" who vulgarly identified human genetics with racism and fascism. A fatal role in this was also played by some philosophers, in particular Kol'man, who published a pogrom article under the title, "The Black-Hundred delirium of fascism and our medico-biological science."[10] Glushchenko also always made sharp attacks on human genetics.

Kol'tsov fortunately was not arrested, but the witch hunt against him had a clearly provocative and slanderous character. The many years of hounding hastened the death of this scientist who, toward the end of his life, lost the institute created by him, his journal, and his good name, which he greatly valued and which must, without fail, be restored to him.

KOL'TSOV, SCIENTIST AND PATRIOT

Kol'tsov died in 1940, and in the following years, as we have seen, the Lysenkoites did their best to defame him and bury in oblivion his name and his truly enormous contribution to the development of Soviet biology. But among the numerous slanderous articles, which continued after Kol'tsov's death, when Lysenko and his entourage occupied all the key positions in the agricultural sciences, a brilliant article devoted to his memory is to be found. Written by Astaurov, Kol'tsov's pupil and friend, and filled with almost inexpressible grief, it illustrates brilliantly and convincingly Kol'tsov's attractive moral makeup and life history. Only a courageous man of high principles would have published such an article, and Astaurov, himself, was later to walk a difficult path.

"Kol'tsov," wrote Astaurov, "was one of the most progressive professors of Tsarist Russia. His great popularity with students was due not only to the brilliance of his gifts as a lecturer, his deep humanity, love of youth, and invariable readiness to help meet the needs of students, but also to the fact that students saw in him an implacable foe of all stagnation, red tape, routine, and obscurantism. From his pen came the book, *To the Memory of the Fallen*, dedicated to the student victims of the bloody events of 1905. The book appeared on the day of the opening of the First Duma and was immediately confiscated."[11]

This book, published by Kol'tsov in 1906 at his own expense, was indeed confiscated and destroyed by the censors. But some copies have been preserved to the present time.[12] It was with deep emotion that I turned over its pages. Some professional revolutionaries could rightfully envy the boldness and revolutionary ideology of its author. On the title page, below Kol'tsov's name and designation of assistant professor of Moscow University, appears the following:

To the Memory of the Fallen

Victims among Moscow students of the October and December days. The income from this edition is designated for committees in the aid of the imprisoned and amnestied.

On the second page the list of the thirty-six fallen students appears, framed in black. The one hundred pages of the book contain an accurately documented description of the brutalities of the Tsarist autocracy in suppressing the uprising of 1905. The following quotation will illustrate:

"Do not weep over the dead bodies of the fallen fighters." Were the students who fell victims to the October and December days fighters? If the student Volkov, torn to pieces in church for protesting a pogrom-inciting sermon, who sold his life dearly when surrounded by soldiers, was a fighter, then the students Lopatin, Grigor'ev, and others were first of all martyrs. They were killed because they were students and therefore stood for freedom. They were killed for beliefs and convictions attributed to all students, which, indeed, practically without exception, they do hold.

"Do not weep over the dead bodies of the fallen fighters!" Yes! There is no need to weep, or rather there is a need not to weep! The memory of these fighter-martyrs can be befittingly honored only by continuing the cause they believed in and died for, the cause of liberation of Russia.

And this was written in 1906, at the height of reaction, when Russia was covered with gallows. It was written by a man who, in 1937, was unjustly labeled a "reactionary" and a "man-hater," labels which were posthumously kept in the official press until very recently. However much calumny and dirt came from the pens of the same people who also blackened the bright name of Vavilov and his comrades-in-arms, Soviet scientists will not forget the name of Kol'tsov, his brilliant discoveries, his honesty and steadfastness, and his struggle for the development of Soviet science.[13]

CHAPTER 5

The Agronomy Debate of 1935-1938

VIL'YAMS AND LYSENKO

THE COMPLETE domination of genetics, breeding, and agrobiology by Lysenkoism was inseparable from an analogous process in agronomy, where the ideas of Academician Vil'yams were established in supremacy. The two scientific schools were always closely linked. In 1936 and 1937, during the debates on breeding and genetics at the LAAAS sessions, special messages from Vil'yams were read. In them he emphasized the parallel between his fight against his "anti-grassland" opponents and Lysenko's struggle against "reactionary" trends in genetics. The support was reciprocated, and after Vil'yams' death in 1939 he was canonized as one of the holy founders of the unified materialistic agrobiology. For illustration, Lysenko himself may be quoted:

The teachings of Michurin and the teachings of Vil'yams are different aspects of one materialistic biology dealing with theoretical problems of agronomic science and with practice. Therefore these teachings, ignored, not recognized by the old idealistic, reactionary biology, under conditions of Soviet agriculture became the basis of our agronomy, and fused into a single agrobiological science. . . . Contrary to the reactionary theory of decreasing soil fertility, Vil'yams' doctrine of soil development and its basic feature of fertility, which reflect correctly, from the dialectic viewpoint, the laws of soil development, gave agronomy the possibility of restoring and improving fertility conditions. This doctrine is the theoretical biological foundation of the grassland system of agriculture.[1]

Now our agricultural science is counting up the sad results of the unchallenged position of Vil'yams' system in agriculture. And at the same time the demagoguery and repressions by which the system forced its acceptance in 1933–1937 are being revealed.

It may be appropriate to give some examples of the methods whereby Vil'yams' supporters attempted, in 1935–1937, to force nationwide acceptance of the grassland system, although it was never subjected to experimental tests before or after its adoption. The Vil'yams system was based entirely on unsubstantiated, abstract speculations in soil science, which at that time were questioned by the majority of our soil scientists.

Vil'yams took a negative view of any attempt at experimental comparisons of his system with any other types of crop rotation. An episode described in the newspaper *Belgorodskaya Pravda*[2] is characteristic. A conversation between Ponedel'nikov and Vil'yams regarding the setting up of an experiment to compare the grassland with the intertillage system is cited: "Vil'yams asked, 'Why do you need intertillage rotation?' Ponedel'nikov replied: 'For comparison, to see which is better.' 'You know,' replied Vil'yams instantly, 'when Lenin was establishing the Soviet regime in Russia, he did not agree to leave on the Ukraine the hetman Skoropadsky[3] in order to compare which regime is better.' "

Long before Prezent and other members of the Lysenko group, Vil'yams took the route of making slanderous accusations of sabotage against his scientific opponents, and of eulogizing himself as the only representative and interpreter of correct methods of socialist agriculture. Labeling his opponents "anti-grasslanders," he attempted to give this term a sinister connotation that was, at the time, equivalent to "anti-Marxist." He wrote:

The grassland system is a historical necessity for socialist agriculture. Only this system can ensure the further flowering of collective and state farms. That is why it has received both impudently open and artfully concealed opposition from the so-called anti-grasslanders. Under cover of pseudoscientific expressions by the "min-

eral agricultural chemists," a battle against the grassland system
was mounted by the enemies of the people, who infiltrated into
agricultural administrative organs.[4]

Such sharp polemic with "mineral" and "formalist-deduc-
tive" agricultural chemists (under which classification Pryanishnikov's followers were understood to fall) Vil'yams
passed off as a manifestation of revolutionary proletarian
vigilance.

Several noted scientists lost their heads (literally) in the
dispute with Vil'yams in the early thirties, a circumstance for
which Vil'yams received credit, rather than blame, for a long
time. Thus as early as 1935, in connection with Vil'yams'
fifty-year jubilee as a scientist, his pupils Avaev and Zheltikov
wrote:

The enemies of the proletarian state (Doyarenko, Vol'f, Kovarsky,
Rudnev, and others) burned with class hatred against Vil'yams.
They understood that the bolshevik scientist, Vil'yams, better than
anyone else, was able to expose their wrecking machinations in
agronomy. That is why one of them [Vol'f] tried with the stroke
of a pen to wipe out the works of Vil'yams—unsurpassed in soil
science and agricultural technology—proclaiming them to be anti-
Marxist and unacceptable in a socialist structure. These features
clearly show that the scientific front is the front of class struggle:
Vil'yams' position on this front is that of a bolshevik scientist with
inherent revolutionary vigilance.[5]

Having removed their basic opponents at the beginning
of the thirties, the Vil'yamsists supposed that the way was
cleared for adoption of their grassland system. According to
their unsupported promises the crop yields then would be
increased at a fabulous tempo, even without substantial development of the fertilizer industry. Vil'yams did not dissipate
his talents on trifles: he promised collective farms yields of
80 to 100 centners per hectare as a minimum result of using
the grassland system.

VIL'YAMSISM[6]

In 1937 the grassland system reached the level of a state problem, and the first draft of a law to adopt it throughout the country was prepared. A brief note on the features of the Vil'yams system may not be amiss.

Without any factual basis, Vil'yams considered fine-textured, lumpy soil to be the only kind that is fertile, and soil texture to be the most important factor for good crops. According to him, a soil with indiscernible horizons or a weak profile could not produce good yields even with added fertilizers and adequate irrigation. Hence Vil'yams considered it useless to fertilize that type of soil, which, according to him, constituted most of the tilled land in the country.

His claim that, merely by including in the rotation a 30 to 40 per cent mixture of legumes and cereal grasses (for induction and maintenance of soil texture), yields could be increased tenfold was pure fantasy: behind those figures there were no experiments, no data. They were arrived at from abstract consideration of water-holding capacities of different kinds of soils. And yet there were people who believed him and oriented the whole of the country's agriculture along this unscientific and irresponsible path.

The foregoing illustrates the essence of the differences between the Vil'yams and Pryanishnikov schools. The latter insisted on the development of mineral fertilizers, one-year planting of clover without cereal grass admixture (thus improving the nitrogen balance of the soil), and the intensification of agriculture by introduction of high-yielding varieties in the rotation, as was done in Western Europe. This method had historical and practical foundations, backed by extensive factual material from experiments and experience. Pryanishnikov insistently pointed out that the development of chemical industry and chemical fertilizers was highly important for

the defense needs of the country. (For example, superphosphate production results in production of sulfuric acid;
thus the manufacture of nitrates and explosives is based on
the same technology.)[7]

Vil'yams, on the other hand, proposed not to develop the
fertilizer industry; to expand clover planting to two to three
years running, and only in mixtures with timothy and other
cereal grasses (thereby reducing the nitrogen-fixing effect of
clover); and to reject the use of various agricultural equipment (for instance, harrows and cultivators), which allegedly
destroyed soil texture.

Other differences between the two men were apparent.
Pryanishnikov's path was that of a real scientist and patriot.
Vil'yams, on the other hand, was a cabinet theorizer, dreamer,
and fanatic who, under cover of loud phrases about the
fatherland and socialism, concealed the aim of establishing the
supremacy of his own ideas in science and in practice by all
available means. His supporters followed the same road.

It should be noted that, potentially, Vil'yams was an outstanding scientist. A physical ailment, partial paralysis, from
which he suffered for twenty years, left a deep mark on the
development of his scientific activities and on his psychology.
Because of it, Vil'yams was confined to a small plot of ground
near his house, which was located next to the TAA department of soil science, of which he was the head. His ailment
made it impossible for him to conduct laboratory and field
experiments, turned him into a sermonizer, and removed his
thoughts from reality without, however, removing his megalomania and the desire to command. In addition, he was highly
uncritical of people, so that, while Pryanishnikov assembled
a galaxy of real scientists, Vil'yams collected about him opportunists, toadies, and dogmatists capable of anything but
serious scientific work. In the last years of his life—that is,
precisely the years dealt with in this narrative—his physical
condition deteriorated to the extent that he was no longer

responsible for his actions and for what appeared under his name. The opportunists in his entourage took advantage of this fact.

ENEMIES OF THE PEOPLE

How, then, did Vil'yams advance his system? How did he succeed in overcoming the resistance of his opponents? How was he able to hypnotize the planning organs into accepting on faith his fantastic promises of 100 to 160 centners per hectare yields of wheat merely from decomposition of roots of perennial cereals? Some think the answer lay in some magic properties of Vil'yams' personality, his skill in speaking and writing, his ability to charm, and his charismatic appeal to youth. This was perhaps true in part. But behind the dialectic facade of his theories lay concealed their intellectual bankruptcy; behind his apparent use of dialectics lay demagoguery; and his aspiration to set hearts on fire was combined with a calculating talent for slandering, discrediting, and defaming his scientific opponents. Vil'yams and his school were people who knew how to exploit the tragic atmosphere of the reigning personality cult for their own ends. Some typical examples will illustrate the nature of the struggle between Vil'yamsists and the proponents of scientific, rational agriculture.

First of all, in connection with the discussion of projects for introduction of correct rotation systems, which opened in 1937, Vil'yams applied pressure on the Department of Crop Rotation of the Commissariat of Agriculture, already shaken by unceasing arrests. (In 1937 two successive commissars of agriculture, Chernov and Eikhe, were arrested.) Vil'yams wrote:

The men now heading the planning of crop rotation in the U.S.S.R. Commissariat of Agriculture either do not understand or for a long time would not see all the fallacy of the postulates behind the plan advanced, not by them, but by the saboteur Vol'f. They covered up the obviously harmful and, on his part, the deliberately destructive activity by the indisputably correct government directive regarding the unsoundness of decreasing the acreage of cereal crops.[8]

In the same year (1937), Vil'yamsists moved against the Pryanishnikov school by accusing a group of his pupils of sabotage. Twelve men from the All-Union Institute of Fertilizers, established on Pryanishnikov's initiative, were arrested, including the director, Zaporozhets. They all were later rehabilitated. A Vil'yams supporter, Usachev, was appointed to the directorship. At an LAAAS meeting he boasted that in the institute "twelve enemies of the people, occupying leading posts, have been exposed." Usachev exclaimed: "And what did we do to liquidate the consequence of sabotage? We unmasked and continue to unmask newer and newer roots of sabotage, we exposed the Trotskyites Sigarkin, Dikussar, and others."[9]

This was not the end of the attack on Pryanishnikov's school. Several months later the issue of sabotage in agricultural chemistry was dredged up again by another Vil'yams follower, Lyashchenko. This slanderer was able to publish a remarkable article in the central press in which the most useful practice of preparing soil maps was denounced as a wrecking activity. Lyashchenko wrote of the Fertilizer Institute:

For a long time a group of enemies of the people operated in the institute. . . . These, if you will forgive the expression, "agricultural chemists" undertook to work out the methodology of map making. Yearning for a kulak economy where from time immemorial they had conducted experiments on fertilizers, these latter-day "agricultural chemists" used all possible means to turn soil maps into a brake against raising yields. . . . The enemies of the people operating in the institute were unmasked and rendered harmless. . . . But sabotage in this area is not yet weeded out. The

Commissariat, the LAAAS, and the Fertilizer Institute do nothing to crush the nests of enemies.[10]

Lyashchenko's article occasioned a plenary discussion of soil maps by the LAAAS section of agricultural chemistry and soil science. In a series of anonymous accounts we read:

The conduct of the chairman of the session, Pryanishnikov, was surprising. Every time a comrade went beyond the framework of purely technical matters and touched on the wrecking activities of the enemies of the people . . . , the chairman would interrupt him.

The plenary session condemned the speech and the behavior of Pryanishnikov at the meeting as being unworthy of a Soviet scientist.[11]

Several months later, the newspaper that had carried these accounts once more favored Pryanishnikov with attention. In an article entitled "Mercilessly to uproot the enemies and their riff-raff from scientific establishments," it said:

The last plenary session . . . provides an example of the attitude of some academicians toward the problem of liquidating the consequences of sabotage. The scientific community remembers that the chairman, Pryanishnikov, openly declared: "It is not the business of the Academy to occupy itself with consequences of sabotage; that is the prerogative of other organs." And the Academy praesidium never even discussed this revolting fact.[12]

The decision of the plenary session was to accept Vil'yams' proposals. They were rather original. The work of map making was to be continued, but the designation was to be changed from soil-agronomic to plain soil maps. Since then, and in fact until recently, soil maps prepared for collective farms gave attention not so much to the nutrient contents of the soil, but to morphological descriptions and characterization of soil texture. Such maps hung in offices of chairmen of collective farms primarily as decorations.

That this kind of dirty slander, which cost the lives of a

number of the workers in the institute, came ultimately from
Vil'yams may be deduced from an informative article published in 1938. Repeating the fabrications about sabotage by
enemies of the people in the institute and about the LAAAS
praesidium's letting the work of wreckers slip by, the article
quotes Vil'yams on the preparation of soil maps as bases for
introduction of the grassland system.[13] It should be noted that
Vil'yams never stinted his unfounded accusations even outside the areas of soil science or agriculture. He was ever
ready to do his bit in the genetics debate, also, without having
even the vaguest notions about the subject under dispute. This
is readily seen from Dvoryankin's article in the newspaper
Timiryazevka, which gives the following details about
Lysenko's visit to the Timiryazev Academy:

> After a chat with comrade Kolesnev, Lysenko visited Vil'yams
> and thanked him for his letter to the session of the Agricultural
> Academy, in which Vil'yams had warmly supported Lysenko's
> theoretical concepts. The friendly talk of the two outstanding
> scientists continued for half an hour. Vil'yams said that he decided
> to send his letter because the controversy on breeding had inten-
> sified not by chance, but as a reflection of the class struggle in
> science. And also, in science, a foe does not retreat from his
> position without giving battle.[14]

As we have seen, Pryanishnikov's school suffered severe
losses in the dispute with Vil'yams in 1936–1937. But despite
these losses it maintained itself and its scientific convictions.
This, the country's foremost agronomic school, was once
more shattered after the death of its founder when, at the
end of 1948, the LAAAS August session gave the full go-
ahead signal to the grassland system. But even then, though
thinned out, the ranks of Pryanishnikov's school did not
waver. He was the founder of Soviet agricultural chemistry
which, as a science, could not have been abolished. There is
not an agricultural chemist in our land who was not brought
up on the classical work of this leading figure in science, a

man with an extraordinary range of interests who made a great contribution not only to agricultural chemistry, but also to biochemistry, plant physiology, agronomy, and plant breeding. He was indeed a genuine progressive scientist, a patriot, and a faithful son of the Russian people.

PRYANISHNIKOV AND VAVILOV

During his long life, Pryanishnikov traveled far and wide in our country. He also went abroad on twenty-five missions, and knew world agriculture from more than just books. Despite the opposition of Vil'yams and his followers, he did much for his country and people and left a rich scientific legacy. Over the years, respect for the memory and labors of this great man grows. He was a courageous fighter for real science, but he was too noble to substitute provocation and intrigue for open struggle. He was defenseless against baseness, and lived through many bitter years, observing the tragedy of Soviet biology and agronomy.

Vavilov, whose fate has already been recounted, was a student of Pryanishnikov's, and they were very fond of each other. Vavilov's arrest shook Pryanishnikov profoundly. Not believing Vavilov guilty in any way, Pryanishnikov obtained an audience with Beria, then the Commissar of Internal Affairs, and energetically petitioned for Vavilov's freedom, offering guarantees of his patriotism and innocence. But Beria turned down the request. After that, Pryanishnikov, together with Vavilov's well-known physicist brother Sergey,[15] obtained an audience with deputy premier Molotov and requested a review of the case and Vavilov's rehabilitation. After being refused, they again appealed to Beria and Molotov for improvements in Vavilov's prison regimen, so that, even though imprisoned, he could continue his scientific work.

In 1941, at the beginning of the war, when Vavilov was already in confinement, Pryanishnikov, who had been evac-

uated, sent a completely unexpected telegram to the Committee on Stalin prizes, nominating Vavilov for a prize for
his creation of the collection of world plants. This noble act
was one of desperation and sorrow, embodying Pryanishnikov's courage in the struggle against arbitrary rule.

VIL'YAMS AND TULAIKOV

Another important agronomic school which opposed Vil'yams
in 1936–1937 was that of the noted scientist Tulaikov, the
organizer and first leader of the All-Union Cereal Institute
in Saratov. Tulaikov was arrested in 1937, and perished because of his opposition to Vil'yams. In the custom of the day,
"Tulaikovites" became a synonym for "enemies of the people"
and was used to achieve the complete annihilation of his
progressive agronomic center.

In the thirty-seven years of his scientific life (1900–1937),
Tulaikov published over four hundred scientific works in the
broad areas covering the agricultural problems of our country.
He clearly showed that Vil'yams' hypothesis greatly exaggerated the role of soil structure in the retention of moisture
and similarly exaggerated the role of perennial grasses in the
development of soil texture. Tulaikov particularly emphasized
their uselessness in drought zones; he insisted on specialization
of farms and on increases in corn planting in the southern regions. He also spoke sharply against substitution, in the
U.S.S.R., of spring wheats for winter varieties, a practice
which had lowered yields because of moisture deficits in the
second half of the summer. Tulaikov also clearly showed up
the scientific falsifications in the works of Vil'yams and his
followers.

In 1962 the newspaper *Sel'skaya Zhizn'* characterized Tulaikov's struggle against the grassland system as follows:

The communist scientist was a courageous fighter in science. He
attempted to defend the progressive methods of agriculture against

banality and dogmatism. The combat with the grasslanders was heated and severe. But his struggle against the faulty grassland system was an unequal one. The scientist became a victim of arbitrary decisions and perished. Only the exposure of the personality cult and the restoration of Lenin's standards of party life allowed the removal from the honest name of the scientist the infamous label of "enemy of the people."[16]

Although Tulaikov perished in the fight against Vil'yams' system, Vil'yams apparently cannot be personally accused of his death. The immediate cause of the annihilation of Tulaikov's school was an article by Stoletov, "Against foreign theories in agronomy," published in the central press on April 11, 1937. In it Stoletov attacked two of Tulaikov's books in which correct ideas on the agricultural development of our country were advanced. In an unobjective and demagogic fashion, Stoletov evaluated those ideas and presented a series of unfounded, foolish accusations. Such "vigilance," concocted out of whole cloth and very characteristic of persons who turned the 1937 tragedy to their own advantage, played a sad role in the fate of a fine scientist.

Stoletov's article was reprinted in the regional Saratov newspaper, *Kommunist*,[17] and a joint meeting of a number of institutes was convened that very day for discussion of it. The next day the same newspaper carried a brief note about the meeting, including the sentence: "Those present were legitimately perplexed by Tulaikov's absence from the meeting." And, indeed, Tulaikov, to whom the article was a complete surprise, had not gone to the meeting because he sensed its pogrom aims. Unlike the geneticists, he was still not used to being hounded, and considered himself a publicly respected man. Unfounded accusations were not yet commonplace to him.

Tulaikov's presentiments proved right. The meeting to discuss Stoletov's article turned into a sanctioned rout of Tulaikov's scientific school.[18]

A newspaper campaign against Tulaikov and his closest collaborators was started. In the summer of 1937, articles with such titles as "Prisoners of pseudoscientific theories," "Root out completely foreign theories in agronomy," "The Saratov hotbed of foreign theories" became common. By the end of the summer the label "wrecker" was sometimes attached to Tulaikov's name. The ominous expressions "Tulaikovism" and "Tulaikovites" made their appearance, signifying the exposing of a whole group and the arrests of others in addition to Tulaikov himself. Thus ended the scientific and public life of the communist scientist, Tulaikov. His physical death followed in 1938 in the Belomor camp.

Toward the end of 1937, Vil'yams was celebrating the "victory" of his grassland doctrine. His triumph was short-lived, for he died in 1939. But in the subsequent years the noisy clique of his pupils and followers took full advantage of the overblown cult of Vil'yams to secure for themselves dominant positions in many responsible posts. These men (Bushinsky, Chizhevsky, Dmitriev, Demidov, Avaev, and others), having contributed nothing either to science or to practice, lived off the exploitation of Vil'yams' unmerited glory.

The beginning of the war temporarily buried the grassland system. The country needed bread and not a specific soil structure with promises of phenomenal yields in eight to ten years. The country needed explosives, gunpowder, acids, all of which were to be provided by chemical industry, the development of which Vil'yams had opposed. He referred to this course as the "useless immobilization of people's billions," and "throwing money to the winds." Fortunately, in the State Planning Commission and in the Council of Commissars there were people who listened to Pryanishnikov's voice, so that by the beginning of the war we had more than a few fertilizer plants. They were rapidly set to work for the defense industry—a worthy contribution of Pryanishnikov's agricultural chemistry to the rout of German fascism.

By then, no one could bring himself to dispute the importance of the chemicalization of agriculture, and Vil'yams' magic system began to be forgotten in the war years. But the oblivion was temporary. After the war, the project was once more dragged into the light of day and forcibly spread through the whole territory of the Soviet Union. Once more Vil'yams' fame was blown up to fabulous proportions, and Pryanishnikov's school again declared reactionary. This happened in 1948, only a few months after the death of Pryanishnikov, who had spent a long and interesting life battling in the service of his people.

Part II

The New Phase: 1946-1962

CHAPTER 6

The Postwar Period

THE FAMOUS AUGUST, 1948, session of the LAAAS was for a long time sorrowfully designated the historical one. It did, indeed, become an event never to be forgotten in the history of science and mankind. It will remain in the annals of human history as an example not only of the senseless destruction of theoretical and practical achievements in biology, but also of the arbitrary and outrageous violation of scientists' convictions. This session will always be remembered as an event which delayed, by many years, the development of agriculture in our fatherland at the whim of a group of ignoramuses.

Immediately after the session, hundreds of scientists, the best and most qualified representatives of Soviet biology, were either dismissed or demoted on the basis of fabricated, slanderous, and perverted accusations of idealism, reactionary views, Morganism, Weismannism, complicity with imperialism and the bourgeoisie, Mendelism, anti-Michurinism, groveling before the West, sabotage, metaphysics, mechanism, racism, cosmopolitanism, formalism, unproductiveness, anti-Marxism, anti-Darwinism, alienation from practice, and the like. In reality these scientists were guilty of one thing only: they did not always, and in everything, agree with the ideas and hypotheses advanced by Lysenko, Prezent, Glushchenko, Ol'shansky, Stoletov, and other members of that group.

Simultaneously, and in the same connection, the opponents of Vil'yams' grassland system were also being dismissed. (Later—1950–1952—still other repressions were imposed on those disagreeing with the concepts of Lepeshinskaya and against the so-called "anti-Pavlovians," a term especially coined for convenience in making accusations.)

The nonsensical anticytological concepts of Lepeshinskaya —revealing an ignorance of even elementary methodology— were declared a basis for Michurin biology, and all criticism of them was banned for several years. The teachings of the great physiologist, Pavlov, were, of course, considered correct, but they by this time had become hypertrophied to the point of absurdity. In this period, persecutions of all those of a different mind, who were denounced as idealists, copied the pogrom methods of the August session of the LAAAS. Such prominent Soviet scientists as Orbeli, Anokhin, Beritashvili, and many others were baited as "anti-Pavlovians" and idealists, and for many years were deprived of normal opportunities to carry on scientific work.

Many excellent genetical, cytological, and physiological laboratories of the country were shut down during this period. The scientific and political prestige of our fatherland, and the immortal cause of socialism suffered greatly from these senseless persecutions. The bourgeois press was provided with material for anti-Soviet propaganda. But most important was the damage to agriculture, medicine, and many branches of the national economy. The extent of the damage is now becoming clear, but the causes are not always understood, and the repair is sometimes entrusted to the very people originally responsible for the harm.

REVIVAL OF THE DEBATE

The events described in the preceding chapters were interrupted by the war. Theoretical arguments were forgotten for a time, to be renewed in 1945–1946 in connection with the publication of an unconvincing article by Lysenko on the absence of intraspecific competition—always one of the cornerstones of Darwinism. Publication of this article broadened the sphere of Lysenkoism and brought it into conflict with the interests of other scientific groups (botanists, morphologists, zoologists, evolutionists), which immediately came forward with critiques of Lysenko's new ideas.

This writer, then a student of the TAA in the Department of Botany (under Professor Zhukovsky), witnessed one characteristic episode at the beginning of this discussion. On November 5, 1945, Lysenko first gave his paper, which denied the existence of intraspecific competition among plants and animals in nature, at a course for workers in state breeding stations. His confidence in the soundness of his argument was so strong that he summoned Zhukovsky and asked him to criticize the unpublished manuscript. Lysenko promised Zhukovsky that he would publish his critical comments alongside the article in the journal *Agrobiologiya*, which he edited. Zhukovsky, a distinguished botanist, a scientist of encyclopedic knowledge, a pupil and comrade-in-arms of Vavilov, accepted Lysenko's challenge in good faith. We young students hotly debated Zhukovsky's manuscript, which he read to us before passing it on to Lysenko. The article contained a solid and convincing criticism of Lysenko's concept; it was interesting, logical, and brilliant.

On reading the article, which he, himself, had originally asked for, Lysenko became enraged and categorically refused to print it in his journal, meanwhile publishing his own article without change or corrections. Zhukovsky decided not to yield, and published his critique in 1946 in the journal *Selektsiya i Semenovodstvo* under the title "Darwinism in a distorting mirror." In reply, a rude and demagogic article by Lysenko, entitled "Do not get into another one's sledge," appeared in *Pravda*. Not only was the title tactless and stupid, but the content was also senseless and malicious. Zhukovsky's counter-reply, submitted to several journals, was not published.

The same journal that published Zhukovsky's original critique also printed an article by Dvoryankin, one of Lysenko's active collaborators, entitled "Darwinism in the Mendelian mirror."[1] Its content was superficial, and consisted mainly of abuse. Some time later, Lysenko once more appeared in *Agrobiologiya* with an article under the heading "Of the distorting mirror and some anti-Darwinians."

Before the polemic, Lysenko's attitude toward Zhukovsky had been rather favorable. But the apt title of Zhukovsky's polemical article apparently wounded the self-esteem of the Lysenkoites. From that moment the persecution of Zhukovsky started. For his defense of Darwinism he was now ranked with the anti-Darwinians and Morganist-Mendelists, although he was an experimental botanist, an expert on cultivated plants, and at the time had no direct connection with genetics.

The beginning of the new debates also changed my personal notions about Lysenko. Up to then, not really knowing genetics, I had viewed the controvery in genetics and Darwinism as a real scientific debate in which, as it appeared to me, both sides deserved respect. But, watching the renewal of the discussion on Darwinism, I understood that the main aim of Lysenko and his followers was anything but elucidation of scientific truth.

The discussion of Darwinism caught the attention of many scientists. It soon became apparent that the position of Lysenko and his followers was weak, far-fetched, and based on few facts. It really bordered on utter falsification of science. It also became clear that neither Lysenko nor his supporters were possessed of sufficient erudition to carry on the debate at the level of serious science.

And then Lysenko once more broke loose with demagoguery and political blackmail, branding everybody who disagreed with his hypothesis as defenders of imperialism. In 1947, in the *Literaturnaya Gazeta*, he published an absurd article which read, in part:

How to explain why bourgeois biology values so highly the "theory" of intraspecific competition? Because it must justify the fact that, in the capitalist society, the great majority of people, in a period of overproduction of material goods, lives poorly.

All mankind belongs to one biological species. Hence, bourgeois science had to invent intraspecific struggle. In nature, they say, within each species there is a cruel struggle for food, which is in short supply, and for living conditions. The stronger, better-adapted individuals are the victors. The same, then, occurs among people: the capitalists have millions, the workers live in poverty, because the capitalists supposedly are more intelligent and more able because of their heredity.

We Soviet people know well that the oppression of the workers, the dominance of the capitalist class, and imperialistic wars have nothing to do with any biological laws. They are all based on the laws of a rotting, moribund, bourgeois, capitalist society.

There is no intraspecific competition in nature. There is only competition between species: the wolf eats the hare; the hare does not eat another hare, it eats grass. Wheat does not hamper wheat. But couchgrass, goose-foot, pastor's lettuce are all members of other species, and when they appear among wheat or kok-sagyz [Russian dandelion], they take away the latter's food, and struggle against them.

Bourgeois biology, by its very essence, because it is bourgeois, neither could nor can make any discoveries that have to be based on the absence of intraspecific competition, a principle it does not recognize. That is why American scientists could not adopt the practice of cluster sowing. They, servants of capitalism, need not struggle with the elements, with nature; they need an invented struggle between two kinds of wheat belonging to the same species. By means of the fabricated intraspecific competition, "the eternal laws of nature," they are attempting to justify the class struggle and the oppression, by white Americans, of Negroes. How can they admit absence of competition within a species?[2]

This thesis of Lysenko (from beginning to end a mixture of social and biological propositions and a deliberate distortion

Right: O. B. Lepeshinskaya.
Below: A. I. Oparin.

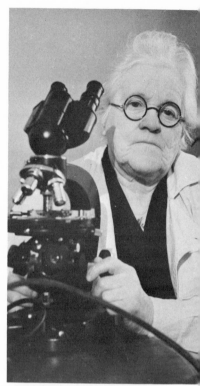

M. A. Ol'shansky

M. B. Mitin

Above: left, G. N. Shlykov; right, S. N. Shundenko.
Below: left, P. P. Lobanov; right, A. S. Musiyko.

of anti-Lysenko criticism for demagogic purposes) is essentially an accusation of Charles Darwin, the real author of the intraspecific competition concept.

Darwinism and genetics were peculiarly juxtaposed, by Prezent, with phases of capitalist development: "Capitalism, in its flourishing period at the crest of its culture, contributed the greatest creation of biological thought—a historical outlook of the organic world—Darwinism. Rotting capitalism, at the imperialist stage of development, gave birth to a stillborn bastard of biological science, the thoroughly metaphysical and antihistorical doctrine of formalist genetics."[3]

This stupid and vulgar demagoguery could not, of course, have scored a serious success; it only increased the opposition of the scientists. Young students manifestly did not support Lysenko at various discussions then held at universities. Particular interest was attracted to the conference on intraspecific competition organized by the biological faculty of Moscow University. It was held on November 4, 1947, in the largest University auditorium, which was filled to the rafters. Speeches were made by Shmal'gauzen, Formozov, and Sabinin, all of whom, in a well-reasoned, logical, and convincing way, demonstrated the complete unsoundness of Lysenko's concept. Not a single Lysenkoite present took part in the discussion despite the chairman's invitation.

Sabinin's speech was greeted with special enthusiasm. Brilliantly and graphically he proved the methodological unreliability of the single experiment on kok-sagyz carried out by a collaborator of Lysenko, which Lysenko had described in the article on "Natural selection and intraspecific competition."[4] All of his conclusions had been based on this particular experiment and on abstract theoretical arguments.[5]

Toward the end of 1947, events took a turn for the worse for Lysenko, the initiator of the Darwin discussion: his authority as a scientist was sharply undermined.

PREPARATION FOR THE
AUGUST, 1948, SESSION

Geneticists were gradually drawn into the Darwinian dispute. This was as it should be, since biology, and especially genetics, had developed abroad exceptionally rapidly after the war, particularly in the United States, and that development had been accompanied by impressive theoretical and practical achievements. Meanwhile Lysenko's concepts of heredity had not changed substantially during that period. It became apparent, shortly after the war, that Soviet science lagged behind that of the United States. It is well known that the party assigned to Soviet science a most important task, which was "to catch up and overcome the achievements of science beyond the confines of our fatherland." Every honest scientist wanted to contribute his share to the solution of this problem. It was only natural that the majority of Soviet biologists came to realize that monopoly and domination of Soviet science by a single group, especially one with dogmatic and demagogic tendencies,[6] were putting the brakes on our development and interfering with our overcoming the lag in Soviet science. With the obvious failure of Lysenko's highly advertised practical measures, scientists became disillusioned with his theoretical concepts. These measures included the planting of winter varieties on unplowed stubble in Siberia, which caused severe damage to Siberian agriculture and evoked sharp criticism in open discussion; vernalization of spring varieties in the south; intravarietal crossing; and late summer planting of sugar beets in Central Asia. The new variety of spring wheat developed for the southern Ukraine by super high-speed methods, and prematurely trumpeted about by Lysenko throughout the land, also turned out to be worthless. (See Chapter 8.)

All the fireworks which, for a long time, had lighted the way of Lysenko and his group toward uncontested supremacy in biology and agronomy, had by 1948 practically fizzled out. Young Yuriy Zhdanov, son of A. Zhdanov, the Secretary of the CC, and at that time in charge of the department of science of the CC, came out against Lysenko in a number of speeches.[7] By then it was clear that the LAAAS, headed by Lysenko, was not functioning in a satisfactory way and had become Lysenko's personal bureaucracy. There had been no elections to the Academy since 1935, and Lysenko had no intention of holding any in a democratic manner, since the majority of members disapproved of the activities of the president.

Lysenko's hope of obtaining new governmental sanctions against geneticists and biologists who disagreed with him began long before August, 1948. In the middle of 1947 he sent a long memorandum to the elder Zhdanov, much of which later formed part of his report at the session. The memorandum in fact was an appeal for help, as may be seen from the following:

On numerous occasions and without foundation, it has been asserted that I have administratively suppressed contrary views in the interest of the scientific views I hold. I can assure you that the situation is exactly the opposite, and of this I can be accused. I was unable (through circumstances beyond my control) to utilize to a proper degree the rights given me by my position, for a greater development in science of the trend I lead and, at least to some extent, to hold back and restrict the scholastics and meta-physicians of the opposing tendency. Hence, in fact, it is the trend represented by the president which turns out to be suppressed, even though until now it always has received support from the leaders of the Government and the Party.

I am literally tormented by the fact that so far I have been unable to inform the Government and the Party about the situation in the biological and agricultural sciences in the country.[8]

This memorandum served to initiate the study, at a high level, of problems touching on the situation in biology. And the balance of the scale for a long time went against the trend "represented by the president."

Lysenko and his groups thus fell upon hard times. In the spring of 1948, Zhdanov raised the question of strengthening the leadership of LAAAS, which assumed Lysenko's dismissal as president. At one of the meetings of the organizational bureau of the CC, Zhdanov subjected Lysenko to severe criticism. Something very extraordinary was required to change the situation, a grandiose rout of the opposition sanctioned by Stalin himself. And this rout was brilliantly organized. It was precisely then that Lysenko and his partisans revived the false notion of class biology and of the necessity for radical, irreconcilable differences in principle between socialist and capitalist biologists. Naturally, Lysenko counted himself and his collaborators as true Soviet biologists, and assigned all his opponents to the ranks of reactionaries and preachers of bourgeois ideology.

Objectively, there cannot be two biologies, any more than there can be two physics, two chemistries, two astronomies. It is possible in social science, however, because there exist on earth two contrasting social systems, socialism and capitalism. But there is only one nature on earth, and biological and genetic phenomena of an organism are realized, studied, and comprehended in one way only, according to the logic of science, not according to one or another political current. Biology, then, is a single science with respect to methods, theories, and problems, although the results of scientific work are applied differently under different social systems. These are truisms of Marxism and of common sense, and they were consciously distorted by Lysenko and his supporters in order to suppress their opponents as well as any criticism of themselves.

It is also well known that at this time the relations between the U.S.S.R. and the United States had deteriorated sharply, and that a struggle, sanctioned by Stalin, was then being organized against "servility toward the West." Everything connected with the United States, Britain, and other capitalist countries was declared reactionary. Difficulties were even experienced in citing foreign authors in articles and books. At the same time, everything Russian, native, home-grown was lauded to the skies, sometimes to the detriment of historical truth. (The fight for priority of Russian and Soviet science is, of course, important if it is carried on intelligently and not used for inflaming passions.) This was the situation exploited by Lysenko, who declared genetics to be a tool of reactionary American imperialism. As we have seen, in 1936–1939, the racism of Hitler's fascism was used as just such a bugbear. Lysenko was able to reach Stalin with this absurd idea and to receive sanction for the organization, to the last detail, of the proposed rout.

The LAAAS session of 1948, with the principal address by Lysenko "On the situation in biological science," was no longer a scientific meeting: it was a one-sided political routing of opponents, which had nothing to do with the real problems of Soviet science and which was exceptionally harmful in its consequences. Its outcome had been predetermined when Lysenko's report had received prior approval of the Politbureau and of Stalin personally.

Let us first examine briefly the basic features of the immediate preparations for the session. Not having a majority among the members of the LAAAS, the last ones of which had been appointed in 1935, Lysenko could not count on a victory. Hence, using Stalin's support, which was based on false information, Lysenko succeeded in securing appointment to the LAAAS, by the U.S.S.R. Council of Ministers, of a large group of his supporters, without election. These appointments, from a list supplied by Lysenko, were made in secret without preliminary discussion of the candidates by the scientific community. This action reflected Lysenko's lack of confidence in Soviet scientists and the Soviet public. It is not superfluous to note that, shortly before Lysenko compiled his list, the Ministry of Agriculture did publish, in newspapers, an announcement of forthcoming elections to the LAAAS, and an invitation to the scientific community to nominate candidates. From the beginning of 1947 the newspaper *Sotszemledelie* began to publish lists of candidates, Academy committees on elections started to work, and the usual preelection activities began.

But Lysenko's nominees had no great success in the course of pre-electoral deliberations; their scientific contributions were considered very modest. In particular, the candidacy of Prezent was rejected. The noted plant breeder, Lisitsyn, in the course of the discussion, proposed Prezent's rejection on two counts: first, because Prezent's basic method of research consisted of citation, and second, because he used too many curses in scientific arguments. As a result of democratic discussions of the nominees, a group of the most meritorious ones was chosen to be presented as candidates at the general meeting of the Academy.

But there never was any voting, since Lysenko, heading off such an event, passed on to Stalin his own list, which had nothing in common with the one discussed by the scientific community. The list of thirty-five included Ol'shansky, Avakyan, Dolgushin, Varuntsyan, Prezent, Greben', Yakovlev, Vlasiuk, Lobanov, Bushinsky, Belen'ky, Demidov, and other Lysenko supporters.[9] Later, Bushinsky, in lecturing to his students, would relate how Stalin underlined his name with a red pencil before approving the list.

The appointment of a large group of Lysenko partisans before the LAAAS session was a rather strange act. Before 1935 there were no LAAAS academicians, nor did the Academy have a constitution. The first group of fifty-one academicians had been appointed by a resolution of the Council of

Commissars on June 4, 1935. At the same time a constitution, which provided for further election of academicians only by a secret ballot at a general meeting, was adopted. No elections were held for the next twelve years. Lysenko deliberately kept the vacancies open: he awaited an increase in the ranks of his supporters. By 1947, because of arrests and natural mortality, the number of academicians had dropped to seventeen. Elections became inevitable. On July 22, 1947, the Council of Ministers enacted a decree (No. 2632) over Stalin's signature authorizing election in October, 1947, of up to sixty full, and sixty corresponding, members of the LAAAS. The decree was not acted upon, for Lysenko could not ensure election of his supporters. On October 7, 1947, a new resolution by the Council of Ministers was passed, postponing the elections to November, 1947. Once more, no action was taken. Only on July 28, 1948, a few days before the opening of the August session, was the decree of the Council of Ministers, dated July 15, 1948, published, *appointing* thirty-five new academicians. But the decree could not by-pass completely the lists of candidates nominated by the scientific community, and previously published. Hence the resolution increased the total number of academicians to seventy-five. The additional vacancies thus created were to be filled by election in September, 1948, from the list of nominees.

But even this decree was not implemented. There were no elections until 1956, when Lysenko left the post of president, and then they were conducted by open balloting. As a result, even today the number of Lysenko partisans in the LAAAS is very high.

Several years after the August session, in connection with Stalin's death, Lysenko wrote that Stalin "personally edited the draft of the report 'On the situation in biological science,' explained to me in detail his corrections, and gave me instructions on delivery."[10] It is thus clear that Lysenko, long before the session, had asked Stalin to sanction the proposed rout of geneticists and other unlike-minded scientists. In fact, Lysenko kept the original text of his report, with Stalin's personal corrections, in his office and used to show it, or a photocopy, to visitors as a mark of royal favor.

THE LAAAS SESSION

The session which opened on July 31 in the U.S.S.R. Ministry of Agriculture Club was, as we have seen, properly prepared. The day after the opening the full text of the extensive report by Lysenko, crowding out other news, was published in all central newspapers. That is to say, the report had a circulation of 60 to 70 million, a figure which up to 1948 had been reached only by materials from government conferences and CEC plenary sessions.

The organization of the session and Lysenko's report called for watchfulness from the start: his opponents were literally compelled to speak at the meeting. It is also characteristic that Lysenko's sensational statement that Stalin had approved his report was saved for a curtain speech. All this bears witness to the fact that the August session was planned and carried out by Lysenko and his confederates not as a scientific discussion, but as a political maneuver for the rout and discrediting of the scientific opposition. This is also evident from the tone of the speeches of Lysenko's partisans, some of which are quoted below.

We are called on here to debate. We will not debate with Morganists, but continue to unmask them as representatives of a detrimental and ideologically foreign and essentially pseudoscientific trend imported from abroad.[11]

In the beginning of the thirties a struggle against menshevizing idealism developed in philosophy. This struggle was not confined to philosophy but touched on other branches of science, and biology in particular. There the struggle involved mainly genetics, since in this field menshevizing idealism found its most brilliant reflection. Recalling the questions around which the struggle revolved, it is easy to see that there is a direct connection between the fight over menshevizing idealism and the discussion of the work of Lysenko. The subsequent phase was a logical continuation of the fight against menshevizing idealism.[12]

The excessively prolonged discussion and the active propaganda of their views by Mendelists-Morganists are causing substantial damage to the ideological education of our cadres. The basic significance of the present session must be in the termination, at last, of this excessively protracted discussion, and of the unmasking and complete rout of the antiscientific concepts of Mendelists-Morganists, thereby creating the basis for further development of Michurinist research and further successes of the Michurinist trend in biology.

The long-term struggle between the two trends in biology has irrefutably demonstrated that the Mendel-Morgan trend in biology is a reactionary, antinational trend, and that it is impeding the further development of biological science and is causing great harm in practice to socialist agriculture.[13]

Stalin's participation in this affair was based on Lysenko's misinforming him about the real situation in biology. Lysenko's report was not a scientific one. He began by saying: "In the post-Darwin period the overwhelming majority of biologists, instead of further developing Darwinism, did all it could to vulgarize it and to stifle its scientific basis."[14] This thesis, as we know, completely negated a nearly eighty-year period of biological research.

The kernel of Lysenko's report was the absurd thesis that in the U.S.S.R. two diametrically opposed biologies existed: on the one hand, the materialistic Soviet, Michurinist; and on the other, the reactionary, idealistic, Weismannist-Mendelist, and metaphysical. The touchstone was the attitude of the scientist toward the chromosomal theory of heredity. Those who believed in it were declared to be reactionaries, idealists, and carriers of the bourgeois influence in Soviet science. Those who accepted, without qualification, the superficial and unconvincing concept of heredity developed by Lysenko were considered materialists, Michurinists, and representatives of progressive science.

The same absurd thesis was repeated at the session by all Lysenko supporters. Many of the orators exhibited a relapse toward the 1937 frame of mind. For example, Mitin, having discovered a statement in a book by Shmal'gauzen that "the cell nucleus is in a state of little mobile and relatively unstable equilibrium," came to the conclusion that Shmal'gauzen accepted the main categories of the "Bogdanov-Bukharin theory of equilibrium."[15] Examples of such vulgarization abound. A few typical illustrations of the statements made during this period, full of demagoguery, idle talk, and self-praise, follow:

Bourgeois genetics has become the fashionable "science" abroad, propagandizing "eugenics" and race politics. Weismannism-Morganism serves today in the arsenal of contemporary imperialism as a means for providing a "scientific base" for its reactionary politics.[16]

The Weismannist-Mendelist-Morganist current in biology is an antinational, pseudoscientific, deleterious current. It disarms practice and orients man toward resignation to the allegedly eternal laws of nature, toward passivity, toward an aimless search for hidden treasure and expectation of lucky accidents. The bourgeoisie is interested in promoting Weismannism, which assumes a political significance through eugenics and various race "theories." Weismannist (Mendelist-Morganist) genetics is a spawn of bourgeois society, which finds the recognition of the theory of development unprofitable because, from it, in connection with social phenomena, stems the inevitability of collapse of the bourgeoisie. Bourgeois society prefers the "theory" of immutability of the old, of appearance of something new only from recombination of the old or by happy chance. This "theory" leads to a passive contemplation of supposedly eternal phenomena of nature, to a passive expectation of accidental variation. That is why Mendelist-Morganist genetics is held in such great esteem in bourgeois countries. That is why this pseudoscience is such a useful tool in Hitler's hands for the promulgation of his monstrous racist theory.[17]

In 1950 Studitsky published an article on "Mendelist-Morganist genetics at the service of American racism." The subheadings in it are representative: "Mendelism-Morganism in defense of racial discrimination," "Morganist genetics against democracy," "Mendelist-Morganist genetics in defense of Malthusianism," "Morganist genetics and fascism." Studitsky, extracting all sorts of delirium from fascist propaganda archives, attempted to equate various obscurantists and fascists with Soviet scientists opposing Lysenko. His conclusions are characteristic:

The rout of the Mendelist-Morganist genetics at the historical session of the LAAAS had great international repercussions. The Mendelist-Morganist pseudoscience, an expression of senile decay and degradation of bourgeois culture, demonstrated its complete bankruptcy. At its roll call it could summon only the lie which reinforced its reactionary sermon on the immutability of heredity. In the light of the tremendous practical and theoretical achievement of progressive Michurinist science, it became completely evident that Mendelist-Morganist genetics has no right to claim to be a science. It became obvious that it owed its development to the interest taken in it by the forces of the international bourgeoisie.[18]

An analogous article by Studitsky was published in the popular journal *Ogonyok* accompanied by irrelevant illustrations of gallows, Ku Kluxers in hoods, etc. The American *Journal of Heredity*[19] reprinted this article in full, with illustrations, and exposed the distortion of quotations from the writings of American geneticists.

Many other supporters of Lysenko wrote in the same spirit. A few more examples follow:

The complete victory of Lysenko's teaching was marked in our days by the crushing ideological rout of the supporters of the reactionary, antiscientific, Weismannist-Mendelist-Morganist trend in biology. This was one of the victories of socialism, of communism over capitalism. The victory in the struggle against the remnants of bourgeois ideology of some scientists in our country was simultaneously a victory against the bourgeoisie in the international arena. The new Michurinist Soviet biology, born of the Soviet regime, exposes ideologically and supplants organizationally the hostile bourgeois Weismannist-Mendelist-Morganist tendency in biology in our land.[20]

In our country there are no longer mutually hostile classes. Yet the struggle of the idealists against dialectic materialists, depending on whose interests are being defended, still has the nature of class war. And, in fact, the followers of Virchow, Weismann, Mendel, and Morgan, talking of the immutability of the gene and denying the effect of the environment, are preachers of pseudoscientific tidings of bourgeois eugenicists and of various distortions in genetics, which provided the base for the racist theory of fascism in capitalistic countries. World War II was unleashed by imperialist forces whose arsenal also included racism.[21]

Weismannism is not a simple current in biology, but a purposeful antiscientific campaign against knowledge, organized and directed by the reactionary bourgeoisie. Hence any unprincipled concession to Weismannism is a concession to reaction. Weismannism was completely exposed in Lysenko's report and rejected out of hand as bourgeois reactionism in biology. The philosophical roots of Weismannism-Morganism cannot be separated from its class nature and its servile role. Weismannism as "physical" idealism is inseparable from Machism or idealism in general. They are all links in the same chain of ideological reactionism.[22]

The author of the last excerpt, who in 1951 found in bourgeois genetics features of all reactionary philosophy (racism, cosmopolitanism, sophism, scholasticism, Machism, idealism, Kantism, etc.) ten years later arrived at diametrically opposite conclusions:

Natural sciences are not part of the superstructure and hence are closer to production than to social sciences and aspects of social consciousness, such as morals, law, etc. Hence it would be wrong if we classified natural sciences on the same principle as we do social sciences, bourgeois and proletarian. The division of, for example, physics into bourgeois and proletarian, or of chemistry, biology, physiology, agronomy, and other branches of natural sciences, is not a Marxist approach. There is only one science of biology, physiology, physics, chemistry, the contents of which are independent of classes and class struggle. Natural science can serve, with its accumulation of facts and its objective laws, feudal, capitalist, or socialist systems.[23]

After the LAAAS session, vulgarization, demagoguery, and slander against Soviet geneticists filled both the scientific and the popular press. The attack extended beyond scientists themselves. Thus Molotov, in a 1948 speech on the 31st anniversary of the October Revolution, repeated and sanctioned the erroneous thesis of Lysenko. The Soviet geneticist Rapoport, well-known for his work with mutagens, which had been followed up in many countries, found himself in difficulties in connection with Molotov's speech. At the meeting of the party bureau he was requested to make a public repudiation of the chromosome theory of heredity. Rapoport attempted to demonstrate the practical value of genetics, but was refuted by quotations from Molotov's speech. "Why do you think that Molotov knows genetics better than I?" he replied. This answer became the grounds for Rapoport's expulsion from the Communist party and dismissal from his post. This leading scientist was then forced to work for several years as a laboratory assistant in a geological institute. At present he is working successfully on mutagens in an institute of chemical physics, but the events described affected his health very adversely.

The erroneous division of U.S.S.R. biologists into two camps and the classification of the proponents of the chromosome theory of heredity as reactionaries and preachers of idealism were spread in the most insistent way through all possible channels. This served as a smoke screen behind which the opponents of Lysenko and of Vil'yams were slaughtered whether they were geneticists, physiologists, morphologists, soil scientists, or medics.

THE CONSEQUENCES OF THE SESSION

Immediately after the LAAAS session analogous meetings were held in other institutions. The Academy of Sciences was the first convert to the new faith. A resolution of an expanded meeting of the AS praesidium supported without qualification the decisions reached at the LAAAS session, and decreed the abolition of a number of laboratories pronounced hotbeds of reactionary Morganism (the laboratories of cytogenetics, botanical cytology, phenogenesis, and others).[24] Then followed a meeting of the party organization of workers in higher education at which Kaftanov, the Minister of Higher Education, called for the country's university staffs to eradicate completely and most rapidly reactionary Morganism and its concrete carriers from institutions of higher learning.[25] Similar resolutions were adopted by the Academy of Medical Sciences.[26] Kaftanov's speech was reproduced as a pamphlet in an edition of 110,000.[27] This document was saturated with demagoguery and slander. Furthermore, Kaftanov and those who directed him were not satisfied with the baiting of living geneticists, but continued to vilify the prewar victims of the genetics discussion. "It is meet to recall," wrote Kaftanov, "the role played in our agrobiological science, by the notorious botanist-Morganist Vavilov, an ardent admirer of the reactionary doctrine of Bateson." Kaftanov also was especially zealous with regard to Kol'tsov. Falsifying, in the manner of Prezent, the sense of Kol'tsov's statements on human genetics made twenty-five years earlier, Kaftanov exclaimed: "There is no need to comment on these man-hating ravings that smell of fascist delirium a mile off. This is the kind of wild fanatic that our contemporary Morganist-Mendelists have for an apostle!" Kaftanov ridiculed the very idea that there are hereditary diseases in man—what kind of hereditary diseases, if you please, can there be in a progressive socialist society, among the leading builders of communism?

In some government departments, ministries, academies, and institutes, menacing orders were being issued, closing laboratories, and dismissing and condemning staff. Special commissions for searching out Morganist-Mendelists and for deciding their fates were created in the large biological and agricultural instructional and research institutions and experiment stations. They included emissaries of the LAAAS, secretaries of regional or city committees, practical agronomists, and the director of each particular institution. Nearly every scientist had to appear before such a commission and declare his attitude toward the new faith.

Within two days alone (August 23–24, 1948), Kaftanov issued a series of detailed orders published in pamphlet form and sent to every institution of higher learning. Order No. 1208 (August 23, 1948), regarding universities, decreed (point 2) the dismissal from Moscow University of those who actively fought against Michurinism, including the professor of Darwinism, Shmal'gauzen, the professor of developmental biology, M. M. Zavadovsky, the professor of plant physiology, Sabinin, the dean of the faculty, Yudintsev, and assistant professors Alikhanyan, Zelikman, Berman, and Shapiro. Similarly dismissed from Leningrad University were the pro-rector Polyansky, the dean of biological sciences, Lobashev,[28] professor Svetlov, and assistant professors Novikov and Arapet'yants. There followed similar lists for the universities of Kharkov, Gor'ky, Voronezh, Kiev, Saratov, and Tbilisi. But that was only the beginning.

Point 6 of the order read: "The Central University Administration and the Administration of Cadres are directed to review within two months all departments of biological faculties to free them from all opposed to Michurinist biology and to strengthen them by appointing Michurinists to them." The order abolished courses and directed the destruction of texts and of books based on Mendelism-Morganism (Sinnott and Dunn, Serebrovsky, Shmal'gauzen, etc.), and elimination of all non-Michurinist research projects.

On the same day, Kaftanov issued a similar order (No. 1210) for zootechnical and veterinary institutes, dismissing Rokitsky, Vasin, and many others, while a lengthy order on schools of agriculture decreed dismissal from the TAA alone of Golubev, Zhebrak, Paramonov, Khokhlov, Borisenko, Konstantinov, and others. This was followed by similar rosters for Kharkov, Omsk, Saratov, and other agricultural institutes.

The next day, still another order (No. 1216/525) from the Minister of Higher Education and the Deputy Minister of Public Health was sent around among the medical institutes. It decreed that such disciplines as anatomy, histology, pathophysiology, pathoanatomy, microbiology, psychopathology, forensic medicine, and psychiatry were to shift to a Michurinist basis.

It would have been ridiculous, of course, to include anything from Michurin and Lysenko in those disciplines; in effect what was done was to eliminate from those courses any references to heredity. Again, lists of dismissed scientists and withdrawn textbooks followed The wave of pogrom orders and decrees continued for several months.

Having come to power, the Lysenkoites attempted to wreck all traces of opposition and everything that might have aided its revival. For instance, there was an order to destroy all stocks of *Drosophila*. All genetic literature was removed from libraries. The TAA library destroyed all genetics textbooks, the books of Shmal'gauzen, and much other literature. In all publishing houses, standing type of books that did not praise

Lysenko was broken up. The purge of books either in press or in preparation began immediately after the LAAAS sessions, on administrative orders.

At this time, with no basis in fact, Shmal'gauzen was counted among Mendelist-Morganist leaders. He was a noted specialist in evolutionary morphology of animals and a pupil of the great evolutionist, Severtsov. Shmal'gauzen was subjected to a particularly violent hounding both at the LAAAS session and later. The strength of the ban on his name is testified to by an episode which I witnessed in 1949. The Sovietskaya Nauka publishing house, for which I was engaged at the time on a small contract job, was reissuing a standard textbook on the identification of higher plants under the editorship of the well-known botanist, Stankov. The senior editor of the publishing house, Gol'tsman, demanded that the numerous references to the name Shmal'gauzen be removed from the text, despite Stankov's explanation that the person referred to was a different man, who died before the revolution—a famous Russian botanist and the father of the Shmal'gauzen defamed by the Lysenkoites.

A protocol (in my possession) of a special meeting of the AS Press, dated August 14, 1948, includes a long list of books withdrawn from distribution and of manuscripts either returned for revision or rejected (including Dubinin's *Evolutionary Genetics*).[29]

Other ministries did not lag far behind. Thus, the Minister of Agriculture, Benediktov, issued an order (No. 1530, October 6, 1948) decreeing cessation of all genetic research in animal husbandry; announcing that there are not nor can there be any lethal mutations; closing the experiment station on distant hybridization, directed by Zhebrak; and prescribing liquidation of all instruction and all research projects not in the spirit of Michurin-Vil'yams-Lysenko. Point 7a directed that all graduate faculties be reviewed, with only those professors "capable of creative development of the teaching of Dokuchaev, Timiryazev, Michurin, Vil'yams, and Lysenko" permitted to have graduate students. Particularly anecdotal was Kaftanov's order No. 543 (May 7, 1949), which directed review of the content of forestry courses to "ensure their being taught on the basis of the materialistic Michurin-Lysenko doctrine of denial of intraspecific competition and facilitation, and of recognition of interspecific competition and facilitation as the basic factor in the evolution of living matter."

Hundreds of such decrees were issued in various ministries, bureaus, boards, publishing houses, universities, institutes, experiment stations, and editorial boards, each seeking to dismiss or condemn someone. Genetics, one of the most important biological sciences, in a matter of days became a state menace. Special emissaries from among Lysenko's closest followers were sent to all large cities and various republics to conduct meetings of biologists and to sanction dismissals of Lysenko's opponents. The clarion call to smash the Morganist-Mendelists and to root out reactionary and pestiferous genetics resounded throughout the country.

Articles on biology and the outcome of the discussion appeared throughout the periodical press. In 1949 even *The Soviet Frontier Guard* published Dvoryankin's article on the reactionary nature (a favorite Michurinist slogan) of the Mendelism-Morganism passing across our borders from abroad.

Meanwhile, under the din of this loud campaign and the noise of unchecked cackling, the "creators" of the new biology, throwing off all restraint, distributed among themselves responsible posts and took over key positions in ministries, academies, institutes, and universities, and on editorial boards and executive boards of party and government organizations. Lysenko followers and closest collaborators, who up to that time had played second- and third-string roles in the sciences, went out for the spoils. They greedily grabbed ranks, posts, scientific degrees, honorary titles, prizes, salaries, medals, orders, honorifics, honoraria, apartments, summer houses, personal cars. They did not just await bounties from nature.

At the same time, baiting of all opponents of Lysenko and

his group, even if they had no relation whatsoever to genetics, was put into effect. Sabinin, a recognized plant physiologist and agricultural chemist, provides an example. He was dismissed by Prezent immediately after the latter was named dean of biology at both the Moscow and Leningrad universities, and for a long time could not find work. After two years of wandering and of material and spiritual trials, with only occasional earnings, he was able, with the aid of friends, to obtain employment in the AS Soils Institute. But Oparin, then heading the AS Biological Section, and who fawned on Lysenko in every way, flatly refused to approve Sabinin's appointment, and he once more became an outcast. He had to leave Moscow and abandon his work on plant nutrition to study algae. But scientific journals would not publish his work. His brilliant, important book on plant physiology, on which he had worked for many years, was withdrawn from publication in 1948, just before it was due to see the light of day. Unable to bear such persecution, Sabinin shot himself in 1951. His suicide was a complete surprise to all his friends, who knew him as an optimist and a man of self-restraint. I talked with him twice during that period, and he amazed me with his boldness and steadfastness. His position at the time was that of an unarmed man facing pirates of science armed to the teeth.

His monograph was published, in part, posthumously in 1955. His pupils arranged to have the book published by the AS Press in 1958, but in 1959 the type was broken up so that the major part of the book (in which Sabinin pointed out that vernalization had been abandoned in the last century, long before Lysenko was born, because of its ineffectiveness) did not appear until 1962. It is now generally conceded that during his lifetime Sabinin was the foremost Soviet plant physiologist.

Despite the mass dismissals of geneticists, the more cruel type of repression was still limited. Dubinin's closest collaborator, Romashev, was arrested. In 1949 Efroimson, an out-standing animal and medical geneticist, was arrested without cause. M'iuge, then a student at the TAA, was arrested as "socially dangerous" merely because he visited his dismissed professor, Paramonov, and presented him with a bouquet of flowers. He was rehabilitated in 1954, as were Romashev and Efroimson in 1955.

After the LAAAS session, leading geneticists were being shadowed by the secret police. As a fourth-year student in botany, under Zhukovsky, I was a witness to one such inci-dent. In 1948 a certain E. had been accepted as a graduate student without examination or competition, by a directive of the Minister of Higher Education. His file, however, was kept at the Ministry and not in the dean's office. According to his tale he had been in the army since 1941 after graduating from a pedagogical institute. In the TAA he worked actively and conscientiously on a Michurinist thesis. Then he suddenly dis-appeared for several months. I met him by chance in 1953, when he was wearing the uniform of a captain in the State Security Service. Later he successfully defended his thesis, and was demobilized. His assignment apparently had been to watch Zhukovsky's school.

Attempts to expose the disgraced geneticists to attack by punitive organs were not rare. Leningrad colleagues have sent me recently an interesting document, a denunciation of a group of well-known Leningrad cytologists and geneticists, written by a Professor V. and found many years later in an examination of archives. V. had replaced Polyansky in a pro-fessorship at the Leningrad Herzen Pedagogical Institute, and tried in every way to calumniate her exiled predecessor and his friends. The denunciation of Polyansky, of Nasonov, the director of the institute, and others concludes:[30]

Nasonov rather graphically characterizes the friendship between his institute and industry. "Before," said he, "it was just like a restaurant; anybody could come and get what he wanted. Now it's like a stock exchange operating on a demand and supply basis." The comparison of a Soviet scientific establishment with some kind of London exchange where speculators and jobbers offer and buy shares shows how incredible Nasonov's concepts of the relation between science and industry are.

At the same time, account must be taken of the fact that Nasonov is one of Polyansky's closest friends. They worked together and fought the Michurinists in the Leningrad University together. They went abroad in 1948 together, they suffered defeat after the LAAAS session together. They met often. In the summer of 1949 Nasonov and Aleksandrov visited, on assignment, the Murmansk station, of which Polyansky is director, etc.

Aleksandrov is also Nasonov's friend and (as in Nasonov's own case) has close ties abroad: his mother and brother live in Palestine (he is a Jew), and his sister in America. The recent Morganist past of these friends, which they have not recanted, their connections abroad, their "scientific" meetings in Murmansk, and the energetic fight put up by their old friends against Michurinist reconstruction—all these undoubtedly are links in one chain, of one organization conducting a political struggle against Soviet science. Nasonov spent a tremendous amount of state money on the maintenance of a whole staff of Morganists, on fruitless "scientific" investigations, causing thereby a notable damage to Soviet science and economy. Is this not service to America! Polyansky for many years was the leader of Leningrad Morganists carrying on a desperate fight against Michurinists. In twenty years he educated thousands of teachers and young scientists in the Morganist spirit. He has spent huge sums of state funds to study *Infusoria*, never turning his research to objects which could have practical use. This is also no small service to our enemies. As director of the Murmansk station, Polyansky probably has access to secret material on the meteorology of our north, on sea currents, maps, data on ice conditions, etc. With friends of the type of Nasonov and Aleksandrov visiting his station, these circumstances assume a special significance. The Murmansk station has a portable radio and can be in touch with foreign countries.

A third friend and collaborator of Polyansky, Kheisin, has also taken up a post not far from our northern borders in Petrozavodsk. They even say that there he has turned into a Finn, and calls himself Heisinen.

I cannot offer documentary proof of the nature of the relations and ties of all these persons, but the facts presented, it seems to me, warrant attention. 15.2.1950. Professor V.

This document, undoubtedly written by an experienced informer, is typical in its slanderous and malicious irresponsibility. Today the absurdity of such unsubstantiated accusations is obvious to all, but in 1950 such base lies brought the persons denounced many unpleasant experiences.

For the sake of the record, Aleksandrov's mother never lived in Palestine, but perished from starvation in Leningrad. His only brother, an old bolshevik, was killed in 1919 by the White Poles. The sister in America is also a product of a sick imagination: Aleksandrov never had a sister.

A number of geneticists were deprived of their scientific degrees in 1948, and a ban on further degrees in genetics of the old school was instituted for a long time. Research in genetics, plant hormones, cytogenetics, polyploidy, etc., was also banned, thereby setting Soviet biology back many years. Thus the monopoly in biology was established, with Lysenko playing the role of the infallible purveyor of scientific truths.

THE LYSENKO CULT IN 1948–1952

Lysenko's cult in these years was blown up to fabulous proportions. He is apparently the only biologist in history to whom the epithet "great" was applied in his lifetime. His portraits hung in all scientific institutions. Art stores sold busts and bas-reliefs of Lysenko (these art works were still available in 1961, at triple discount). In some cities, monuments were erected to him. The State Chorus had in its repertory a hymn honoring Lysenko. In songbooks one could find folk doggerel along the lines:

Merrily play on, accordion,
With my girl friend let me sing
Of the eternal glory of Academician Lysenko.

He walks the Michurin path
With firm tread;
He protects us from being duped
*   by Mendelist-Morganists.*

I remember well an interesting episode—Lysenko's first lecture at the TAA. In that academy, after the LAAAS session, the well-known economist Nemchinov was replaced as director by Stoletov, who had previously worked with Lysenko in the Institute of Genetics. As already noted, a number of outstanding scientists, such as Zhebrak[31] and Paramonov,[32] were dismissed. Together with all his other posts, Lysenko became professor of genetics and breeding, although before that he had never done any teaching.

And now this was to be his first lecture directed to the students. The compliant leadership of the Academy summoned to the lecture the whole staff, which occupied most of the seats, while the students, crowding the hallways, listened to a loudspeaker. The whole street was crowded with personal cars of Ministry executives, including that of the Minister of Agriculture himself. And now the illustrious LAAAS president arrives in his personal ZIS car. An especially summoned brass band begins to play a triumphal march, under the sounds of which Lysenko proceeds through the hailing rows to the rostrum to begin his first lecture. Seeing gray-haired scientists in the front rows of the audience, Lysenko exclaims with exaltation: "Aha! You came to relearn?" I remember little of the content of the lecture—only the assertion that a horse is alive only in interaction with the environment; without interaction it is no longer a horse but a cadaver of a horse; that, when different birds are fed hairy caterpillars, cuckoos hatch from their eggs; that a new cell is not formed from a previously existing one, but near one; that the living body always wants to eat; etc., etc.

THE SPREAD OF LYSENKOISM

The harmful thesis of the existence of two biologies spread into other branches of science in subsequent years. Attempts were made in this direction in medicine (with the prescribed attitude toward Pavlov and "Pavlovians" as a criterion) and in soil science, where all opponents of the doctrines of Vil'yams were proclaimed to be reactionaries. Cybernetics was likewise declared reactionary, and remained underground until 1955. The very word was missing from the last edition of the *Great Soviet Encyclopedia*. Medical investigations of hereditary diseases were put beyond the law.

The effect of the August session on attempts by scientists in certain fields to establish similar situations in other sciences is readily seen from the fact that true concepts were being discredited merely on the grounds that they had been developed in the United States. This murky wave swept partly over physics, fortunately for a short time only. In a collection of demagogic articles, for example, the introduction states: "Since among Soviet physicists the task analogous to the one which has already shown significant results in agrobiology, physiology, and some other branches of Soviet science has not yet been carried out, the authors have to begin from the very beginning."[33] And they began by declaring reactionary and idealistic Einstein's relativity theory ("reactionary Einsteinism"), Bohr's complementary principle, Pauling's theory of resonance, and a number of other concepts that were landmarks in science.

To rout the resonance theory, a special meeting of the AS Division of Chemistry was convened in a clear attempt to copy the LAAAS session. In spite of this, after several years the resonance theory was restored to its rightful position, and only Soviet chemistry suffered a setback because of this session. Trends of this type developed in nearly all sciences.

FURTHER DEVELOPMENTS

Lysenko's own concepts and those of his followers began to assume a misshapen and absurd character. The fraudulent experiments on transformation of one species into another (wheat into rye, cultivated into wild oats and barley, cabbages into rutabagas and rape, sunflowers into strangleweed, pines into firs, etc.) were given wide publicity. Such "discoveries" were reported by the dozen in Lysenko's journal *Agrobiologiya*, and these illiterate, shameful articles were advertised as achievements of progressive science. Support for these mythical transformations was again based on Stalin's authority: "Stalin's teaching about gradual, concealed, unnoticeable quantitative changes leading to rapid, radical qualitative changes permitted Soviet biologists to discover 'in plants the realization of such quantitative transitions, the transformation of one species into another."[34]

In 1949–1951 wide international publicity was given to the fraudulent work of Bosh'yan on the origin of viruses from microbes, and vice versa, on the obtaining of microbes from antibiotics produced by them, and on crystallization of bacteria. Similar publicity attended Lepeshinskaya's work on the origin of cells and even tissues from "living matter." All these were declared Michurinist; hence it was compulsory to accept them. Despite active support from Lysenko, Studitsky, and others, as a result of the work of eighteen review committees of prominent scientists, Bosh'yan was exposed as a falsifier and stripped of his doctor's degree which had been awarded him some years earlier for his "discoveries." Neither could Lepeshinskaya's work find confirmation in spite of support and publicity by Lysenko's group.

Stalin's support was also used in the "solution" of other problems under discussion. Thus, at the very beginning of her book, Lepeshinskaya wrote with rapture that Stalin had read it and approved. Later, after Stalin's death, she recounted in greater detail the secrets of her scientific success:

In these sorrowful days, I cannot help recollecting an incident in my life. It was in a difficult year when malicious metaphysicians, Old Testament idealists, bearers of the most reactionary ideas of Weismannism-Morganism took up arms against my work in biology. Once, when I felt especially wretched and miserable from the endless hostile attacks, the telephone rang in my room. I lifted the receiver and heard such a familiar, such a dear voice, that of Iosif Vissarianovich. . . . Encouraging me with friendly paternal words, Stalin gave me advice. And in his wise counsel there was such crystal clarity, such power of scientific prevision, that my heart stood still with pride. Pride that there is on this large planet a man intimate and dear, for whom all complex questions and problems are an open book, for whom, in all detail, the path of development of Soviet progressive science is clear.[35]

As to Oparin, in an article on Stalin as the inspiration of progressive biology, he simply included him among the founders of Michurinist biology and proclaimed his superficial, youthful article ("Anarchism or socialism") a most important contribution to it. According to Oparin, Stalin, long before Lysenko, asserted that acquired characters are inherited, and that it was precisely these "strokes of Stalin's genius that inspired the Michurinists in their fight against neo-Darwinism as an idealistic perversion of biology."[36]

Yet what was it that Stalin had said in this connection; what were the thoughts that so transported Oparin? It was a single casual, meaningless statement: "The Mendeleev periodic table clearly shows the great significance of qualitative and quantitative changes in the history of nature. This is also shown in biology by the theory of neo-Lamarckism, which is supplanting neo-Darwinism."[37]

INTERNATIONAL REPERCUSSIONS

The August session and the decisions and measures that followed created a very poor impression abroad, considerably damaging the prestige of Soviet science. This was demonstrated by the fact that nearly all foreign members and corresponding members of the Academy of Sciences resigned with appropriate public declaration. One such statement by Sir Henry Dale was made in the form of an open letter to the then president of the Academy, S. I. Vavilov, the brother of the fallen N. I. Vavilov. This letter was published in the Russian-language weekly newspaper *The British Ally*.[38] As I recall, the issue containing it was the last one: the paper was declared to be anti-Soviet, and was closed by demand of the appropriate authorities.

REVIVAL OF THE DEBATE IN 1952–1958

The period of absolute domination of Lysenkoism in Soviet biology and agronomy was relatively short-lived. Immoderate praise and complete suppression of criticism were typical for only four years. In December, 1952, the *Botanichesky Zhurnal*, edited by Sukachev, published two articles in which Lysenko was accused of retreating from Darwinism and from the very doctrines of Michurinism. The first was written by Turbin, up to then one of Lysenko's warmest supporters. The other came from the pen of N. D. Ivanov, who also stood on Lysenko's positions in genetics. Only Lysenko's theory of speciation by saltation was criticized, a theory on an equally low level with his others, and remarkable for its absurdity and lack of authenticity.

Both articles and especially the resumption of the discussion were received by Soviet scientists with tremendous enthusiasm. Dozens of articles from many scientists flooded the editors of the *Botanichesky Zhurnal*. Many were distinguished by great brilliance and polemical talent. The long-contained pressure of thoughts and ideas had apparently found an outlet in spite of the sharply demagogic articles in rebuttal appearing in journals under Lysenkoite control.[39] The sympathies of scientists and of youth were with the *Botanichesky Zhurnal*.

For the first two years the discussion centered on problems of speciation,[40] but also included an article by Sukachev on intraspecific competition.[41] But the logic of the discussion and attempts of Lysenko supporters to brand those disputing them as Morganist-Mendelists naturally led to broadening the front of the debate to include genetics and agrobiology. In essence, all aspects of Lysenkoism fell under examination. The *Botanichesky Zhurnal* rapidly became the most popular biological periodical, and its every issue was awaited with impatience. Its volume and circulation went up, and from a bimonthly it became a monthly. Soon critical articles also began appearing in the publication of the Moscow Society of Naturalists.

Under the influence of the discussion, research in genetics came to life and it again became a lawful science. In the AS, genetics laboratories and groups began to arise, although universities, agricultural institutes, and the LAAAS research system were still under nearly total control of Lysenko supporters.

Soon practical aspects were added to the theoretical ones of the debate. In a number of convincing articles the practical damage to agriculture caused by Lysenkoism was demonstrated. The pseudoscientific work of Lepeshinskaya was debunked in short order. By the end of 1955 more than three hundred scientists had signed a petition requesting Lysenko's removal from the post of LAAAS president and the dismissal of Oparin as secretary of the Biological Section of the AS.

The request was granted. The more moderate Lobanov took the first post, and Engel'gardt replaced Oparin. The positions of Lysenko supporters began to weaken, and the developing discussion essentially was beginning to dethrone Lysenkoism.

The discussion in the *Botanichesky Zhurnal* undoubtedly brought a current of fresh air into our biology and, in fact, uncrowned Lysenkoism in the eyes of scientists in our own land and other socialist countries. It brought Lysenkoism to the verge of total collapse, and exposed its scientific bankruptcy. Unable to continue an honest scientific debate, the Lysenkoites once more resorted to demagoguery and to administrative methods by injunction. At the CC plenary session of December, 1958, Lysenko represented all criticism against him as intrigues of Western imperialists, thus appealing for protection against "imperialist" slander:

It is well known that in the whole world, in scientific journals, and not infrequently in newspapers, in the so-called discussion around Michurinist biology, which the reactionaries of capitalist countries call "Lysenkoism," a lot of nonsense is made up about materialist biology and myself personally. It is clear that the question is not about me but about the materialistic trend of biology related to collective farm practice, which I have upheld and still uphold in my articles. Because of this the reactionaries in science and the journalists of the bourgeois world, especially in the United States, Britain, and other capitalist countries, attribute to me all kinds of sins. All my work in biology and agronomic practice is proclaimed to be a swindle and deceit.[42]

By appealing not to the scientists of his country but to his patrons in the administrative party apparatus, Lysenko and his supporters once more succeeded in evoking administrative reprisals against their opponents. The editorial board of the *Botanichesky Zhurnal* was disbanded at the end of 1958 and reconstituted largely from Lysenko's followers.[43] The Moscow Society of Naturalists was likewise directed to cease all polemics.

Engel'gardt was removed from the leadership of the AS

Biological Section and replaced by Sisakyan. Avdonin, director of the All-Union Institute of Fertilizers and Agricultural Practice, was also removed from his post on the basis of his opposition to Lysenko's methods of preparing fertilizer mixtures and his "biological theory" of plant nutrition. Dubinin was removed from the directorship of the Novosibirsk Institute of Cytology and Genetics.

The Soviet delegation to the 1958 Tenth International Congress of Genetics in Canada had a singular composition. All papers of Soviet geneticists previously submitted, and included in the program of the Congress, were withdrawn. But it was too late to change the printed program. Since the time at which each paper was to be read appeared on the program, members of the Congress waited in silence until the time assigned for the undelivered papers expired. The Soviet delegation was headed by Stoletov and consisted entirely of Lysenko supporters (Glushchenko, Nuzhdin, Kushner, Enikeev, Khitrinsky, and others). They participated in only one of the Congress's twenty sections (on graft hybrids) which, in essence, was arranged for them especially.

The organization of the Soviet delegation, as expected, produced an unfavorable impression on other delegations and gave rise to a resolution passed by the Congress at its closing session. The resolution, published in *Science*, read:

The Permanent International Committee on Genetics Congresses considers it to be its duty to express deep concern over the fact that a number of Soviet geneticists who had submitted abstracts of papers to the X International Congress of Genetics failed to appear in Montreal. The Committee also deeply regrets the absence of representatives at the Congress from a number of other countries. It wishes to express its deepest sympathy and send its warmest regards to all scientists who may have been prevented from attending the Congress by their governments.

The IX International Congress of Genetics, meeting in Bellagio, Italy, in 1953, passed a resolution that Genetics Congresses should not "be held in any country to which it may be expected that scientists would be refused permission to enter on grounds of race, nationality, religion, place of birth, or political associations past or present." The Permanent Committee takes this occasion to extend this policy by appealing strongly to all governments in the world to allow their scientists the right of unimpeded travel for scientific purposes, without regard of race, nationality, religion, place of birth, past or present political associations, and, in view of the experiences at the current Congress, irrespective of whether their scientific views and work are in conformity with any official governmentally shaped policies and ideology. We consider any attempt on the part of governments to interfere on political, ideological, or other grounds with a free pursuit of science and free dissemination of scientific information as a serious violation of the basic principles of research. We appeal to the learned academies and scientific societies of all countries and to the United Nations and its organizations to exert all possible influence to persuade all governments to adhere to the principles outlined here. Their violation will, no doubt, spell the end of scientific freedom and therefore also of scientific progress.

As may be seen, the followers of Lysenkoism placed their personal prestige above that of Soviet science and country. Deliberately and antipatriotically they provided grounds for criticism of our country and the Soviet government, and tried to take advantage of the criticism for their own ends, without taking into account the fact that such criticism could do real damage to the socialist ideal of scientific progress and freedom of scientific discussion. Criticism from abroad, even if justifiable, was desirable for them, because it helped them to fight off criticism from their own compatriot Soviet scientists.

The events of 1958 had a significant, though not very strong, effect on our biology. Critical analysis of the theoretical and practical propositions of Lysenkoism was virtually discontinued. But the development of experimental trends in genetics and molecular biology continued in our country, thus preparing the basis for a renewal of debate.[44]

CHAPTER 7

The Two Trends up to 1963

IN THE EARLIER CHAPTERS, in examining the genetics controversy of 1936, we have seen the extent of the factual and theoretical material then at the disposal of the Lysenko group. Yet the evaluation of a new trend at the point of its origin is not necessarily objective: the new frequently seems less attractive than the old. Now, however, twenty-five years have gone by[1]—a long time for science—at least long enough to allow a new trend to become established and to prove itself in other ways than by an administrative rout of its opponents.

In spite of the decisions of the "historical" session of the LAAAS in August, 1948, which declared genetics to be an unproductive pseudoscience and reactionary Mendelism-Morganism, advances in genetics did not cease. The decisions of the session could not be implemented throughout the world, although the stenographic report of the proceedings was rapidly translated by Soviet publishers into German, English and French in 1949, and sent from the Soviet Union to all other countries. This unique volume was also translated into languages of friendly socialist states, some of which, unfortunately, adopted the Soviet "experience" of persecution of genetics. But by no means did the whole world accept on faith the postulates of the new doctrine, and investigation of the "hereditary substance" continued in many laboratories. This research proceeded at headlong speed, exerting its influence on the neighboring disciplines of biochemstry, biophysics, cytology, and others. Nearly every year brought news of important discoveries, and the mechanism of heredity became increasingly understood.[2]

It was an exciting saga of discoveries, within the framework of "Morganism-Mendelism," but Soviet science was for a long time on the outside because of the activities of a small group. It cannot be said that Soviet scientists made no contribution, but theirs was relatively modest because they lacked the technical and methodological conditions for experimentation on the necessary scale. Such work was impossible without actual rebirth of genetics in the U.S.S.R., without revision of curricula, without preparation of appropriate cadres, without creation of new laboratories and institutes, all of which met violent resistance from Lysenko's supporters.

Only recently have first-class laboratories been established in the U.S.S.R., with research teams capable of developing these trends in genetics and molecular biology at the level of world science (Engel'gardt, Khesin, Spirin, Alikhanyan, Rapoport, Olenov, Bresler, Shapot, Neifakh, Astaurov, Dubinin, and others).

After 1948 the methodological level of biology in our country dropped sharply. This opened the way for a large number of people incapable of real and serious creative work in science, and with a personal interest in continued persecution of genetics and biology, to receive scientific degrees and positions. There arose a large, rather influential, and noisy clique of biologists and philosophers who made praise of Lysenko and criticism of modern attainments in biology and genetics their main profession, which was all they were capable of. (They included Prezent, Dvoryankin, Feiginson, Khalifman, Varuntsyan, Platonov, Nuzhdin, Ol'shansky, and others.) Their task was the defamation of all opponents of Lysenko, no matter where they appeared. Editorial boards of journals and newspapers and responsible posts in other institutions either sponsoring or in charge of scientific investigations were filled with like-minded people who saw their calling as the suppression and muffling of all that contradicted Lysenko and his entourage. In fact a separate, large sect appeared, with a specific organization and a particular dogma violently resisting the truly progressive development of biology.

This sect would periodically capture a number of ministerial posts, and for a long time held certain key positions in the AS Biology Section, in the LAAAS, the Committee on Higher Degrees, the academies of Union republics, the "Znanie" society, and in the agricultural section of the Union of Societies for Cultural Links Abroad. The sect blocked informational channels on biology and agricultural science leading to the CEC, and made captive most scientific institutes and journals in agriculture and biology. The positions and power of these people were not based on the development of science but on its falsification and stagnation, on dogmatism, on blind faith in the infallibility of Lysenko and his postulates.

In the fifteen years after the 1948 LAAAS session, representatives of this sect, who had at their disposal all the necessary conditions for scientific work and who occupied all key positions for ensuring the influence of science on agricultural production, made not a single recognizable theoretical discovery, nor took one step forward toward the understanding of hereditary mechanisms. And, as a result, Soviet biology lagged behind, for example, that of the United States.

In the name of what did Soviet biology make these enormous sacrifices? In the name of what did we for so long grant our opponents, the enemies of communism and socialism, a monopoly on such a broad front of science? Did we not react sensitively to the successes of other countries in physics, chemistry, cybernetics, space exploration? We followed their theoretical and practical achievements, we assimilated their experience in order to be ahead in the historical rivalry of the two systems. Why, then, did we permit a group of people to carry out a completely opposite line in biology, a line of ignoring, silencing, falsifying, misinforming about everything learned abroad concerning practical and theoretical aspects of heredity and variation? Is it possible that this was justified because the trend in genetics created by Lysenko and Prezent had brought us such joy through its colossal theoretical achievements that beside them everything done in other countries paled?

To answer these questions, it is appropriate to examine the development of the genetical concepts of this trend and to review the theoretical discoveries with which these concepts enriched the Soviet nation in the period following the LAAAS session.

MICHURINIST THEORY

The "new trend" brought nothing new on the nature of heredity and variation during this period. This was no accident, for the very character of the new formulations about heredity and variation at the dawn of the genetics debate indicated that they did not contain any potential for further development. It is impossible to accumulate proof of a primary hypothesis that states: "Heredity is the property of the living body to demand certain environmental conditions and to react in a certain way to them." It is only possible to repeat this incomprehensible thesis as a revelation, fully acceptable for all times and all peoples. The creators of the new genetics asserted that heredity is a property characteristic of all particles of living matter. This property cannot be reduced to the terms of chemistry and physics, it is not analyzable. It merely has to be comprehended, and whoever has comprehended it does not need to recognize hereditary substances. This was precisely the thesis formulated by Lysenko and Prezent, and precisely the way Feiginson represented the issue in his article, "Living nature has its own laws."[3]

I have examined very carefully the contribution to theoretical science made by this trend in recent years and have found in it nothing new leading toward an understanding of the nature of heredity. Such understanding was presumably established in Lysenko's original work, after which all energy, all experiments, all theoretical constructs of the sect were directed toward the single goal of "disproving" the chromosome theory of heredity, defaming the new theories on the role of DNA in hereditary transmission, and retarding the penetration of chemical, physical, and cybernetic methods into biology. *The basic activity of Lysenko's followers in the theoretical field both then and now consists of misinformation and criticism, and, as before, they consider their main service to be the struggle against their opponents.*

This, for example, is what members of the group said in 1948–1954 about genes, when their existence had already been proved incontrovertibly, even though their role in cellular metabolism was not completely clear:

Cytogenetics is collapsing. It is not for nothing that Morganists invent offhand, in addition to genes, "plasmagenes," "plastidogenes," and similar terms to draw a veil over the theoretical and practical rout of Morganism. . . . Mendelism-Morganism has fully exposed its gaping emptiness; it is rotting also from within and nothing can save it now.[4]

The hereditary substance, as against living matter, no more exists than caloric or phlogiston.[5]

No special hereditary substance exists any more than does the substance of combustion, phlogiston, or the substance of heat, caloric.[6]

In the past, to explain the supermaterialism of living phenomena, vitalism advanced concepts of entelechy or vital force. Its current variety, in the guise of Morganism, resorts to genes, codes, and templates in order not to lose its scientific aspect. But, as we know, changing terminology does not change the substance. And, in substance, entelechy, template molecules, vital force, genoneme are all synonyms. No matter what contrivances Morganists use, they cannot help but reveal that their only purpose in juggling the new terminology is to camouflage the idealistic essence of their doctrine and to cover undisguised idealism with a scientific sauce.[7]

And here is what the pillars of Lysenkoism asserted in 1961–1963, when the mechanism of gene action on the molecular level had already been discovered, and biology had emerged at the forefront of the natural sciences: "The assertion that there are in an organism some minute particles, genes, responsible for the transmission of hereditary traits is pure fantasy without any basis in science." This is the sound of Prezent's voice, and it rings, alas, from the pages of the journal *Biologiya v Shkole*,[8] which for thirty years disoriented Soviet schools in matters of biology.

The hypothetical connection of the empty abstractions [of the gene theory] with specified substrates—chromosomes, DNA—declared to be the "material carriers of heredity" does not confer on these abstractions material content, any more than superstitious deification of objects makes the superstitions materialistic.[9]

And here is an editorial, from a leading journal, very responsibly entitled "The 22nd Congress of the Communist Party and some problems of biology":

It is regrettable that the lesson taught by nature itself and by the whole development of modern biology did not benefit many representatives of formal genetics. They are attempting to fit new facts into modernized . . . old theoretical ideas. For instance, the representatives of modern genetics identify the DNA molecule with the gene, thereby conferring on it all the weaknesses and number of superstructures. And the more of them there are, the elucidation of the nature of heredity and interferes with the clarification of the real role of DNA in a living system. The history of science tells us that unconfirmed theories cannot be saved by any number of superstructures. And the more of them there are, the more obvious becomes the bankruptcy of the theories which they are called on to support.[10]

But all records for profanation and falsification of science have recently been beaten by the professor of philosophy, Platonov, in his book with the loud title *Dialectical Materialism and Problems of Genetics:*

Among bourgeois scientists there are not a few who sold their body and soul to their masters. They are trying faithfully to serve the bourgeoisie. Some of them, fulfilling the class order of monopolies, create the atom and the hydrogen bomb, invent new poisons, various means of bacteriological warfare, and other tools for mass destruction. Others move from scientific activity to direct participation in the apparatus of the bourgeois state. Still others specialize in distortion of scientific data in the spirit of idealism and mysticism.[11]

And it is in this last group that Platonov places geneticists. We also learn from him that:

. . . the reactionary tendencies inherent in Weismann-Morgan genetics from the moment of its origin have not dried up at the present but rather become reinforced. This is witnessed, for instance, by the trend of the corpuscular theory of heredity and the associated aspiration of some Morganists toward restoration of the shaken faith in the creation of the world.[12]

And here is how Platonov describes the history of the struggle between the two trends in genetics. Misrepresenting the fight of the "innovators," Lysenko, Ol'shansky, and others, against the "idealists" and "metaphysicians," Vavilov, Kol'tsov, Serebrovsky, and others, he writes:

A substantial blow was suffered by Weismannism-Morganism in the course of the struggle of the Communist party against the menshevizing, idealistic, philosophical current which distorted Marxism and revived one of the most damaging dogmas and traditions of the Second International, the separation of theory and practice. Among the menshevizing idealists together with philosophers (Deborin, Sten, Karev) were to be found scientists, in particular, geneticists (Agol, Levin, Levit, Serebrovsky). This is why the rout of menshevizing idealists also seriously undermined the positions of Weismannist-Morganists in our land.

In turn, the foreign leaders of Weismann-Morgan genetics strengthened their attacks on the Darwin-Michurin doctrine. The world bourgeoisie mobilized all ideological means of struggle against Marxism and those scientific theories which serve as a basis and consolidation of the dialectic-materialistic outlook. In particular, Weismannism-Morganism with its theory of an immortal hereditary substance was widely utilized. With the aid of this doctrine, attempts are made to justify the exploitation of workers, colonialism, and racial discrimination. At the same time it is used for proving the proposition that the moving force of social development is not the manufacture of material goods, not the class struggle, but the hereditary substrate, above all, of great personalities.[13]

Filling his whole book with this kind of political demagoguery, defiling the memory of outstanding Soviet scientists who perished for their convictions as a result of similarly unfounded accusation in the period of the personality cult, Platonov did all possible to keep Soviet science from knowledge of the newest attainments in biology. He undoubtedly felt that the most recent discoveries in genetics undermined the foundations of demagoguery which had supported him and his like for the last twenty-five years, and tried by all means to put a brake on this process. In fact, Platonov offers a choice to his readers—either genetics or Marxism and dialectical materialism. By counterposing Marxism and the newest achievements of theoretical and experimental biology, Platonov distorts the progressive, creative spirit of the teaching of Marx-Lenin.

Numerous examples of such falsification can be cited. They included not only direct lies and distortion of facts, but also some more subtle techniques: attributing to genetics views and concepts fifty to sixty years old; attributing views and pronouncements of individual geneticists to genetics as a whole; consciously confusing philosophical views of foreign scientists with scientific ones; hushing up, and sometimes crediting themselves with, the achievements of genetics.

But even this rich arsenal of techniques became ineffective. In spite of bans, in spite of shortage of cadres, in spite of revision of curricula, genetics based on the chromosome theory of heredity and on recognition of the reality of genes as the material factors of inheritance began to revive rapidly in our country. It penetrated our science through all possible channels—chemistry, physics, mathematics, biophysics, radiobiology, breeding, botany, zoology, medicine—and this invincible movement is becoming ever more apparent. Scientific and popular-science journals, as well as the regular press, now carry articles on genetics, on the discovery of the chemical nature of genes, on control of heredity by artificial mutagenesis, on the fact that the notorious substance of heredity, previously declared to be nonexistent, actually exists in the chromosomes of cells.

And, as had happened before, the creators of the "new biology" attempted to stop this process through administrative channels, along lines of political provocation, and by misinforming party and government circles. This was clearly apparent in the administrative ban on a large scientific conference on experimental (basically agricultural) genetics convened by Leningrad University in the beginning of 1961. The ban was due to Lysenko,[14] who suddenly discovered a large number of his scientific opponents listed in the program. Over one hundred papers dealing with current and most important questions in genetics had been submitted. The cancellation of the conference only two or three days before its scheduled opening caused many scientists who had arrived in Leningrad for it to return home.

Particularly energetic in his attempts to put the brakes on progress in our biology and agronomy was the president of the LAAAS (1962–1965), Ol'shansky. In his published articles and speeches he did not advance any really constructive ideas about the development of our science and our agricultural practice. And at the same time he zealously attempted to denigrate all work of Soviet geneticists, as if the revival of genetics was the biggest danger for agriculture. Ol'shansky and his cohorts, particularly, persistently tried to prove that genetics is contradictory to the thesis of the party program on the leading role of environment in the development of the living world (a thesis included in the program through a proposal by Lysenko).[15]

In general, in talking of the inauspicious contributions of Lysenko's followers, to be fair, it must be pointed out that they formed a relatively small group of theoreticians. But after 1948, a great many other scientists (plant physiologists, biochemists, plant breeders, botanists) joined Lysenko. In their various specialties, these men often carried out useful and necessary research with no direct bearing on genetics. They merely shared Lysenko's views on heredity, absorbed during their school days. They repeated Lysenko's criticism of modern genetic theory without essentially understanding it, without knowing the history of genetics, its methods, and its recent discoveries. The Lysenkoites take credit for the work of the scientists in various fields, attributing their results to the influence of Lysenkoite ideas. This is, of course, deliberate misrepresentation.

CHAPTER 8

Lysenko's Agrobiology

THE THEORETICAL ASPECTS of the controversy were touched on in the preceding chapter; but it is the practical accomplishments that must decide the issue. It is often stated that perhaps, as armchair or laboratory scientists, the Lysenko group lags behind the Morganists in some ways, but that a comparison of the practical achievements of the two groups favors the Lysenkoites. After all, it is said, Lysenko and his followers are in close touch with the practical application of research to problems of agriculture; they settle disputes in the field, and not with useless fruit flies.

This is a widespread point of view and, unless it is analyzed, final judgment is not possible. Victors, as the saying goes, are not judged and, if our agriculture, our industry, our medicine have gained from the liquidation of genetics and from a monopoly by the new doctrine, the need for radical change, perhaps, does not exist. Let us examine, then, the outcome of the practical recommendations of Lysenko and his followers.[1] Some of the techniques and methods to be reviewed have no real connection with genetics. But genetics, as such, disappeared to a considerable degree from the conglomerate of practical and theoretical propositions of Lysenko's agrobiology, which was opposed to genetics. We must therefore examine the complex as a whole. Since most of the agricultural practices and methods are no longer in use, but have become a matter of history, they will merely be summarized.[2]

VERNALIZATION

In Chapter 1 we described how Lysenko was catapulted to fame on the sensationalized alleged discovery of vernalization.

Yet, as Sabinin had pointed out in his book on the physiology of plant growth and development (see Chapter 6), analogous experiments had been carried out in Russia in the middle of the last century with the same results. The reports on them, in Russian agronomic journals, had been long forgotten. Similar experiments had also been carried out in other countries. The century-old formula for the technique, little different in principle from Lysenko's, was given by an American, J. H. Klippart, in the annual report of the Ohio State Board of Agriculture for 1857:

To convert winter into spring wheat, nothing more is necessary than that the winter wheat should be allowed to germinate slightly in the fall or winter, but kept from vegetation by a low temperature or freezing, until it can be sown in the spring. This is usually done by soaking and sprouting the seed, and freezing it while in this state and keeping it frozen until the season for spring sowing has arrived.[3]

Originally vernalization was proposed as a way of sowing winter varieties in the spring, although this was obviously a hopeless project. It was then applied to spring varieties which, of course, had no need of it, and it did shorten their vegetative period by a few days, with alleged beneficial effects on yield. But spring varieties were not sown extensively in the southern Ukraine. It now became necessary to use them, in preference to the higher-yielding winter forms, to prove the effectiveness of vernalization, especially since Vil'yams' grassland system demanded it. The prominent plant breeder and experimenter, Konstantinov, carried out a five-year (1931–1936) experimental check on the effectiveness of vernalization at many experiment stations (54 plots) and on many varieties (35), and came to the absolutely reliable conclusions that vernalization, most of the time, does not raise yields.[4]

However, Lysenko and the agronomist Utekhin pounced sharply on Konstantinov, practically accusing him of sabotage, after which there were no volunteers to conduct further experiments attempting to verify the efficacy of the method. Konstantinov's data showed that the mean yield of vernalized wheat was 960 kilograms per hectare, while the controls yielded 956 kilograms. The 4-kilogram difference was not statistically significant. Lysenko could not deny these results; he could only counter with his own, as a rule unreliable, experiments. Nevertheless, in replying to Konstantinov he made a definite threat. He warned that there had been many cases in which experimental data had been disproved by collective farm practice. Wrote Lysenko: "Konstantinov must give thought to the fact that, when such erroneous data were swept away from the field of scientific activity, those who failed to understand the implications of such data, and insisted on retaining them, were also swept away."

Later, vernalization died a natural death. Abandonment of the method was somehow officially explained by Lysenkoites on the grounds that highly technical agricultural equipment permitted the sowing of spring forms in the shortest time.[5] Yet vernalization is precisely the method which demanded sowing in supercompressed periods of time, with the least delay threatening the loss of the seed material. In fact, vernalization of spring varieties (as well as potatoes) was abandoned because the considerable labor and expense required were far from paid for by the insignificant yield increase.

The saga of vernalization did not, however, pass without trace in agricultural science. One of its most significant contributions, applied in all further work of Lysenko, was the development of the questionnaire method for ascertaining the efficiency of one or another measure. This new method was of such importance in the flowering of Lysenkoism and the production of agronomic eyewash in general that it deserves special attention.

The technique of the method is extremely simple and may be illustrated by an early article by Lysenko, "A preliminary communication on vernalized sowing of wheat in collective and state farms in 1932,"[6] written while the method was still being developed. In this article the results of vernalization were being evaluated from reports of 59 collective and state farms. These farms had been sent instruction on vernalization, and several types of questionnaires, which were eventually filled out and returned by the respective chairmen and agronomists. The questionnaires covered all that was necessary: the size of area sown to vernalized seed and the extent of increase in yield. These were the basic data for Lysenko's claims. Later this method embraced thousands of collective farms, and led to the sensational official communications about the millions of kilograms of grain that the country received from vernalization.

Yet in no case were there the replications essential to experimentation, which could be subjected to statistical analysis, nor were there indications of possible differences in soil fertility between areas devoted to vernalized and control seed. There was no qualified staff to conduct experiments on many of the collective farms. The chairman bore no responsibility for the figures entered on the questionnaire, which was one of dozens that he had to fill out from various organizations. Yet under the conditions of preliminary noise and propaganda surrounding vernalization, and those of a harsh struggle against the "anti-vernalizers," who were ranked with the kulaks, most of the chairmen and agronomists preferred to fill out the questionnaire with figures indicating modest gains from vernalization. Negative results in such a situation usually were hushed up. In spite of the obvious unreliability of this method of calculation, it is very handy for pure propaganda: "From the fields of thousands of collective farms come reports . . ."; "Production experiments in hundreds of collective farms have shown . . ."; etc.

A recent instance demonstrating the unsoundness of this method may be cited. A method for spraying superphosphate solutions from airplanes was adopted throughout one of the

Central Asian republics. It was assumed that the superphosphate would be absorbed through the leaves. According to the report of the Cotton Institute, the increase in yield from spraying amounted to several centners per hectare throughout the republic. Yet the gross yield for the republic remained the same. As an investigation by a special committee demonstrated, the computation of the gains was based on the questionnaire method, the group leaders entering whatever figures they wanted, since nobody checked them. The questionnaire method inevitably produces such results under conditions of advance propaganda and pressure from above, as had been demonstrated by the whole history of measures proposed by Lysenko, from the introduction of vernalization to the present. A serious criticism of the method may be found in Lisitsyn's speech at the 1936 LAAAS session.[7]

NEW VARIETIES

The second sensation of Lysenko's career occurred in 1935. In *Yarovizatsiya*[8] and a number of other publications and newspapers, the following telegram from the Odessa institute, addressed to the chief of the agricultural section of the CC (Yakovlev), the Commissar of Agriculture (Chernov), and the president of the LAAAS (Muralov), appeared:

With your support our promise to produce within two and a half years by hybridization a variety of spring wheat for the Odessa region, which would be earlier-maturing and more resistant than the regional variety Lutescens 062, has been fulfilled. Four new varieties have been obtained. We have 50–80 kilograms of seed of each. On the basis of this work the question of review of the scientific bases of breeding self-fertilizing plants has arisen. We have come to the conclusion that prolonged self-fertilization leads to degeneration of many varieties of cultivated plants. We are developing the methodology for prevention of the harmful effects of prolonged self-fertilization by growing elite seed from artificial

S. S. Chetverikov.

V. R. Vil'yams

Below: left, N. K. Kol'tsov;
right, B. L. Astaurov.

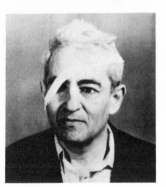

Top left, G. A. Levitsky; right, N. P. Dubinin in Mendel's garden.

Center left, I. A. Rapoport; right, N. V. Timofeev-Resovsky.

Lower left, A. S. Serebrovsky; right, A. R. Zhebrak.

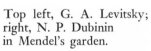

intravarietal cross-fertilization. Degenerate varieties will be bio-
logically renewed. . . . We promise to produce data from June 20,
1935, to July 20, 1936, on the practical effectiveness of renovation
of varieties. Simultaneously, we shall carry out all preliminary
steps for rapid adoption of this measure in the practice of state
and collective farms. Our theoretical postulates, not yet verified in
practice, give us reason to believe in the tremendous practical effectiveness of renewal of seed of a self-fertilized variety. This work
has first priority in the program of the institute. . . . We rely on
your further leadership and support in our new undertakings.

The telegram was signed by Lysenko, by the director of the
institute (Stepanenko), the secretary of the party committee
(Kirichenko), and the chairman of the workers' committee
(Lebedev).

The telegram was sent for sensational purposes and psychological effect: there was no urgency about the communication,
and a letter would have sufficed. The statement about the new
varieties was mere bragging; a variety, by definition, requires a
three-year testing period by the state. Lysenko sent the telegram in order to submit the seed to the variety-testing system,
basing his statement on his own results without any statistical
analysis. Later, as is known, these "varieties" failed the tests.
Three of them were rejected in the very year of submission,
1935, and only one, 1163, on Lysenko's insistence, began to
be adopted in 1936. But even it failed shortly. By the end of
1936 the foremost Soviet breeders, Konstantinov, Lisitsyn, and
Kostov, wrote in a joint communication:

The grain of 1163 is too floury, and according to Lysenko makes
poor bread. These defects Lysenko has promised to remedy rapidly.
Furthermore, it is susceptible to smut. If we take into account that
the variety is not yet ready, that it has not yet been subject to
varietal testing by the state, the question naturally arises, why is
such a nonapproved variety being propagated at such a rate. We
shall hardly straighten out seed growing in the Union if varieties
not yet ready, not yet having a right to be called varieties, are
going to be rushed into production in such an anarchical way.[9]

As might have been expected, the variety turned out to be poorer than the standard ones and was soon forgotten. The plant-breeding sensation was a bluff, but the three- to four-year propaganda accorded it in the press made Lysenko famous as an innovator in the super-rapid production of new varieties. At the same time, Lysenko's extraordinary recommendations that selection from crosses can be started in the F_1, before segregation has occurred in later generations, created much confusion in plant breeding. Proof of the erroneousness of this method came after several years, and it was discarded by nearly all breeders.

"RENEWAL" OF VARIETIES

The promise of adoption of the "theoretically expected" but "practically as yet unproved" method of renewal of self-fertilized seeds by intravarietal crosses turned out to be a more serious matter. To verify the effectiveness of this purely theoretical and completely unfounded idea would be a long and arduous affair. Hence in 1936, at the LAAAS session, Lysenko had already demanded adoption of the method by "at least 50 to 70 thousand collective farms," which would involve the services of some 800 thousand collective farmers.[10]

(It should be noted that self-fertilizing plants had existed in nature for millions of years and had not degenerated.)

Outstanding plant breeders—Vavilov, Konstantinov, Lisitsyn and others—argued against the method, but Lysenko was implacable: he demanded that all self-fertilizers be cross-pollinated. He insisted on emasculation of all wheat, and on formation of an army of collective farmers to remove the anthers from the spikes of wheat with tweezers. The wheat would then be fertilized by wind-borne pollen of neighboring plants of the same variety (with inevitable contamination by other varieties). Thus would all seed production be reformed. The only guarantee of success was provided by citations from Darwin. All critics of the method were immediately denounced as anti-Darwinists (to stick labels on opponents was part of being successful). The method was widely advertised before its adoption. It reached a point at which Yakovlev, the chief of the CC agricultural section, in his 1937 report on the reconstruction of seed production, equated intravarietal crossing with the production of new varieties and considered it necessary to pay Lysenko the same royalties per hectare of sown "renewed" seed as were received by breeders who had produced new regional varieties. The effectiveness of the method in 1938–1939 was determined in the usual way. The questionnaire method of assessment gave a positive answer; serious scientific experiments by experiment stations, a negative one. But the complexity of the whole procedure and its economic ineffectiveness finally caused this technique to die out, too.

INTERVARIETAL CROSSING

Even more absurd was the method that grew out of the one described above—intervarietal pollination of cross-fertilized crops, such as rye. According to Lysenko, such intervarietal pollination does not produce varietal hybrids, but does increase yield through the stimulating effects of foreign pollen.

The description of this "discovery" is given in a book published in 1949 by Lysenko's closest collaborator, Dolgushin:

The tests of intervarietal crosses of winter rye, carried out on many experiment stations and, in the last ten years, at Gorki Leninskie, the LAAAS experimental base, are fairly widely known. The methodology of these tests differed from those conducted with wheat only in that rye, being a cross-fertilized plant, need not be emasculated. Diverse varieties of rye planted in neighboring plots were cross-fertilized as clouds of pollen were carried across the whole planted area during flowering. The seed from each plot was harvested separately, sown, and so on, for ten generations.

For comparison, elite seed of pure varieties not subjected to cross-varietal pollination were sown. Thus every year there were plots of different varieties sown with pure seed, and plots with seed produced by successive cross-varietal pollination for one, two, three, etc., years. These experiments demonstrated that, for up to ten years, the latter seed as a rule yielded 1 to 3 centners more than did the controls. Furthermore, it turned out that, in spite of the continuous fertilization by pollen of foreign varieties, the majority of varieties retained their typical characteristics.

The experiments with rye initiated in 1936–1937 served as a basis on which Lysenko could secure repeal of the law calling for a kilometer-wide isolation zone between plantings of rye varieties. This purely Mendelian law had done much harm to rye seed production. Excellent plots of land had been mercilessly removed from seed production merely because another variety of rye was growing nearby, and its pollen could reach the neighboring variety.[11]

However, this "method" also did not distinguish itself. Hybridization between varieties occurred, of course, and pure varietal planting, the basis of seed production, became impossible. Varieties became contaminated and disappeared. The method was adopted in practice in 1948, but after a few years had to be abandoned. Even Yur'ev, who always supported Lysenko, noted in an article entitled "From the practice of selection and seed production of cereals"[12] that free intervarietal pollination leads to the disappearance of varieties and to the lowering of yields, and therefore cannot be used in seed production.

SUMMER PLANTING OF POTATOES

The method of summer planting of potatoes in the south of the U.S.S.R., proposed by Lysenko to check the so-called potato decline, received wide notice before the war. The decline of the vegetatively reproduced potato is an international disaster. As has been incontrovertibly proved, it is connected with virus diseases which spread, over a period of many years, in the vegetatively reproducing clones. In 1934, on the basis of purely abstract considerations, Lysenko proposed a new explanation of decline, as a process of "phasic aging" of tubers maturing under hot summer conditions. With summer planting, tubers are formed during the cooler autumn, and this, in Lysenko's opinion, would prevent decline. The viral nature of the disease was completely rejected as a mere concoction, without any checkup.

It may not be amiss to note that the novelty of summer planting is itself a moot point. On the shores of the Mediterranean, summer planting has been used ever since potatoes were brought from America in the sixteenth century, because there is a better guarantee of moisture in the last half of the summer. Agronomy textbooks of the last century also carry descriptions of the method.[13] Linnik's article[14] devoted to the history of the subject gives similar information and also points out that the method has been in use for a long time in the lower reaches of the Dnepr.

But, all in all, this is not the point. If Lysenko's proposal had, indeed, aided the prevention of decline, it would not be necessary to enter into questions of priority. In fact, however, the fight against decline was greatly hindered by his erroneous concepts. The successes in increasing yield on small areas in 1934 and 1935 were chance effects. No reliable data on tests were ever published. To this day the propaganda and advertising of summer planting of potatoes contain only prewar data, and no serious economic accounting is so far available. The pattern of precipitation (a droughty second half of the summer) in many southern regions of the U.S.S.R., as it became clear later, is unfavorable for summer planting, and the conservation of seed material until the middle of summer presented difficulties. As a result the method was not retained in practice, but the importunate adoption of the Lysenko theory of decline produced a great lag in our country in the practical work of developing antiviral measures in the battle against the disease. Even in the face of this, our virologists solved the problem of diagnosing affected tubers before it was solved abroad.

In most European countries, methods for control of decline are now based on detecting the presence of the virus, selecting virus-free tubers, and propagating and selling healthy planting material. The prolonged ignoring of these methods and the disorganization of breeding work with potatoes (the change to vegetative hybridization led to a sharp lowering of the production rate of new varieties) caused the spread of virus diseases, so that in the last twenty years the problem of decline has no longer been one of the south only, but also of the central part of our country.

WINTER WHEAT IN SIBERIA

The planting of winter wheat in Siberia on stubble not plowed under after the harvest of spring wheat, which produced such a noise during the Patriotic War, also turned out to be unsuccessful and unprofitable.

The use of winter wheat and rye in Siberia has an earlier history. In January, 1939, the government charged the LAAAS to produce, within two to four years, frost-resistant varieties of wheat and rye for growing in Siberia. The task, a very difficult one, was actually unrealistic, but it was assigned on the basis of repeated assertions by Lysenko that his methods made it possible to produce frost-resistant varieties of any kind within two to three years. In the 1939 discussions sponsored by the journal *Under the Banner of Marxism*, Lysenko boastfully announced that he would fulfill the task by the deadline set by the government. He said:

If these varieties are not produced in the time allotted, an economic measure will fall through. Who will be responsible? I do not think it will be Mendelism or, in general, Darwinism, but primarily Lysenko, as the leader of the Agricultural Academy and as an academician in the section of plant breeding and seed production. Hence, if the Mendelists, mobilizing their science, would give even a hint as to how to obtain a variety of rye in two to three years and a variety of wheat in three to five years that are adapted to the rigorous Siberian conditions, could it really be that I would refuse them? Three years are not that distant, and nearly a year has already passed since the assignment was made.

As was to be expected, however, production of frost-resistant varieties turned out to be no easy matter. Unable to accomplish this with the help of "re-education," Lysenko proposed his famous method of planting nonresistant, southern winter varieties in Siberia on soil with stubble that had not been plowed under—once more without any serious experimental tests.

The theoretical foundations of the scheme were simple. First, lack of plowing would presumably preserve soil texture which, according to the doctrine of Vil'yams, would ensure soil fertility. Second, the plant roots would be less likely to be destroyed by frost in compact soil. These calculations unfortunately did not prove correct and the method, having been used on hundreds of thousands of hectares, was abandoned immediately after the war because of extremely low yields and sometimes complete destruction of the crop by frost.

Ignoring precise physiological information on the nature of frost resistance proved to be costly to our country. The adaptation of southern winter varieties to Siberian conditions without prolonged selection did not, of course, succeed, and the whole shady enterprise soon collapsed. However, neither Lysenko nor his followers ever admitted their error.

In 1946 a discussion of this planting method was held in the pages of the newspaper *Sotszemledelie,* which aided considerably in turning the events into past history. The discussion had an interesting character: workers from Lysenko's institutions demonstrated the method's effectiveness; practical workers produced directly opposite findings. One chairman of a collective farm entitled his article, "To use the method is not to thresh or winnow."

The discussion on the subject also demonstrated that among agricultural scientists and specialists was a stratum of unprincipled, sharp dealers capable of any sort of falsification in order to prove the validity of any assertion by Lysenko, no matter how absurd. This was a circumstance which the party press was subsequently forced to recognize. Thus an editorial in a party paper, under the title "Principles in scientific work," read:

It also happens that the recommendations of a leading scientist fail under actual conditions of practice, but scientific workers lack the courage to admit it . . . practice has proved that recommendations [for Lysenko's method] are completely inapplicable under the conditions of the Omsk and other Western Siberian regions. Nevertheless, members of the Siberian Agricultural Research Institute in Omsk, in order to please Lysenko, and ignoring obvious facts, proved the unprovable on the plots of the institute, under hot-house conditions, and stubbornly branded as scientific conservatives the conscientious agricultural specialists who looked facts in the face. As a result, in the Omsk region alone, in the course of several years, tens of thousands of hectares of winter wheat were sown according to this method, and failed to return even the amount of seed originally expended.[15]

Incidentally, there were even hotheads who proposed that the system be used throughout the country.

SUGAR BEETS IN CENTRAL ASIA

The same inglorious end awaited another worthy contribution of Lysenko to the agriculture of our land during the Patriotic War. It was his suggestion for summer planting of sugar beets in Central Asia. This persistent proposal, made without any preliminary testing, was carried out in 1943 and 1944 on tens of thousands of hectares at once. These absurd plantings in parched soil were attempted several times on enormous areas, in the middle of the torrid Central Asian summers, and each time the shoots perished despite Lysenko's assertions of the feasibility of this measure, in the newspapers and in the 1944 collection of his papers.[16] Later editions of his works, however, omitted the articles on summer planting of beets.

TUBER-TOP PLANTING OF POTATOES

It is known that during the war, in addition to the methods just described, Lysenko also proposed a sometimes verifiably useful technique for planting the tops of potato tubers (the rest was used for food). It goes without saying that, in wartime, this method was occasionally effective, and to propagandize it was, of course, a direct duty of the president of the Agricultural Academy. But the authorship of the method, for which Lysenko received a Stalin prize, is in grave doubt. The point is that it was described not only in Pryanishnikóv's book in 1931,[17] but also in the 1905 cookbook, *A Gift for the Young Housewife*, by Elena Molokhovets.[18]

Incidentally, there are other innovations dubiously attributed to Lysenko, such as breaking off the tops of cotton plants to reduce bud drop. This method is described in a book published in 1896, a pamphlet in 1926,[19] and has long been used in the United States.

It is impossible to write of the practical aspects of Lysenkoism in the postwar period without bitter irony. It was with such irony that Pryanishnikov used to view many of Lysenko's discoveries. It was he who coined the remark about the "oblysenie"[20] (baldness) of agricultural science.

CLUSTER PLANTING

The first and costliest of Lysenko's postwar enterprises was closely connected with his "abolition" of intraspecific competition. According to Lysenko, Darwin invented this competition when the book of the reactionary, Malthus, happened to fall into his hands. The single unreliable experiment with kok-sagyz, which purported to prove the absence of competition within a species, was rapidly applied to trees. But once again there was no attempt to verify the notion: advertising was substituted for experiments. The government decree on tree planting in the steppe regions was issued in October, 1948, and by spring of 1949 Lysenko had already prepared instructions for cluster planting of oak and other species, thus negating centuries of experience in afforestation.

According to these instructions, clusters of thirty to forty acorns were to be planted. Thirty trees would arise from each cluster, and twenty-nine of them, according to Lysenko's theory, would, without mutual oppression, placidly die, filled with noble self-sacrifice for the prosperity of one fortunate shoot which they guarded, battling like soldiers with the surrounding grass. This new "law of species life" was termed "self-thinning-out" by Lysenko, and did not deny that the majority of plants in a cluster must perish. This was not the result of crowding, however, but for the glory of the species. "It must be emphasized," wrote Lysenko, "that self-thinning-out or the death of individual saplings in the group occurs not because they are crowded, but for the express purpose of ensuring that in the future they will not be crowded."[21]

The French scientist, the communist Marcel Prenant, described his impressions of a talk with Lysenko about this law. In 1957 he wrote:

In 1948 I was already amazed that Lysenko denied the existence of Darwinian intraspecific competition. At that time the *Literaturnaya Gazeta* published an interview with him on the subject. A translation of it appeared in an issue of *Europe* after the account of the LAAAS session. The text was so strange that I attributed it to some mediocre journalist, until Lysenko repeated it to me word for word in the course of a discussion with which he favored me in 1950.

I allowed myself to put a question to him: "I admit that young trees should be planted in a cluster; they may thus be better protected at first; but is it not necessary to remove some of them after a few years?" "No," replied Lysenko, explaining: "They will sacrifice themselves for one." "Do you mean," I replied, "that one will turn out to be stronger and the others will weaken or perish?" "No," he repeated, "they will sacrifice themselves for the good of the species," and he entered into a long and very hazy discourse, completely overwhelming me with a "materialistic" explanation which would have been acceptable to Bernardin de Saint Pierre, and which was very close to a belief in divine Providence.[22]

The law of self-thinning-out has to be amended, Lysenko recently announced at a meeting of front-rank agricultural workers of the Moscow region: only plants not yet cultivated obey it. Those that have been domesticated, and placed themselves in man's hands, abandon the law; why should they thin themselves out when man has machines to do it for them? It was no accident that corn was the first plant freed from the law's operation: under a high density of clusters, it produced no ears.

Nevertheless, it was precisely the law of self-thinning-out that was used by Lysenko and Ol'shansky as the basis for establishing field-protecting forest belts. Forest plantings on huge areas refused to obey the law, however, and perished as a result of the rejection of the concept of intraspecific competition for moisture and space, taking with them hundreds of millions of rubles, and paying no attention to the articles of Lysenko and Ol'shansky, which told of the beautiful state of forest belts planted in clusters.

The losses caused by use of the system, according to the computations of the former deputy Minister of Forestry, Koldanov, ran to about a billion old rubles.[23] In 1954, at the All-Union conference of foresters, the cluster method was almost unanimously voted down as bankrupt. Yet even here Lysenko was able to cover up the tracks of his errors. During the visit of the members of the government to his experimental base in 1962,[24] he demonstrated to the leaders of the Soviet Union, as proof of the correctness of his view, a fine stand of trees planted by the cluster method in 1949. But it should not be forgotten that what was wanted in 1948 was not the creation of forest belts near Moscow, in a forest area with adequate moisture, but on the treeless steppes in a droughty zone. Hence his demonstration as proof of the efficacy of cluster planting was mere eyewash.

It may be incidentally noted that the vitalistic idea of self-thinning-out of plants for the sake of the species as a whole was far from original. In 1923 the well-known Russian botanist, Liubimenko, had already published a book, *Individual and Society in the Plant World*, in which he advanced the same considerations in a much more thorough way. He wrote, for instance: ". . . the millions of individuals which perish for lack of space are essentially sacrificed not in the interest of the dominant trees, but in the interest of the pine forest as a whole."

Perhaps we should not have succeeded in establishing Liubimenko's priority had not Prezent subjected the idea of self-thinning-out to violent criticism in 1932. Citing the above quotation in the brochure already noted (Chapter 1, note 4), Prezent wrote:

True enough, this is poor consolation for the millions of dying trees, but such is the logic of the vitalist Liubimenko, who wants to shield the "dominant" trees and represent the loss of millions of plants as a beautiful death for the sake of the whole. . . . Does it not seem to you that the trend of Liubimenko's discourse resembles that of the mensheviks who, while recognizing the existence of classes and class struggle, still claim that the exploitation of workers by capital is not for the purpose of enrichment of capitalists but for the prosperity of the national whole . . . ? And does it not seem to you that the very "botanical" thought of a certain whole, standing above the interests of individual plants, is based not on botanical materials but on the corresponding bourgeois class aims?

Yet sixteen years later, when exactly the same ideas on the practically conscious self-thinning-out of plants were advanced by Lysenko in a considerably more absurd form, Prezent forgot his harsh conclusions and became a warm propagandist for these, according to his own definition, bourgeois class aims.

TRANSFORMATION OF SPECIES

The fantastic theory of a saltatory origin of one species from another without intermediate forms occupied a special place in Lysenko's work from 1948 on. This theory had a number of practical implications: Lysenko's ideas on plant nutrition and use of fertilizers (saltatory origin of microbes required by plants) were based on it, as well as his notions about the futility of ordinary methods of controlling weeds, which arise spontaneously from the cultivated plants themselves.

All collaborators of Lysenko began a somewhat original contest in his journal, *Agrobiologiya:* Who would detect most transformations? In nearly every issue of the journal from 1950 to 1955, articles appeared in which were seriously reported transformations of wheat into rye and vice versa, barley into oats, peas into vetch, vetch into lentils, cabbage into swedes, firs into pines, hazelnuts into hornbeams, alders into birches, sunflowers into strangleweed.

All of these communications were utterly without proof, methodologically illiterate, and thoroughly unreliable. The authors had one leading thought—to please Lysenko, to support by every means the theory advanced by him, to keep the Lysenko trend from being discredited. Lysenko's own conception was simple enough. "Under the action of external environment," he wrote, "which is unsuitable or little suitable for a given species, particles of a different species for which the conditions are more suitable arise in the body of the plant. From these particles, rudiments (buds or seeds) are formed which develop into individuals of the other species."[25] This unproved explanation, worthy of the worst examples of seventeenth and eighteenth century natural philosophy, embarrassed even some philosophers used to adjusting their concepts to any Lysenko ideas. This embarrassment was, for instance, apparent in an article in the journal *Voprosy Filosofi*[26] which, while defending the fantastic inventions of Lysenko, was nevertheless forced to note that the actual process of formation of "particles" of one species in the body of another had not yet been sufficiently investigated, and hence Lysenko's assertion must still be considered only a scientific hypothesis.

Of course, no serious person believed in such transformation, on top of which the discussion of the problem for many years proved the absurdity of such ideas. Yet Lysenko even here would not admit his obvious error, and in August, 1961, he repeated his thesis, characterizing it as an important achievement of Soviet materialistic biology. Moreover, on May 25, 1962, an article in *Sel'skaya Zhizn'* by Feiginson, one of the theoreticians of Lysenkoism, demanded the revocation of the doctor's degree of a scientist who previously believed in the origin of rye from wheat but later began to doubt this possibility.

It should also be pointed out that, at the 1948 LAAAS session and later, propaganda was used to present the question of origin of species in this manner as the way to creation of new, useful plants discovered by Lysenko. Yet, through the years of the saga, out of dozens of transformations no new species appeared. Only previously known forms arose—firs, pines, peas, alders, barley, etc. (including, sometimes, well-known cultivated varieties). This, of course, was no accident. Neither old nor new forms can arise in such a manner. The appearance of old forms can be demonstrated by using methodological tricks, but new ones cannot be produced by such techniques.

And once more, despite its manifest absurdity, the theory was not original. At the end of the seventeenth and the beginning of the eighteenth centuries, in John Ray's time, naive transformationism held the view that one species occasionally can give rise to another.

AGRICULTURAL CHEMISTRY

To recount all of Lysenko's practical "achievements" which failed the test of time would take a separate, long book. For example, it would be interesting to give the details of Lysenko's contribution to methods of fertilizer application, but they can be discussed here only in a bare outline.

The matter started with a suggestion, made in 1950, for a method of preparing special organic-mineral granules by mixing humus or manure with mineral fertilizers in a rotating barrel. Several years later, when practice rejected the use of such granules, organic-mineral mixtures, now to be obtained without the aid of a barrel, were proposed for use in small doses. They were expected to produce high yields—contrary to the reactionary law of input-output and therefore the no less reactionary law of conservation of matter and energy.

Fertilizer experts may be interested to know how, despite categorical objections from agricultural chemists, Lysenko for many years proposed to mix superphosphate with lime before applying it to the soil. This procedure is absurd because it transforms superphosphate into an insoluble form, tricalcium phosphate. What happens then is that the superphosphate is converted into phosphate, the raw material from which it is originally made in chemical factories, so that, instead of being applied to the soil, it might as well have been shipped back to the factory.

Also typical was Lysenko's suggestion that manure should

be applied to the soil only after it turns to humus—this was Vil'yams' favorite dream. But the trouble is that the most valuable component of manure, nitrogen, meanwhile evaporates into the air. But then, according to Vil'yams, it is only organic matter that counts.

The use of small doses of organic-mineral mixtures according to Lysenko's method was sharply criticized by agricultural chemists, and in particular by Sokolov at a 1956 meeting of the LAAAS devoted to discussion of the results of Lysenko's fertilizer methods.[27] Two excerpts from Sokolov's speech follow:

[Lysenko] pointed out that in my report, according to his opinion, there is no biology, that I am, of course, not a biologist and am even a poor chemist, and that chemical science must be developed as much as possible. With the latter, I am pleased. As to what kind of chemist I am, that is up to chemists to decide, but I do wish to say a few words about biology. Apparently we have two kinds of biology. There are biologists who for many years carry out experiments and obtain results which any investigator can reproduce anywhere, whether it be in the Soviet Union or the Chinese People's Republic. The results are the same because the experiment is repeatable, carried out according to recorded methods and under conditions guaranteeing the reliability and correctness of results. . . . But in experiments of these biologists there are no miracles. No matter how much I have watched these biologists, never in their experiments has rye turned into wheat, a warbler into a cuckoo, etc. Such phenomena are lacking among these biologists.

But then apparently there is another biology, and in that sense I do not care to be a biologist. I do not want such miracles in my experiments. And even if it began to seem to me that my rye was turning into cornflowers, it wouldn't be a bad idea if my collaborators advised me that it was time I retired, that the time had come. There are no miracles in this world! I do not want to be such a biologist, and I share the position that I am not a biologist, but in a different sense from that of [Lysenko].

The second excerpt recounts a visit to Lysenko's experiment station, Gorki Leninskie:

We were shown how well the organic-mineral mixtures work. Very well, but it would be good to see a neighboring plot where other methods of fertilizing were used for comparison. This was impossible. When we asked to see replications, they were not shown to us; apparently there were none. Finally, looking at the plots, I discovered some on which the plants growing particularly poorly were labeled, indicating the triple mixture[28] recommended by Lysenko. Of course, our attention was not drawn to those plots. I pointed out that in these experiments there were plots on the triple mixture in which plants grew well, and others where they grew poorly. So what happened? We left, and three days later in this auditorium Avakyan appears with masses of paper-wrapped plants. He pours them onto the table in front of the chairman and says: "Last time it was found that on some plots the triple mixture does not work. We went to the field, dug up the plants, and it turned out that the technician had made a mistake; he had not applied the triple mixture, but the label remained."

If experiments are made without replication, the results depend on the work of the technician. Is it necessary to characterize these experiments more vividly? All this happened in this auditorium and in Gorki Leninskie. I consider that such experiments should not be undertaken; they are a sheer waste of time.

The effectiveness of Lysenko's method of using organic-mineral mixtures had already come under discussion in 1955 at a special meeting of the Technical Council of the U.S.S.R. Ministry of Agriculture. Notice of it appeared only in the TAA newspaper.[29] The results of some one hundred experimental tests were discussed, and they all showed the lack of foundation for Lysenko's proposals and their economic worthlessness. Lysenko did not dispute the conclusions of the Technical Council: he ran to complain. A phone call to the Minister Matskevich, and the decision of the Technical Council was not confirmed.

The results of application of Lysenko's methods in this area were the usual ones: newspapers and questionnaires told of increased yields; reports of experiment stations indicated less effective results and economic unsoundness as compared with the scientifically based recommendations of agricultural chemistry. But the circulation of newspapers is great, and they provided Lysenko with a smoke screen until he invented the so-called manure-earth composts.

These composts had actually been known for a long time, and were used in vegetable growing, especially in hotbeds and greenhouses. But the earth component comprises only 15 to 20 per cent, and is added to improve the physical properties of the compost and as an absorbent. Lysenko, however, proposed the use of 80 to 90 per cent of earth in the compost for use in the field.

According to Lysenko's theoretical proposals, earth mixed with manure, watered, and enriched with chemicals acquired the properties of manure, and he immediately began to implement his suggestion. Neither he nor his associates was embarrassed by the fact that, under the system, means of transport would have to be overloaded to carry useless ballast, i.e., earth, around the field from one place to another. They were not embarrassed by the fact that the effectiveness of fertilizing drops while costs rise sharply under this method. Neither were they embarrassed by protests of agricultural chemists, since nobody published them. After all, any measure connected with Lysenko's name must be immediately adopted and must appear in official speeches. Whether it is good or bad is of only minor concern.

VEGETATIVE HYBRIDIZATION

Vegetative hybridization is the doctrine that grafting one plant onto another, which ensures the transfer of heredity by the sap, is equivalent to sexual hybridization. The significance of vegetative hybridization in biology is convincingly attested by the fact that more than three hundred people have received scientific degrees for experiments on it, and some became professors and even members of the LAAAS. The only things lacking in agricultural industry are the vegetative hybrids themselves, with the exception of a few tomato varieties of disputable origin. With such an army of scientists proving the existence of vegetative hybridization, with the enormous volume of work in this area, and the great amount of advertising proclaiming this method to be equal to and perhaps more promising than sexual hybridization, a few kinds of tomatoes in twenty-five years is less than a modest result.

It should be pointed out that serious and precise experiments by many scientists have failed to prove the possibility of transfer of hereditarily stable properties from stock to scion.[30] Tomatoes have a complex heredity. Every variety is a result of hundreds of prior crosses, and the effect of the stock may be to reveal or activate some concealed characters. In experiments with plants of nonhybrid origin, results of vegetative hybridization are always negative when carried out under properly controlled conditions.[31]

BRANCHED WHEAT

Who does not remember the preliminary advertising of branched wheat, which promised so much—100 to 150 centners per hectare and an agricultural revolution? This wheat, however, turned out to be much poorer than ordinary varieties, in both yield and disease resistance, in spite of the fact that all saw its huge spikes in Lysenko's own hands on the pages and covers of many periodicals.

In fact, the ancient Egyptians had tried unsuccessfully to grow this wheat widely even before our era. It has also been known from time immemorial in other countries, and rejected throughout a millennium of agricultural practice. Yet Lysenko brought it back. This was hailed as an achievement by newspapers, magazines, the radio. There was no end to promises, and work on branched wheat was made mandatory at most of the country's breeding stations. Dolgushin concluded his book on Michurinist methods of selection and seed production (see note 11) with a veritable poem about branched wheat, exclaiming:

Let us imagine a variety of wheat which will produce spikes weighing not one gram, but three, four or five times more. Such a form may be found in the already existing spring branched wheat, on which work of mastering methods for its production is in progress. Agronomic techniques are being investigated, and work is being carried out on hybridization for the creation of divers new forms of spring, as well as winter, wheats with highly productive spikes. In raising hybrids of this branched wheat, methods of Michurinist agrobiology are used. And the work is under the immediate direction of the president of the Lenin All-Union Agricultural Academy, Academician T. D. Lysenko, the head of Soviet agrobiological science, which is opening up for us limitless wide spaces for creative work for the good of our beautiful Homeland.

The end of all this ballyhoo was joyless. The branched wheat would not branch under ordinary growing conditions, its spikes were smaller than those of standard varieties, and its yield half as large. The miraculous wheat was susceptible to every disease, and its grain contained half the protein found in standard varieties. It was not even possible to make bread from its flour—the gluten content was insufficient. The din raised for many years ceased, but the losses were never tallied. The whole affair was the result of the obvious plant-breeding illiteracy of its initiators, who escaped even the slightest reproof: after all, they were apparently announcing another new victory over nature.

PLANT AND ANIMAL HORMONES

Lysenko's school has to its practical credit not only discoveries of new phenomena but also the debunking of old. One of his closest collaborators, Avakyan, for instance, abolished plant hormones, declaring them to be an invention of idealists. To this date he manages to insist on this, even though plant hormones are widely used in the practice of plant and fruit breeding. "It can be unerringly stated," declared Avakyan authoritatively, "that the hormonal theory of development is the same Mendelism-Morganism, that is, the same formalism and metaphysics in physiology."[32]

He was echoed by the more petty falsifiers, apparently also aspiring to be innovators. Moshkov, for instance, wrote: "Hormonal events are probably not inherent to plants. The hormonal theory of development, once in vogue, is in fact a mirage, which should be finished off as soon as possible."[33]

This achievement of Lysenkoism has by now been forgotten, and the State Planning Committee now establishes quotas for chemical factories for the production of synthetic plant hormones for agriculture.

In animal husbandry, hormonal stimulation of superovulation in sheep and other species had been developed by the Morganist M. M. Zavadovsky, and should be revived. The preparation worked out by him was widely used to raise significantly the production of caracul and other skins derived from newborn lambs. However, when Prezent and his patrons seized power in Moscow University, they shut down Zavadovsky's laboratory, dismissed him, and broke up the type for a large monograph written by him which was ready for the press. The use of his method was stopped. Zavadovsky, realizing its practical significance, appealed to the Minister of Agriculture, Benediktov. He, however, refused to aid the scientist, justifying his refusal on the grounds that there was already a shortage of foodstuffs, so that experimental increases in fertility were an empty venture. Seven or eight years later, after visiting Britain, Benediktov described, in a pamphlet, the hormonal method of inducing superovulation used there, and recommended its adoption at home.[34] By then Zavadovsky was dead, and the minister did not know that the English had successfully used the preparation developed by him.

INBRED-LINE HYBRIDS

Lysenko and his associates have long boasted of their struggle for many years against adoption in the U.S.S.R. of hybrid corn derived from crosses between inbred lines. Since this was an undoubted achievement of the genetics of reactionary Morganists, it had to be abused and defamed in spite of the demonstrable effect of hybridization on the agriculture of the United States and other countries. Lysenko, Prezent, Ol'shansky, Feiginson, Nuzhdin, and others spent twenty years attempting to stifle the development of this method in the U.S.S.R. They drove Vavilov's pupils, who continued the work, underground, declaring all the success of the technique abroad to be mere propaganda, blown up by capitalists for their own gains at the expense of the simpleton farmers who had not read the works of Lysenko.

The story of defamation of inbred-line hybrids began as early as 1935. Speaking at an LAAAS meeting in Odessa, Lysenko subjected inbreeding by self-fertilization to a sharp but unfounded criticism of little competence. "Is there a single variety in the world," he asked, "including corn, which was developed by inbreeding and which is in wide use? Yet inbreeding has been going on for a long time; in America corn has been inbred for twenty years."[35]

In this connection Vavilov provided the information on the brilliant success of hybrid corn and its wide adoption in the United States where, by then, 5 per cent of all areas under corn was planted to the hybrids, and their use was rapidly increasing. He pointed out that the practical Yankees would not be likely to adopt the method had it not increased yields. Yet in his concluding statement, replying to Vavilov, Lysenko turned the figures around, using a purely polemical trick without regard for the essence of the matter, clear to all:

More convincing is Vavilov's example with corn breeding in America. As is known, America is the birthplace of inbreeding, and the method has been basically worked out on corn. Vavilov stated that the Americans are a practical people and would not throw away money to no purpose. In defense of inbreeding he pointed out that, in America, some 5 per cent of the area devoted to corn is planted with hybrids derived from inbred lines. I do not understand in what way the practicality of Americans is demonstrated by this example: is it the fact that this "good business," the theory of inbreeding, is used on 5 per cent of the area, or is it that 95 per cent is sown with varieties of corn developed not by inbreeding, but by ordinary mass selection, i.e., a method completely opposite to inbreeding.[36]

After 1935 the area planted to hybrid corn in the United States increased rapidly. At the 1939 discussion sponsored by *Under the Banner of Marxism*, Vavilov stated that hybrid corn in the United States occupied 10 million hectares. Three or four years later, 100 per cent of the corn grown in the United States was of hybrid origin. But this did not modify Lysenko's original negative position; only the character of his critical argumentation changed. It became overly familiar and demagogic.

Feiginson, at the 1948 LAAAS session, assured the Soviet public that hybrid corn was the current swindle by the Morganists: "The Morganists proposed some complicated technical methods to produce hybrid corn (preliminary self-fertilization and selection of inbred lines), which make it difficult for large-scale use. This apparently serves the interests of the capitalist seed firms, since the methods proposed by the Morganists are inaccessible to ordinary farmers."[37]

Other Lysenkoites, Glushchenko, Ol'shansky, and Dolgushin, wrote in the same style. The latter said:

Enforced self-pollination of cross-fertilized plants is the so-called
inbreeding, a method of the Morganist-Mendelists which made so
much noise because the Mendelists had nothing to brag about except their skill in producing plants in some way changed and, as
a rule, deformed. This "achievement" of theirs they passed off as
mastery over the process of morphogenesis. What would the plant
world become if morphogenesis did, indeed, follow this path![38]

The same thesis was energetically defended by other Lysenkoites. This anti-inbreeding campaign continued until 1954
when, at one of the CC plenary sessions, after a careful study
of American experience, a resolution was passed directing
quick adoption of this progressive methodology in the
U.S.S.R. Had there not been the unproved, unfounded, tendentious, and simply ignorant propaganda by the Lysenkoites,
the method could have been adopted in 1938–1939 when it
was insistently proposed and plans for its organization were
prepared by Vavilov and his collaborators.[39] Thirty to fifty
billion kilograms of corn is the minimum loss sustained by
our country from the twenty-year anti-inbreeding campaign.

SODA BATHS

The wealth of proposals and pseudo discoveries of Lysenkoism is veritably inexhaustible. Among the attainments of this
home-grown school and its branches is the highly original
doctrine of Lepeshinskaya, who pronounced the great Louis
Pasteur a reactionary and an idealist. For a century, grateful
mankind had been rightfully proud of the name of that scientist, until Lepeshinskaya proposed her own candidacy to
supplant it. The proposal was warmly supported by Lysenko,
Sisakyan, Oparin, Zhukov-Verezhnikov, Bosh'yan, Nuzhdin,
and other representatives of the new biology, who eagerly
welcomed another prophet in their midst. In short order a
special meeting of the Committee on Stalin prizes was con-

vened in order to award Lepeshinskaya, without delay, a prize of 200,000 rubles for her great discoveries: mutual transformation of cells of plants and animals, spontaneous generation of *Infusoria* in broth of hay, formation of cells from egg albumen and of blood vessels from egg yolk.

The extraordinary award of a Stalin prize to Lepeshinskaya for her book on the origin of cells from living matter[40] was even more unexpected, since three years earlier, in 1946, it had been rejected by the biological section of the Committee. Lysenko was the only one who had voted for it then, so that the rejection had been virtually unanimous.

To believe all her rubbish voluntarily was of course difficult. Hence the U.S.S.R. Minister of Higher Education, Stoletov, issued a special order[41] which obliged all institutions of higher learning to believe Lepeshinskaya's teaching. The order was entitled: "On the reconstruction of scientific and educational work in histology, embryology, microbiology, cytology, and biochemistry in the light of O. B. Lepeshinskaya's theory of development of cellular and acellular forms of living matter." We have already touched on the orders of the previous Minister, Kaftanov. The new one followed the same path. He repealed all previous curricula and texts on cytology, histology, embryology, biochemistry, microbiology, general pathology, and oncology, and demanded that the new ones be based henceforth on Lepeshinskaya's teachings. The founder of some branch of science is usually considered a great scientist: the Minister's order declared Lepeshinskaya's teachings to be basic principles of all biological and medical science.

Lepeshinskaya's daughter surpassed even Bosh'yan who, as may be recalled, "discovered" the process of crystallization of bacteria. In her experiments the crystals turned not only into bacteria but also into the simplest animals, *Infusoria*. Lysenko was made particularly happy by these discoveries. He wrote an article about them and provided the elder Lepeshinskaya's book with a preface. And well he might have been happy. After all, Lepeshinskaya once more refuted the chromosome theory of heredity and helped in the construction of the theory of interspecific transformation.

Success inspired Lepeshinskaya, and she decided to bring happiness to mankind with still another discovery: she found an original method of rejuvenation, prolonging man's life and conquering old age. This discovery was the famous "soda baths."

A bag of soda in the bath and old age retreats, dissolving in the alkaline solution. The results of this discovery, propagandized in newspapers and periodicals, were not long in coming. Soda temporarily disappeared from stores and pharmacies, and polyclinics had to cope with a stream of the rejuvenated suffering from the naive faith in the healing powers of drinkable soda. On the occasion of one of her speeches, Lepeshinskaya, without noticing the hidden irony in the question, acknowledged that it was sensible to introduce soda into the body even by way of an enema. This provided a way of prolonging life even for that major part of mankind which still has no private baths.

ALTERATION OF SOILS

And then there was the promising method of agriculture proposed by the favorite of Vil'yams and Lysenko, Bushinsky. He suggested that land should be plowed not to a depth of 20 centimeters, as is usually done, but of a meter, turning the infertile strata, usually ordinary clay, up to the surface. It was a majestic sight—a powerful tractor dragging behind it an enormous plow making a ditch large enough to lay an oil pipe, while on the next trip around it would be covered up and a new ditch dug next to it. This treatment yielded no crops; but, since it was designated "the radical alteration of soils," it was guaranteed to be successful. (After all, "radical alteration of soils" does sound impressive.) Luckily, this foolish venture, which lasted some years, fell with a crash just as Bushinsky had decided to recommend his method to collective and state farms.

All this is now past history. Knowledge of the past, of course, is important in evaluating trends, but their fate is usually decided by the present and future. What, then, remains today to the credit of the "new" genetics? First, some new varieties, created, according to the official version, exclusively on the basis of Lysenko's teaching. And second, the high butterfat-yielding herd of cattle on the farm of the AS Institute of Genetics and a promise to increase butterfat content by 1 per cent in the whole Soviet Union. Let us examine these claims.

SPRING AND WINTER WHEAT

First, we may consider the plant-breeding achievements so intensively discussed in the course of the recent celebration of the jubilee of the Lysenko Odessa Institute of Plant Breeding and Genetics.[42] The discussion centered on the production of a series of good varieties by Lysenkoite plant breeders (Yur'ev, Kirichenko, Remeslo, and others) through "education." An examination of the data shows, however, that *the fundamental method in producing all these varieties was the classical plant-breeding method of individual selection.* New characters are in most cases created by classical hybridization. The methods of "education" (such as prewinter planting of spring forms) only provide the necessary background for selection, which is the same method used in Vavilov's time and which is still used in plant breeding throughout the world. Arguments about assimilation of the fall condition, of change of heredity under the influence of agronomic conditions, and so forth, are just a coating to give a Lysenkoite appearance. The effect of all these factors in securing one or another result has never been proved by anybody; it has just been announced.

That the main role in the transformation of one form into another is played by hybridization and selection in a changed environment is amply evident from the description of the methods of re-education found in accounts of the work of plant breeders.[43]

We are happy with any success in Soviet plant breeding; a good variety is a good variety, regardless of whether it was produced by a Lysenkoite or a "Morganist." But when even a minor practical achievement is used first of all to advertise and establish a monopoly for one method of breeding, the success is no longer a success. And there was precisely this tone to the din recently raised in connection with the new varieties of the Odessa Institute. Its director, Musiyko, after reviewing his attainments in a jubilee article, wrote: "The Michurinists, on the basis of strictly controlled experiments in genetics, breeding, and seed growing, step by step pressed speculative, dogmatic, formal genetics, unmasking its theoretical bankruptcy and its practical unproductiveness."[44]

One could name a good many Soviet plant breeders (Tsitsin, Zosimovich, Lebedeva, Lutkov, Sakharov, and others) who, in difficult circumstances, obtained excellent results, but whose achievements are hushed up, to the detriment of Soviet science, only because these scientists do not belong among Lysenko's followers.

In discussing the overblown publicity crediting Lysenko followers with a monopoly in obtaining successful results, it should not be forgotten that numerous excellent varieties are produced annually in the United States, Sweden, Britain, Canada, the Federal German Republic, the German Democratic Republic, France, and other countries, where all plant breeding and seed production are now based on cytogenetics.

D. N. Pryanishnikov

B. E. Raikov

N. M. Tulaikov

I. I. Shmal'gauzen

Above: left, N. N. Semenov; center,
V. N. Sukachev; right, P. N. Konstantinov.

Below: left, V. D. Dudintsev; center,
V. A. Engel'gardt; right, N. A. Maksimov.

THE JERSEY CATTLE EXPERIMENT

Special attention should be paid to the latest advertised measure—the increase in butterfat content of milk by crossing
Jerseys (6 to 7 per cent) with our ordinary local breeds. We
shall not go into the two hundred-year-old, unpromising history of the use of Jerseys for crosses in various countries.
Nor need we give the history of the idea in the U.S.S.R.,
first advanced by the well-known animal breeder, Kislovsky.
At his suggestion the Ministry of Agriculture bought a number of cows and bull calves of the ancient Jersey breed, from
which Kushner (apparently in 1954 or 1955) selected two
young bulls for Lysenko's experimental farm. For several
years there has been so much noise in the press about these
experiments that it might be thought that the problem has
been solved. In fact, however, the noise is the usual preliminary
self-advertising. The experiment is designed to last several
years, and publicity about success and future prospects must
be carried on from the beginning. Beyond that, as we have
seen, importunate propaganda, especially from above, ensures
positive results for the questionnaire-based evaluation of effectiveness and encourages the hushing up of negative results.

In his presidential address in August, 1961, Lysenko said
that his experiments on butterfat originate in the "law of the
existence of a biological species," formulated by him, and
even more so in "the law of transformation of nonliving
matter (food) into living matter by means of the latter." The
first law we have already seen as applied to the plant world:
voluntary death of the weaker members of the species in the
name of the good of all, i.e., self-thinning-out. But this "law"
apparently did not apply to domesticated species, and how it
works to maintain high butterfat content in crosses with low
butterfat cattle is not known to us. It would seem that the
best way to use this law would be to remove from herds the

cows with milk of low butterfat content—a simple selection process of culling inferior producers. Such culling is apparently being carried out, but on what scale has not as yet been made public.

The law of the existence of a species, according to its discoverer, manifests itself first of all in the species doing all it can to flourish. This is why, perhaps, the law is reflected not only in the self-thinning-out but in other acts of higher consciousness on the part of biological structures. One of these becomes significant in animal husbandry. It is Lysenko's conviction that a hybrid zygote develops traits not in accordance with the Morganist laws of segregation and dominance and recessiveness, but in the way most profitable to itself.[45] To popularize, Lysenko sometimes expresses the law as: "The zygote is no fool." But how is this manifested in connection with butterfat? It turns out to be a very simple matter. If the bull is genetically large and of high butterfat, and the cow mated to him is small, high butterfat milk content will not be transmitted. The zygote feels that a large calf (because of his father's heredity) would have difficulty in emerging from a small cow, and hence it chooses to develop in the maternal direction, which is of benefit to the species. But, in crossing a small bull of a high butterfat genotype with a large cow, the zygote, foreseeing no problems at calving, can calmly develop along the line of his sire's high butterfat heredity. This is helped by doubling and tripling the normal food consumption of the gestating cow, since increasing the growth of the fetus tends to push it farther in the direction of the properties of the father. Lysenko's basic publications on his theoretical ideas in this area, and the book (1961) and article of his collaborator, Ioannisyan,[46] clearly demonstrate that it is this teleological principle that underlies the hope that the high butterfat inheritance from a Jersey bull would continue to be preserved in further crosses. To make it absolutely clear that there is no misunderstanding of the initial postulations in the experiment, we may cite Lysenko's own statement:

Jersey cows usually weigh 350 to 400 kilograms, while the cows we have on our farm, both purebred and others, weigh 550 to 700 kilograms. We surmise that the zygotes, the embryos from crosses of large cows with bulls of small breeds, will, with abundant nutrition, develop along the lines of the small breed.[47]

As it happened, the calves in this case were intermediate in size (30 to 31 kilograms). The explanation was very simple: 20 of the kilograms (typical for Jerseys) were due to the calves' "choosing" to develop in the Jersey direction, and the remainder were not the result of heredity but of the abundant feeding of the mothers.

It should be noted that crossbreeding with imported Jersey cows and bulls had been started independently of Lysenko, on other farms in the U.S.S.R. some ten years ago, without any great noise. Perhaps because concentrates were in short supply, or maybe because the zygotes were more stupid, the inheritance of different traits in the hybrids was intermediate, and proportional to the percentage of Jersey genes they carried.

As to the other, even more general, law of transformation of nonliving into living matter, on which these experiments were based, it could be stated, we think, in a simplified version as: "Food, if it is nonliving (which is not always the case), is assimilated by an organism only when it is eaten." It is not too clear how Lysenko's experiments are based on this law, but apparently the point is that, for hybrid cows to produce rich milk, they should be fed, the more the better. If it were possible to use the phenomenal standards of feeding in collective and state farms that are used by Lysenko on his farm, we might be able to put into practice his methods of increasing butterfat content of milk. But by the time this is possible—and it is hard to say when that will be—

there will be enough milk in the country so that the failure of increasing butterfat percentage as a result of using Jerseys will not grieve anyone.[48]

CONCLUSIONS

Before summarizing the chapter, it may be appropriate to show the ways in which representatives of the Lysenko sect ascribed to themselves the achievements of others. One of the most interesting methods was found by Greben', the leader of the zootechnical wing of Lysenkoism. He used the technique of Gogol's hero Chichikov in acquiring "dead souls." One such dead soul was the great Soviet animal husbandman, M. F. Ivanov, who died in the same year that Lysenko and Prezent announced their attack on modern biology.

Ivanov took a favorable view of genetics, and in the mature period of his activity successfully used its principles in the creation of new breeds of livestock. At the 1948 session of the LAAAS, however, Ivanov was proclaimed a founder of Michurinism, and in the posthumous edition of his works, Greben', the editor, carefully removed from all articles and books all sections, paragraphs, and sentences in which Ivanov spoke well of genetics or used genetical terminology (combinations of genes, genotype, phenotype, heterozygosity, mutation, lethal gene, etc.). Ivanov was thus repainted into a Lysenkoite. Greben' continued this falsification while acting as a scientific consultant for Elagin's biographical novel and the mediocre film made about Ivanov.[49]

In ending this part of the book, we do not wish to evaluate or draw conclusions from the various issues discussed. Facts must speak for themselves. We have shown first of all what methods the Lysenkoites and Vil'yamsists used to gain recognition for their ideas. Distortion of facts, demagoguery, intimidation, dismissal, reliance on authorities, eyewash, misinformation, self-advertising, repression, obscurantism, slander, fabricated accusation, insulting name calling, and physical elimination of opponents—all were part of the rich arsenal of effective means by which, for nearly thirty years, the "progressive" nature of scientific concepts was confirmed. Lysenkoism could be maintained only as a result of "political" provocation, colored in different hues depending on the historical situation. There were no other effective proofs of its concepts, and any relatively free discussion (such as took place in 1936, 1946–47, and 1953–1958) put Lysenkoism in mortal danger.

Analysis of the content of those discussions has shown that they are sufficient proof of Lysenkoism's bankruptcy, of its detachment from world science, of its sectarian nature. The analysis also shows that it is impossible to fight Lysenkoism by methods of academic discussion and scientific argument. Lysenkoism does not recognize any criticism from without, any critique by representatives of other scientific trends.

We have shown here how Lysenkoism attained its supremacy, and this we consider the most important point. Only a scientifically bankrupt doctrine would use such methods; correct theories spread and win recognition primarily because they are correct. False concepts can be imposed temporarily on science only by demagoguery, repression, and suppression; correct ideas and theories develop and find support in spite of any suppressive methods. *The demonstration of the ways and means that secured the imposition of Lysenkoism on our science for so long is, then, a demonstration of its scientific bankruptcy.*

We have paid particular attention to the fate of many scientists who perished tragically during the period of the personality cult because of their participation in the debate described. This side of the controversy deserves very careful study.

Looking back on our biological and agronomic science, we see much to be proud of and much to regret. It is very easy

to establish who were actually guilty in causing the great lag
in our biology and agricultural science—a lag which is felt
more acutely every year, and which has had dire effects in
many branches of our economy.

It is difficult to reconcile oneself to this situation and to
bear it. In understanding the causes of the situation that was
created, one begins to understand even better, and to respect
the courage and high principles of such foremost scientists
and patriots as Vavilov, Kol'tsov, Sabinin, Tulaikov, Karpechenko, Pryanishnikov, and many other Soviet scientists
who have defended and are defending the dignity and purity
of Soviet science.

It is not on ethical grounds alone that one finds it impossible
to be reconciled to the situation. The turn of events caused,
and is still causing, immeasurable damage. Direct losses from
the failure of one or another measure can be calculated. Indirect harm resulting from failure to use many available measures is more difficult to establish. And even harder to compute
is the damage caused by the inadequate preparation of cadres
in schools, in agricultural, biological, and medical institutions
of higher learning, in the areas of genetics and breeding. In
secondary schools, millions of children still learned, from the
stereotyped text on Darwinism by Veselov, that Morganist
genetics is unproductive and reactionary, that it was begotten
of the bourgeoisie, that acquired characters are inherited, and
so forth. This falsification was continued in university biology
textbooks. Even in the modern text on breeding and seed
growing of field crops designed for agronomic institutes (by
Maksimovich), and the text on genetics of animals (by Vsyakikh), genetics and the bases of breeding were set forth only
in accordance with Lysenko's ideas, and all that is related to
real genetics was either defamed or ignored. Even the regulari-
ties of segregation of hybrids, as necessary for breeders as
air, were not discussed—only in order to avoid writing about
Mendel, whose data cannot be disproved. In the section on

foundation material, Vavilov's name is not mentioned. The Soviet stage in the development of breeding of field crops begins with Lysenko.

And such misinformation extends beyond agriculture. Twenty-five successive classes of physicians have been graduated from medical school without the slightest notion of the laws of heredity.

We have previously mentioned Astaurov's article depicting the fair image of the Soviet scientist and patriot, Kol'tsov. The end of the article is symbolic, and we should like to quote it in concluding this chapter, because the lifelong motto of Kol'tsov is equally characteristic of all the scientists to whose memory this book is dedicated.

"All his life," wrote Astaurov of Kol'tsov, "was consonant with the words of his favorite poet, the words which he more than once declaimed with warm feeling as his life motto, in solemn and joyful moments:

> *Just as this lantern will flicker and pale*
> *In the face of the bright rise of dawn,*
> *The wisdom that's false will grow dim*
> *   and will fail*
> *Before mind's perpetual light.*
> *All hail to the sun! Let dispersed*
> *   be the night!*"[50]

Part III

The Last Phase: 1962-1966

As already noted, the preceding chapters were written in 1961–1962, a period in which Lysenkoism
occupied a dominant position in our biology and
agronomy, at least organizationally. It also maintained its supremacy in the systems of secondary and
higher education and was unconditionally supported
politically and administratively. In view of these conditions there seemed to be little likelihood that such
a manuscript could be published. It was therefore
written as a critical and historical essay intended to
influence public opinion through verbal discussion in
various places and at various levels and, particularly,
to draw attention to the facts and possibly to evaluate the existing situation.

Lysenkoism was undoubtedly a definite historical
phenomenon; it was actively and skillfully implanted
in connection with a number of other events at a
higher level. It was not a normal stage of scientific
development, but rather a symptom of a very serious
disease. And it is natural that the gradual "crowding-
out" of Lysenkoism, beginning with October, 1964,

was also a reflection of historical events that the eye-witnesses must not leave unstudied and undescribed.

The years 1962–1966 were tempestuous for Soviet biology. This period began with the strengthening of Lysenkoism, which received exceedingly wide-spread state and political support, in many ways approaching the August, 1948, situation. Khrushchev gave Lysenko broad and concrete help somewhat more often than had Stalin. Essentially, the head of the party and of the government became a direct advocate of Lysenkoism, responsible for carrying out his pseudoscientific recommendations. So close were the links between Lysenko's and Khrushchev's activities that the turning point in the latter's fate in October, 1964, was also the radical turning point in the fate of Lysenkoism. The remaining chapters examine the course of those events.

CHAPTER 9

The Events of 1962-1964

THE AS REVIEWS LYSENKO'S WORK

THE CRACKING of the genetic code and the discovery of the mechanisms of protein synthesis and self-reproduction of hereditary macromolecules, accomplished in 1961–1962, shook up the scientific community throughout the world. Biology became the center of universal attention. The popular press presented these accomplishments as a current sensation, and the readers, accustomed to the various happenings in space exploration, and having lost track of the number of artificial satellites, readily switched their interests to the science of greatest import to mankind. As a result, in the few months at the end of 1961 and the beginning of 1962, the funding of biological research increased (in the United States, for example, three- or fourfold), and the new fields of biology—molecular biology, molecular genetics, molecular biophysics, and others—rapidly assumed a dominant position.

Against the background of this overwhelming progress in biology, with its avalanche of discoveries indicating new possibilities and tremendous practical potentialities, the lag in Soviet biology stood out sharply. The yoke of Lysenkoism became particularly burdensome as this pseudoscience continued seeking to suppress the new shoots inevitably sprouting in our science. The control of biological literature by the supporters of Michurinist biology was so tight that for four years (1959–1962) there was scarcely a single article in the Soviet press openly critical of Lysenkoism. It was impossible to publish genetics articles as such during that period, and they had to appear in periodicals devoted to chemistry, physics, or mathematics. No direct critique of Lysenko himself got past editorial boards or the censorship. At the same time, periodicals and the popular press continued to propagandize the significance of the work of Michurinists for agriculture and the national economy.

Nonetheless, the backwardness of our theoretical biology became so obvious that some decisions had to be made as pressure on the AS and other scientific administrative organs became stronger and stronger. On May 11, 1962, the AS praesidium called an organizational conference on molecular biology, at which Engel'gardt made a substantial report on the state and prospects of this branch of science. He very vividly emphasized the fact that the new discoveries in molecular biology were not an isolated event, but represented a shift of all natural science, and marked the most important development in the study of nature in the twentieth century.[1] The conclusions of the report were warmly supported by all participants of the conference and, as a result, a permanent Scientific Council on Molecular Biology was established. Since the program adopted by the conference, calling for the creation of new institutes and laboratories, was a procedure requiring governmental decrees, the AS praesidium established a special commission to prepare them. The commission went to work quickly, and its working subcommittees, with the approval of the AS praesidium, began review of research in the AS biological institutes. The AS Institute of Genetics, headed by Lysenko, fell within the bounds of such review. At the end of June, for the first time in twenty years, the Institute was visited by a group of scientists with a mandate to examine, investigate, and report its findings. The group included representatives of biology, physics, chemistry, and even medicine.

The commission carefully reviewed the research under way at Gorki Leninskie, carried out a series of interviews with Lysenko, and at what was planned as the penultimate meeting on July 10, 1962, decided almost unanimously to pass a vote of censure on the state of affairs in the institute and the level of research under way. The censure was to be formally voted on at the last meeting and communicated to the AS praesidium. But, on the evening of July 12, all members of the commission were notified by telephone that the last meeting had been canceled and the commission dissolved. All of its materials were sequestered by the CC, and their fate remains unknown.

THE NEW DECREE

The causes of this turn of events were obvious. On July 11, 1962, Khrushchev and other party and government leaders visited Gorki Leninskie. The next day the central press carried front-page photographs of Lysenko next to Khrushchev, among the leaders of the country, either on the dairy farm or amid a rich stand of grain. The photographs were accompanied by news stories relating Khrushchev's approval of all the work of Lysenko and his followers. Khrushchev noted that "The attainments of Michurinist biology are the result of the persistent struggle of scientists and practitioners: they are our national property and the property of the Communist party. These practical achievements aid in the creation of abundance of agricultural products and in the solution of the problem of Communist construction in our land."[2]

Immediately after the visit, the AS commission charged with preparing decrees on the development of molecular biology ceased to exist. Instead, another commission was created to prepare a quite different decree calling for the orientation of Soviet biologists toward facing life and strengthening the bonds of biology and practice, with Lysenko's achievements as a model for other areas. Lysenko and a group of his followers were included in the commission although it was headed by Kirillin, in charge of the CC section on science, who at that time took a neutral stand. The commission included some opponents of Lysenko, and therefore could not bring in a one-sided report. Rather, a compromise might be expected, involving at least temporary common consent of the opposing currents, to be presented to the higher administrative levels.

The commission worked a long time in an agony of contradictions. On many issues no agreement could be reached. Several deadlines passed, and still the commission could not produce a definitive report. Finally, those at the higher governmental levels lost their patience and, instead of the large commission, an editorial group of seven was organized, representing the basic administrative agencies involved (CC, the Ministry of Higher Education, the Ministry of Agriculture, the Committee on Coordination of Research, the AS, the LAAAS, and the Academy of Medical Sciences). On the basis of previous protocols and proposals, this group drafted the text of the final project. It was accepted by the CC and the Council of Ministers and published in the central press.[3]

The project was, indeed, a compromise, calling for development of all trends and the whole complex of biological science. Although the development of Michurinist biology was particularly emphasized, the achievements and significance of other, anti-Lysenkoite, currents were also noted: the formulation, indeed, gave legal scope for return to real genetics. A series of research tasks for genetics was outlined in a long list of fundamental problems of biology, medicine, and agricultural science, and possibilities for genetics to exist side by side with Michurin biology were also opened in the sphere of education.

In the resolution, neither "Morganism" nor "Mendelism" was mentioned, and no names were named. This was very important. Yet the agricultural department of *Pravda* placed next to the text a front-page photograph of two Lysenkoites (Kirichenko and Garkavyi) amid tall wheat at the Odessa institute (on which Lysenko's name had been conferred in 1948). This was in January, during snowstorms and frosts, and fields of wheat were hardly an appropriate illustration to the text, particularly since no explanation of the photograph was given. Presumably it was a symbolic illustration of the model—of the pattern to be emulated in linking science with practice.

A compromise with genetics, however, could not satisfy such men as Lysenko, Ol'shansky, Prezent, and other members of the group. There cannot be two different valid truths regarding the same phenomena of nature. Darkness is incompatible with light. Development of real genetics, its penetration into education, the opportunity presented to youth to choose between the two concepts by comparison and evaluation of their respective merits, were not acceptable to the Lysenkoites. They could not accept a truce, for the struggle against world science was their means of existence. And it was natural that they noticed only the part in the government decree that approved their trend and dealt with their successes, and used it to broaden their monopoly and to support further criticism of classical biology.

Almost immediately after publication of the decree, a long article by Lysenko appeared. Occupying two columns, it was entitled "The theoretical bases of directed changes in heredity of agricultural plants."[4] Lysenko had been published before in *Pravda* and in *Izvestiya*, but simultaneous appearance in both of the central newspapers was no ordinary publication: it meant that Lysenko's article had come to both papers from the CC with directions to publish without review or editorial changes. The article created a distressing impression. In it Lysenko repeated his old and severely criticized proposition about transformation of one species into another; about the errors of Darwin, Morgan, Weismann; about his concept of heredity; and so forth. This time he added his new laws of transformation of nonliving into living matter and of the life of the species (see Chapter 8). Once more he denied the existence of a hereditary substance and the role of DNA in inheritance. In the year 1963, the year of wide interest in the problems of the genetic code, protein synthesis, chromosome action, and so forth, the directive article of Lysenko was a scandalous anachronism attempting to turn Michurin biology back to its 1937 and 1948 levels.

Lysenko's supporters quickly tried to reinforce their position by administrative measures. A session of the LAAAS was convened on March 5–7 to discuss the government decree on biology, at which a report on the objectives of the Academy was made by its president, Ol'shansky.[5] He obviously wanted to have the session approach the 1948 one in significance and, under cover of the decree, he demonstrated in his report the triumph of Michurinist biology over the reactionary Morganism-Mendelism.

According to Ol'shansky, until the appearance of the Michurinist trend, biology had developed only in the nineteenth century: "In the beginning of the twentieth century its path of development was barred by Mendelism-Morganism." Then the president of the LAAAS described the history of the unmasking of Morganism and the triumph of the ideas of Michurin and Lysenko, who ensured the fulfillment of a socialist reconstruction of agriculture. Ol'shansky stated directly that it was Lysenko who had created the materialistic concepts of Michurinist biology. According to Ol'shansky the theory that the gene is a DNA molecule merely made doubly clear the defects of Morganism; and the promises of geneticists to gain control over biochemical mechanisms of variability are worthless, since Michurinist biology had long ago learned how to control variation and is constantly creating new forms of plants and animals required by our practice. Much attention was paid in the report to practical attainments and especially to butterfat content, earth-compost fertilizers, and the polemics with Western and Soviet geneticists.

Those participating in the discussion of the report were mostly Lysenko followers,[6] and the resolution adopted called for LAAAS to be, as before, the center of the Michurinist current in biology. Combined with Lysenko's article, noted above, and other articles by Lysenkoites (including philosophical ones), the session clearly demonstrated how the compromise decree of the CEC and the Council of Ministers was utilized for a further attack on classical biology and the reinforcement of the Michurinist monopoly. At the same time, as a result of the decree, opposing procedures strengthening real science were also initiated. Financial support of scientific institutions was increased, imports of scientific equipment were started, and the experimental and organizational possibilities for biological research were broadened. Publication of translated monographs and books was intensified. They disclosed the status of scientific advances abroad and had a decisive influence on young scientists who obviously were not disposed to swell the ranks of Lysenko's followers. Yet geneticists could not openly reply to their critics: the ban on a critical analysis of Lysenko's views still remained in force.

LENIN PRIZES

Among many other works, two by Lysenkoite scientists were nominated for Lenin prizes in 1963: that of Musiyko on hybridization of corn, and of Remeslo on the production of new wheat varieties by "re-education." Both were moot. Musiyko had fought for many years against adopting the practice of hybridization between inbred lines, and advocated instead intra-line crosses of clearly inferior quality. At the same time the method of re-education used by Remeslo raised severe doubts and was not repeatable by others. Actually, Remeslo used ordinary selection, and his arguments about re-education were merely a means to attract special attention and gain Lysenko's patronage.

Ol'shansky was the rapporteur on these works before the committee on Lenin prizes, of which Lysenko was a member representing agriculture (he was the only biologist on the praesidium).[7] The discussion did not go smoothly. Some committee members expressed grave doubts regarding the value of the works, and by a secret ballot on April 11, 1963, they were rejected. Ordinarily the decisions of the committee are confirmed by the U.S.S.R. Council of Ministers and published on April 21, Lenin's birthday. But by Saturday, April 13, the storm broke. Khrushchev demanded categorically that the whole committee of over a hundred be immediately reconvened to review its negative decision. An extraordinary meeting was called for April 15. There, objectors trying to substantiate their objections were interrupted or not given the floor. The voting this time was in favor of Musiyko and Remeslo, who thus became Lenin prize laureates to the glory of Michurinist science.

THE NEVA DISCUSSION

In the beginning of April, 1963, in the third issue of the Leningrad literary and social-political magazine *Neva*, there appeared an article by Zh. Medvedev[8] and Kirpichnikov entitled "The perspectives for Soviet genetics." It was published as a result of the initiative of the editor-in-chief, Voronin, and a member of the editorial board, Khvatov, who decided on this step after a careful study of the situation in biology. Together with a popular account of the basic theoretical and practical achievements of genetics, the article contained a clear-cut critique of Lysenkoism and its attempts to isolate Soviet biology from world science.

The authors wrote in their conclusions:

How, then, did it happen that in our country the development of modern genetics was so long delayed? Why did we for so long yield to the capitalist countries this large and productive area of the scientific front under the excuse that genetics is a bourgeois science? After all, we do not talk of "bourgeois physics," "bourgeois chemistry," "bourgeois physiology"! On the contrary, in these and other fields of knowledge we follow carefully the work done abroad and attempt to use rapidly all that is new and interesting. Beyond that, we try to ensure successful development in the U.S.S.R. of modern research in all scientific disciplines. Only in biology certain people still try persistently to draw a line between Soviet and world science and to ignore all work done by representatives of scientific currents different from their own.

The answers to the questions posed seem to us to be very simple. It could have happened only in the environment of distortions observed in the era of the personality cult. The attempt to isolate Soviet biology from world science is a harmful remnant of the personality cult, an alienation from reality, a fear of openly and honestly admitting and correcting previous errors.

As was to be expected, the article did not fail to attract the attention of Lysenkoites. The first response came in an article, "The ideological front of the struggle in modern genetics," under the authorship of Vsyakikh, Vlasov, and Brigis.[9] As an epigraph, in large type, the article carried an excerpt from Khrushchev's comments at his meeting with writers on March 8, 1963: "Peaceful coexistence in the area of ideology is treason against Marxism-Leninism and betrayal of the cause of workers and peasants."

The tone of the article was in the style of the ideological struggle of 1948:

The biological front of the battle is not only the battlefront of a Soviet scientist to further technical progress; it is the battlefront of Soviet ideology versus bourgeois ideology. There cannot be peaceful coexistence on this front. . . . Medvedev and Kirpichnikov want to convince the readers of *Neva* of the nonclass basis of genetics in order to shield the genetics of Weismann, Mendel and Morgan. . . . The Mendelist-Morganist trend in genetics is essentially idealistic in nature and, no matter what guise it is in, it has fenced itself in by scientific terminology and fabricated "laws."

This is not changed by the attempts of the Weismannist-Morganists to disguise their ideas in the form of science and materialism
by calling genes (the imagined particles of an imagined hereditary
substance) materialistic . . . since such structures do not have and
cannot have the property of heredity.

THE CC PLENARY SESSION

The June, 1963, plenary session was planned to include discussion of the problems of literature, art, party propaganda,
and others, which arose primarily as a result of the revelations
of the personality cult and related phenomena. But the usual
aspirations of the Lysenkoites to give their continuing debate
on genetics an ideological coloration bespoke the fact that
they would also use this plenary session to strengthen their
positions. And such attempts, indeed, took place. Ol'shansky
and Lysenko, through the agricultural secretary of the CC,
Polyakov, tried to include in the basic report by Il'ichev a
number of propositions regarding the ideological, reactionary
nature of Mendelism-Morganism. However, at a preliminary
discussion between Il'ichev and the AS leaders, it was decided
to omit the propositions from the basic documents of the
session. And, in the broad and long discussion at the plenary
session, critical words were uttered against Lysenko's opponents only once, and that was in the speech of the Secretary
of the Moscow committee of the party, Egorychev, condemning the manuscript of the first draft of this book. Background
material for this part of Egorychev's speech had been provided by the secretary of the TAA party committee, Step-
anov, who, in July and November, 1962, organized special
study sessions of the manuscript, declaring it to be antiparty,
antiscience, and anti-Soviet.[10]

Egorychev said:

Soviet science is developing at unprecedentedly rapid rates. The
Marxist-Lenin philosophical formulation of the basis of the newest

discoveries is of the greatest significance in the correct education of scientific cadres for successful development of all branches of science. Lenin has taught us that "without a solid philosophical formulation, no natural science, no materialism can withstand the struggle against the attack of bourgeois ideas."

Many scientists, forgetting this directive by Lenin, take an uncritical attitude toward bourgeois scientific concepts. Thus, for instance, Medvedev, in the past a senior scientific worker in the TAA department of agricultural chemistry, prepared a monograph on *Biological Science and the Personality Cult*. In it the fundamental questions of development of Soviet biology are interpreted incorrectly, Michurinist science is defamed, and bourgeois research, which is not consistently materialistic, is lauded to the skies. Rebuffed by the collective of the Academy, Medvedev did not lay down his arms, but shifted his base to the Kaluga region, and wrote a book [published by the Medgiz][11] on *Biosynthesis of Proteins and Problems of Ontogenesis* containing similar errors. Behind the screen of pseudoscience, ideological dislocations are sometimes hidden! Unfortunately we still publish too few books and serious philosophical studies attempting to comprehend the advances in natural sciences, and which would aid in the unmasking of views foreign to us.[12]

Egorychev's speech was printed in full only in Moscow papers, and had no serious consequences, although two curious episodes in connection with it are worth relating. At the time, I did, indeed, work in Obninsk in the Kaluga region, in the Molecular Radiobiology Laboratory of the U.S.S.R. Academy of Medical Sciences Institute of Radiobiology. A highly placed official from the Kaluga region was present at the CC plenary session. Having heard of Medvedev, who "did not lay down his arms but shifted his base to the Kaluga region," he telephoned Kaluga and ordered Medvedev's base to be shifted some place farther away. A search for Medvedev was immediately initiated by telephone among various scientific institutions, and he was located in Borovsk in the Institute of Livestock Biochemistry and Physiology, some 30 kilometers from

Obninsk. It was a different Medvedev, but he happened also to be a biochemist and a graduate of TAA. An order for his dismissal followed. The institute directors, summoned to Kaluga several days later, understood the reasons for it, and explained that this Medvedev had no connection with the books mentioned and was a quiet and calm person. By the time the real author was found, passions had abated considerably. Furthermore, by 1963 Lysenkoism no longer had support in medicine, and the Academy of Medical Sciences was undertaking decisive steps for the rebirth of medical genetics.

The second book mentioned by Egorychev had a sadder fate in 1963. Two weeks before the plenary session, all of the issue was removed from circulation at the order of the CC ideological commission, barely two to three days after it had been consigned to the distributing agency. The CC agricultural secretary, Polyakov, who always complied with all Lysenkoite requests, and Utekhin (a former leader in vernalization), in charge of the department of agricultural sciences, attempted to procure a resolution of the CC secretariat to liquidate the collected press run. This project found no support in the AS or in the Academy of Medical Sciences. After prolonged debate and review, it was decided to tear out of the book the section critical of Lysenko, replacing it by a general discussion, naming no names. This was done, so that the book now exists in two versions: a few copies contain direct criticisms of Lysenko and Prezent; several thousand others, only an indirect critique. Because of print-shop errors, there are also versions halfway between the two forms.

REBIRTH OF MEDICAL GENETICS

The resolution of the CC and the U.S.S.R. Council of Ministers was, as noted, many-faceted, and in particular it provided a basis for the restoration of medical genetics in the

U.S.S.R. Medical genetics, by its very nature, could not be Michurinist, and to restore it required the recreation of general genetics. It was impossible to ignore this need. The praesidium of the Academy of Medical Sciences carried out a series of conferences in 1963 and on July 24 adopted a resolution "On the state and perspectives of development of research in medical genetics." It took note of the acute lag of the U.S.S.R. in this area, and of the economic damage connected with the rout of medical genetics in 1937 and 1948, and laid the responsibility squarely on the shoulders of the creators of Michurinist biology. It was impossible to conceal this, in spite of the attempt by Zhukov-Verezhnikov, who had seized the leadership of the study group on medical genetics, to whitewash the existing situation.

The resolution could not guarantee rapid change, but it did propose a series of measures (textbooks, gathering of statistics on hereditary diseases, professorships, laboratories, courses, genetic counseling, conferences, missions abroad, etc.) which could become the basis of a gradual revival of general and medical genetics. It thus reinforced the official recognition of "Morganism-Mendelism" as a practical and theoretically essential branch of biology.

The legality and necessity of restoring genetics, at least in medicine, to Soviet science were becoming a reality. This situation was unacceptable to the representatives of Michurinist biology, but their sphere of practical action in medicine was limited. In October, 1963, an article by Pavlenko appeared, "Neopositivism—the arms of reaction," which attempted to return genetics to the 1948 level.[13] The author asserted that the chromosome theory of heredity "brought untold harm to genetics," and that the ideas of Morgan and Mendel "directed genetics into the river bed of idealism." The article was full of harsh fulminations against Morganism and neo-Morganism (molecular genetics), and concluded that medical genetics can develop only on the basis of the ideas of Michurin, Lysenko, and Pavlov.[14] But this was an isolated attack which appeared ridiculous against the background of the general trends of development in medical genetics.

MICHURINISM REINFORCED

The events of 1963 in any case demonstrated that the monopoly of Michurinist biology was on the way out. The popularity of the representatives of this trend dropped sharply, while the real genetics was beginning to receive ever greater opportunities for development in different branches. Michurinist biology, protected from criticism in the press, nevertheless was subjected to criticism in numerous debates and conferences and at meetings of scientists, writers, journalists, and students. Among the Michurinists themselves, numerous contradictions arose, and it became apparent that decisive steps to halt this process were necessary in order to put the fear of God into the unlike-minded, in order to protect Lysenko and his comrades-in-arms from constant criticism. The arsenal of Lysenkoism contained many tried-and-true methods of attack from the past, to which its representatives once more resorted, despite the change of circumstances.

On August 18, 1963, the newspaper *Sel'skaya Zhizn'* published a long article by Ol'shansky, "Against falsification in biology," which three days later was reprinted in an abridged form in *Pravda*. In it Ol'shansky energetically publicized the alleged Michurinist advances and once more aspired toward the establishment of a complete monopoly by Michurinist biology in Soviet science:

Michurinist biology comprises all the valuable, tested scientific propositions established by previous biology. At the same time it has as an organic component, the genetical and biological propositions elaborated by Lysenko, which found a highroad in agricultural practice, as well as the numerous works of biologists and breeders in the mainstream of understanding biology as a science dealing with a qualitatively peculiar form of motion of matter. The Michurinist trend rejects all mechanistic and idealistic concepts of "classical genetics," including the currently fashionable chemical version.

Ol'shansky expressed in his article the idea that the decisions of the 1948 LAAAS session were irrevocable so far as Soviet biology was concerned. He attacked the Atomizdat publishing house and the Moscow Society of Naturalists for publishing papers on "classical genetics." According to him the *Neva* article was slanderous in character and was received with bewilderment by the scientific community: "Every Soviet scientist understands of course that peaceful coexistence of materialism and idealism in science cannot be. That is why the Michurinist trend is decisively rejecting all reactionary concepts of genetics."

But the style chosen by Ol'shansky for his article was not suitable for the 1963 environment. The Soviet scientific community had become more mature, and the methods and tactics chosen by Ol'shansky by then worked against him.

An important event in our biology was the publication in 1963 of the first native texts on scientific genetics in twenty-five years: Lobashev's *Genetika*, published by the Leningrad University; and Efroimson's *Introduction to Medical Genetics*, which appeared a little later under the imprint of Medgiz. Both books were on a high scientific level and were immediately sold out. Wide circulation was also enjoyed by a pamphlet of the World Health Organization, which included recommendations, by an international committee of experts, on human genetics studies in medical institutions, colleges, and for continuing education of physicians. Thus the question arose of introducing the teaching of genetics in universities and medical schools, from which it had been absent since 1948.

THE FEBRUARY CC PLENARY SESSION

The plenary session of the CC was convened in the Great Kremlin Palace on February 10, 1964, to discuss "The intensification of agricultural production on the basis of widespread utilization of fertilizers, irrigation, complex mechanization, and the adoption of scientific advances and front-rank experience for the attainment of most rapid increase in agricultural production." As we have already seen, in the past Lysenko always attempted to use the agricultural CC session for reinforcement of his positions and attacks on his opponents. This was also to be expected on the current occasion since scientific issues were on the agenda of the session. Indeed, agricultural science was in the main represented at the session by Lysenkoites. The main report was made by the Minister of Agriculture, Volovchenko.[15] Although he noted that Lysenko had made sterling contributions to science and practice, he did not choose to develop this thesis nor to recommend adoption of anything concrete from Lysenko's contributions (even though Lysenko had recently publicized in every possible way his method of increasing the butterfat content of milk and his earth-compost fertilizers). Neither did Volovchenko refer to "reactionary Morganism." Thus the opening of the plenary session was not satisfactory to the creators of Michurinist biology. They therefore, in short order, took measures to correct the situation. First, Kalistratov, the director of Lysenko's experimental farm, took the stand to advertise the butterfat program. He was followed by Ol'shansky and then by Lysenko himself,[16] who noted with deep resentment Volovchenko's omissions with respect to butterfat and compost evaluation. "This," reminded Lysenko, "is not a mere detail: these methods are of great significance in increasing yields and dairy production throughout the Soviet Union. . . . We have formulated a general law about the life of a species, a law subsuming all other biological and genetic laws."

Lysenko then told how this most fundamental law of nature aided him in raising the butterfat content of milk. This method, according to him, must be adopted on all U.S.S.R. farms, which must switch to Jersey crosses, using bull calves from his experimental farms. Lysenko reminded his audience that, on Khrushchev's initiative, the U.S.S.R. Council of Ministers had already adopted an implementing decree, but that for some reason the Ministry of Agriculture was dragging its feet.

Lebedev was then given the floor for purposes of condemning Morganism-Mendelism. He demanded the banning of Morganism from curricula and severely criticized Lobashev's textbook of genetics. At the final session the First Secretary of the CC, Khrushchev, appeared with an extensive speech. In it he devoted a lot of attention to Lysenko, whom he advanced as the ideal Soviet scientist, and insistently recommended adoption of his methods in practice. Said Khrushchev:

It is one thing to listen to a speech, in which a man can serve you a platter very well, but he cannot show you anything in the field. Yet a field is like a book: you can read where and what fertilizers were used and what results were obtained. And so comrade Lysenko has shown in practice that his methods produce high yields of grain, beef, milk. I was then the Secretary of the Moscow party committee, and recommended [his methods] to collective and state farms. And those who used them with knowledge did obtain high yield increases.

This, then, is science, and you can see that, even then, Lysenko presented a due-bill in the debate which developed in the speeches of several comrades at the present sessions. . . . Who wishes to use Lysenko's method cannot lose. Go this year and look at his wheat. I am sure that as always he will have a good crop.

Look at the corn on his farm, look at the sugar beets. . . . It is from such scientists that we can learn. (Applause)[17]

This was powerful support of Lysenko and a completely nonobjective evaluation of his practical recommendations. Khrushchev was also ready to liquidate all native breeds of cattle and switch completely to Jersey crosses, all on the basis of unfounded recommendations of Lysenko, the opposition to which Khrushchev clearly saw.

In less than a month Khrushchev appeared with a new long speech at a conference of the leaders of the party, Soviet, and agricultural organs, and once more paid considerable attention to Lysenko and his recommendations.[18] At the same time one of the orators at the March plenary session, Lebedev, published a long article, "In the old manner," containing a harsh critique of Lobashev's text. According to Lebedev,

Soviet science has long discarded the reactionary husk of Weismannism-Morganism. But the remnants are, alas, still with us. . . . The book *Genetika* is a new attempt to resurrect in biology the old idealistic, metaphysical Weismann-Mendel-Morgan ideas of genetics. It is here that the isolation of theoretical investigations of some scientists from the needs of socialist agriculture are manifested. . . . Lobashev's book contains his lectures to the students in the Faculty of Biology. Students from other institutions, including pedagogical ones, also use this book in studying genetics. Without proper experience, they apparently accept on faith all that Lobashev writes. These graduates become either scientific investigators or schoolteachers of biology. It is easy to imagine what harm using this book as a text does to biology and the education of youth.[19]

At the same time Ol'shansky requested the CC to ban Lobashev's book and have it removed from all libraries. A special commission was set up to study this issue.

THE AS ELECTIONS

Elections to the AS were set for June, 1964. Although the Biology Section had some unconditional supporters of Lysenko, they were only corresponding members (Avakyan, Nuzhdin). The full members who at one time had supported Lysenko (Sisakyan, Oparin, Pavlovsky) by 1964 preferred to remain neutral. But the mid-1964 situation favoring Lysenko permitted him to prepare a project to augment his forces in the AS Biology Section and to make it the same kind of stronghold of Lysenkoism that the LAAAS became through Ol'shansky. At Khrushchev's initiative, the government created an unprecedented number of vacancies in genetics: three full and two corresponding members. It was clearly understood that Luk'yanenko, Pustovoit, and Nuzhdin were to be elected to the former posts and that Remeslo would become one of the corresponding members. Luk'yanenko and Pustovoit were deserving practical breeders, members of the LAAAS, and the evaluation of their scientific merits presented no problem. Neither of them was a geneticist, and they were unsuitable for election to the AS as such. But both had received wide publicity for years, and had recently been elected to the Communist party together with the cosmonauts, without having to go through the stage of candidate. To oppose their election to the AS was useless. Remeslo and Nuzhdin, however, were a different matter: both were unprincipled, active supporters of Lysenko, and the latter in particular was an exceptionally unpopular personality.

Remeslo was voted on three times—an unprecedented situation. He was, nonetheless, rejected. The intensive election campaign on Nuzhdin's behalf bore fruit. The Biology Section voted for his election, but a confirming vote of the AS general meeting was necessary. Until then, there had been no instance of a scientist's being elected by a section and failing to be confirmed by the general meeting. But this time, members of other sections—biochemistry and physiology, and physics—decided to rectify the mistake perpetrated by their biological colleagues. Two excerpts from the stenographic account follow:

ENGEL'GARDT: Among the candidates for the vacancies in genetics, we find names of people well-known throughout the land as having made contributions of considerable significance to agricultural practice and to breeding. We look at these names with respect, and their merits raise no doubts in anyone's mind. But also among the candidates in genetics there is, at least in my opinion, a reason to depart from the recommendation of the committee and the opinion expressed by the vote of the appropriate section. I have in mind the candidacy of Nuzhdin. I am here in an embarrassing position: after all, some ten years ago we elected Nuzhdin as a corresponding member in the Biology Section. In the natural course of events his promotion would be normal. But the question arises, has Nuzhdin kept pace in this period with the advancement of science? I know of no practical contributions he has made that are comparable with those of other candidates in the same category.

It is hence clear that our judgment here must be based on the theoretical and experimental work of Nuzhdin. The problem of developing experimental genetics in all its modern aspects is one of utmost importance for our country, because at all costs we have to overcome the essential lag which has developed in this area in the course of recent times. I see no basis for supposing that the election of Nuzhdin would aid in the solution of the problem. . . . Thumbing through several annual indexes of the leading journals in genetics for the last few years, I found no mention of Nuzhdin's name. And even without indexes, had such work been in existence, it would have been known to us.

In a word, it is clear that the AS would not gain, in the person of Nuzhdin, a scientist who could raise the level of genetical research and turn it in the direction of the main line of development of contemporary genetics. I must therefore disagree with the evaluation of the section of General Biology, and hence cannot consider Nuzhdin's candidacy as meeting the requirements expected of the highest-ranking scientists of our land.

SAKHAROV: I shall be brief. We all recognize that the scientific reputation of a member of the Soviet Academy of Sciences should be above reproach. And now, in discussing Nuzhdin's candidacy, we must approach this issue with great attentiveness. In the document passed around it says: "Nuzhdin had paid much attention to the problems of the struggle with anti-Michurinist distortions of biology, constantly criticizing various idealistic trends in the study of heredity and variation. His general philosophical works, in connection with the further development of the materialistic teaching of Michurin and other outstanding figures of biology, are widely known not only in our country but also abroad."

It is a matter of scientific conscience for each of the academicians who will vote as to how to interpret what is really hidden behind this struggle against anti-Michurinist distortion and for the further development of the philosophical works of outstanding figures in biology, and so forth. I shall not read the excerpt a second time.

As for myself, I call on all those present to vote so that the only "ayes" will be by those who, together with Nuzhdin, together with Lysenko, bear the responsibility for the infamous, painful pages in the development of Soviet science, which fortunately are now coming to an end. (Applause)

PRESIDENT KELDYSH: . . . I do not think that we can approach . . . the election from this point of view. It would seem to me inappropriate to open up here a discussion on the problems of development of biology. And from this standpoint, I consider Sakharov's speech tactless. . . .

LYSENKO: Not tactless, but slanderous! The praesidium . . .

KELDYSH: Trofim Denisovich, why should the praesidium defend itself? It was Sakharov's speech, not the praesidium's. It is not supported, at least by me; I don't know about the praesidium, but think it would not support it, since the praesidium discussed the resolution on biology of the CC and Council of Ministers and will carry on in the spirit of that resolution. I think that, given Trofim Denisovich's protest, we can discuss the incident which just occurred, but this is not the time. I think we should concentrate now on the candidacy.

LYSENKO: At least, if not the meeting as a whole, does the praesidium support Sakharov's statement? You said you did not, but what about the praesidium?

Lysenko's question remained unanswered. But, when the vote was taken, it was found that 126 members voted against Nuzhdin and only 22 or 24 for him. The vacancy remained unfilled.

KHRUSHCHEV TO LYSENKO'S AID

When the rejection of Remeslo and Nuzhdin by the AS was reported to Khrushchev, it evoked a sharp reaction from him.

The AS president was summoned for an explanation. A memorandum of explanation to the CC was also demanded of Sakharov, one of the outstanding Soviet physicists. The memorandum was written in a very sharp tone, further irritating Khrushchev. At a reception, Khrushchev made some harsh statements about the Academy, accusing it of entering politics. The Soviet people do not need such an Academy, he said. And although Mikoyan modestly reminded him that the Academy of Sciences was created by Peter the First, nevertheless, on Khrushchev's order, a commission was formed to look into the possibility of reforming the Academy as a "Committee on Science." A series of plenipotentiary commissions was created to review the work of the AS biological institutes. The review committee on the Institute of Physicochemical and Radiation Biology, headed by Engel'gardt, included Lysenko and Kirillin.

From the standpoint of agriculture, the end of the summer of 1964 was unfortunate both in Siberia and the virgin lands. It may be recalled that, in 1963, for the first time in the history of the country, large amounts of grain to feed the population had to be bought from Canada, Australia, the German Federal Republic, the United States, and other countries. But 1964 did not bring any serious improvements, and in some respects aggravated the difficulties. This, in Khrushchev's opinion, called for new reorganization and for a new plenary session of the CC. Toward the end of the summer a draft of another report by Khrushchev on the reorganization of agriculture and the raising of production levels was circulated among different agricultural institutions and regional committees. Having prepared the report, Khrushchev first went abroad and then on vacation in Sochi on the Black Sea. The plenary session was planned for November, 1964.

We shall not go into a detailed analysis of this last report of Khrushchev which, so far, unfortunately, remains unpublished. Its basic idea was for the transfer of the general centralized Ministry control of agriculture to specialized committees, boards, and trusts dealing with individual crops. One such projected trust or board would have dealt with Lysenko's proposals on compost production. Lysenko's opponents were severely criticized in the draft of the report.

The discussion of Khrushchev's memorandum, beginning in August, 1964, coincided with a sharp intensification of aggressive activity by Lysenko's group. An article on "The theoretical insolvency and practical unproductiveness of formal genetics," signed by twelve authors from different cities, was published in the *Vestnik Sel'skokhozyaistvennoy Nauki*.[20] Morganism and the chromosomal theory of inheritance were again censured in a harsh and rude manner as "the developing antiscientific campaign against materialist science and the decisions of the party and government." Ol'shansky published an article entitled "Against misinformation and slander" in which he attacked Efroimson for his 1957 articles, as well as Shchepot'ev, and the author of this book.[21] Commenting on the manuscript of the first two parts, he wrote:

Lately a voluminous memorandum compiled by Zh. Medvedev, full of dirty inventions about our biology, has been circulated about. If the vicious content of the *Neva* article was covered by external decorum, the memorandum is written in familiar, insulting tones. Substituting marketplace gossip for facts, Medvedev, with one stroke of the pen, crosses out the achievements of Soviet breeding in the creation of new varieties of plants and breeds of animals. ... Along the way, in a haughty, mocking manner he "overthrows" the theoretical tenets of Michurinist biology. All these fabrications and fairy tales would appear as an empty farce if the author, in his lampoon of Michurinist science, had not resorted to political slander which can only provoke anger and disgust. Arbitrarily, and contrary to historical truth, in discussing certain well-known events during the personality cult period, Medvedev arrives at the monstrous conclusion that the scientists of the Michurin persuasion are to blame for the repressions suffered by some innocent scientists in that period.

It is clear to all that this is no longer a farce. It is dirty political speculation. And it is the more necessary to bring this out in the open because Medvedev's political speculation is apparently having an effect on some ill-informed and simple-minded persons. How else can one explain the fact that at an AS meeting, Sakharov, an engineer by specialty, permitted himself an insulting public attack on Michurinist scientists in the style of anonymous letters circulated by Medvedev? Has not the time come to pose the question to Medvedev and similar slanderers: either prove your vicious accusations by facts or answer to the courts for the calumnies spread by you. It goes without saying that they cannot support these accusations by facts, since no such facts exist.

The slanderous attacks against Michurinist biologists, the attempts of individuals to defame the attainments of Michurinist biology are not only insulting to Soviet scientists but also damage the development of biology. They are grist for the mill of those interested in weakening the materialistic positions of Soviet science. Such "criticism" does much harm to the effort to educate youth in the spirit of a materialistic understanding of the development of the organic world, and interferes with the mobilization of Soviet scientists for the solution of the tasks they face.

The same newspaper on September 11, 1964, carried an article by Remeslo, who warmly supported Ol'shansky. And in October, 1964, *Sel'skaya Zhizn'* once more came out with a harsh article, "Far away from production," in which the AS Botanical Institute was taken apart for its struggle of many years' standing against Michurin biology. Simultaneously, behind the scenes of various committees and subcommittees reviewing the work of biological institutions, preparation for the CEC plenary session went on, for the purpose of using the current radical reorganization as a means for the complete suppression of opponents of Michurinist biology.

CHAPTER 10

The End of Lysenkoïsm

KHRUSHCHEV'S RESIGNATION

THE MEETING of the CC praesidium that decided
Khrushchev's fate and that of his economic and agricultural
policies began on October 12, 1964. Khrushchev himself was
in Sochi on that day. But on October 13 he was urgently
summoned to Moscow to participate in the meeting. On October 14, in the evening, the CC plenary session unanimously
voted to relieve Khrushchev of the posts of Chairman of the
Council of Ministers and First Secretary of the CC. The
country learned of this on October 16 when the announcement
and the appropriate decree of the praesidium of the Supreme
Soviet were published.

The protocols of the meeting have not been published, but
this was hardly necessary for Khrushchev's contemporaries.
Any serious-minded person knew and had endured the main
defects of Khrushchev's activities: petty tyranny and sub-
jectivism; endless reorganizations; unconcealed amateurism in
dealing with industry and agriculture; the ridiculous division
of regional party and Soviet organs into industrial and agricultural ones; nepotism in ruling the country and in making
foreign policy; and many others.

If there were positive aspects to Khrushchev's activities, they
nearly all belonged to the period 1953–1956. In more recent
years the tone of his behavior and leadership had become more
erroneous and unpopular.

The country accepted the events of October 12–14 calmly
and with satisfaction. Everybody understood that the worthwhile undertakings of Khrushchev's regime which had taken

root and brought fruit would continue to be fruitful. This was the majority reaction. But Moscow geneticists had become aware of the pending major change even before Khrushchev resigned.

On October 13, the noted geneticist Rapoport, bedeviled at the end of September and beginning of October by various review commissions, and expecting instant dismissal (not the first in his life), received an urgent telephone call from a highly placed leader in the agricultural section of the CC. On behalf of the CC, Rapoport was being approached with a very strange assignment: to prepare within twenty-four hours a full-page article on the achievements of genetics for the news-paper *Sel'skaya Zhizn'*.

Rapoport replied that he could not complete such a serious article so fast, and that in any case the newspaper, noted for its pogrom publications and Lysenko sympathies, would hardly be likely to publish it. The caller responded to these objec-tions by saying that Rapoport could count on any help he needed and that a stenographer would be sent to his apart-ment from the CC office. The reply to Rapoport's further question, as to whether Mendel and Morgan could be men-tioned in the article, was affirmative. In an hour or two a stenographer arrived, and the work was in full swing. The ar-ticle, some twenty-five typewritten pages, was ready in about thirty hours and was sent to the CC.

As far as can be judged, there were some among the leader-ship who wanted to have the article appear before the official announcement of Khrushchev's resignation. On October 13 it was not yet clear when this was to be made. But the events moved so rapidly that by the time Rapoport's article was re-ceived, through the CC, by the editors of *Sel'skaya Zhizn'*, i.e., on October 15, the basic resolutions had already been adopted by the plenary session, so that the political sensation forestalled the genetic one. The communique about the plenary session was published on October 16. Rapoport's article, which created a sensation among biologists, did not appear until October 21. It occupied a full page, but the paragraphs praising Mendel and Morgan were cautiously omitted by the editors.

As became known later, at the CC praesidium meeting on October 12–14 and the CC plenary session on October 14 in which Suslov made a report, many examples of Khrushchev's activities deserving of extreme censure were discussed, including his unconditional support of Lysenko and, in particular, the episode involving the attempt to elect Nuzhdin and Remeslo to the AS, with Khrushchev's subsequent desire to invoke sanctions against the Academy. Also severely criticized was Khrushchev's unauthorized, personal order to shut down the TAA when he found out that it included scientists critical of his agricultural policies. The order was immediately revoked and, by October 16, measures had been taken to restore that agricultural educational institution, the oldest in the country.

THE REVIVAL OF GENETICS AND THE ELIMINATION OF LYSENKOISM

As we have seen, the newspaper *Sel'skaya Zhizn'* was the first to start paying off a long-standing debt to Soviet science. There was an element of egoism in this. It also demonstrated an utter lack of principle: most editors understood the pseudoscientific nature of Lysenkoism and the absurdity of persecuting genetics. Hence in the new situation, when boldness became safe and sensationalism, the soul of the press, possible, nearly all newspapers—central, regional, and those devoted to special subjects—started ordering articles on genetics. One of these, entitled "No, truth is untouchable," deserves special mention.[1]

It was written by Dudintsev, the author of the widely known novel, *Not by Bread Alone*, which in its time had an important influence on Soviet literature. The article had originally been written in September and October, 1963, a year before the article by Rapoport. It wandered from editor to editor for more than a year, and was accepted for publication everywhere. But, when it came to typesetting, the influential hands of Lysenko, Ol'shansky, Sizov, and others, with the help of agencies controlling the press, prevented its appearance. The means were simple and unfailing, and were based primarily on the editors' cowardice. Although an editor could take personal responsibility for publication, he usually sought approval of a superior. This usually meant that the material would be brought to the attention of Lysenko's highly placed patrons. As a result, not only would the article fail to see the light of day, but note would also be taken of its author: at the right opportunity he would be reminded of what he should do. I have in my possession three different versions of proof sheets of Dudintsev's article, as well as the last one, which was eventually read with satisfaction by millions.

The article is devoted to a discussion of a talented Soviet breeder and geneticist, Lebedeva. Under difficult conditions, working without pay and without a position, she produced a number of valuable resistant varieties of potatoes by the use of polyploidy and distant hybridization. And it was only because she was a real geneticist and a brave person that Ol'shansky's friend, Sizov, the long-time director of the AIPB, persecuted her for years, constantly denigrated her results, and interfered with the adoption of her varieties.

Dudintsev vividly shows that the representatives of Michurinist biology were in fact a group which, above all, treasured its position and was prepared to bar the road to anything new, useful, and valuable if it contradicted the dogmas of Lysenkoism—dogmas in the name of which whole branches of science had been abolished.

Why (asks Dudintsev) did Sizov take up arms against [Lebedeba]? Why, having become director, did he fire her from her unpaid post, even though the fruits of her labor continued to serve the institute honestly? . . . The scientists with whom I talked explained to me confidentially: Sizov is an opponent of research on polyploidy because it was discovered by experimental genetics, which Sizov came out against, declaring it to be a bourgeois, idealistic, harmful science, categorically unacceptable to us. I know, from Sizov's published works, that he actively opposes experimental genetics and does not believe in its practical attainments.

Well, he is free to have his own scientific convictions. But if this is the reason why he blocked Lebedeva's discoveries for ten years, it tells me that in Sizov's scientific and moral baggage there are vulnerable spots.

Comrade Sizov! The progress brought to the breeding of potatoes by Lebedeva's hybrids says: natural science which discovers new, indisputable, material facts and which provides valuable practical material cannot be dismissed as bourgeois. . . .

It is known that nature provides society with its material treasures in an indifferent way. The only departure from nature's and science's indifference comes about when we ourselves, misguided by irresponsible and illiterate judgments, reject the riches offered by nature through science.

This is what we are witnessing here. Breeders from bourgeois countries are after Lebedeva's polyploids. One request for them follows another. Those abroad know what to do with this valuable material. I have heard that a capitalist also likes a good potato. And it goes onto his plate in an indifferent way: it does not care who will eat it.

Rapoport's article was not intended for discussion. It merely publicized genetics and indicated the legality of that science from now on. Dudintsev's essay opened a new page in the debate. It showed up those responsible for the difficult years of our science, their lack of principles, their egoism and cynicism, their dependence on political demagoguery. It showed the losses, both moral and economic, that the country had suffered because of the situation. And it was clear to the reader that the facts disclosed by the writer were a mere drop in the ocean of injustice surrounding Soviet geneticists and biologists, and that behind the persons mentioned stood mightier powers, against whom it was still necessary to do battle long and persistently.

By the end of October, every Moscow newspaper had held editorial conferences on biology, on measures for its improvement, and on publication of popular articles on genetics. They were ordered by the dozen, and many of them appeared in November, 1964.

On Saturday, October 24, a representative of the Moscow committee of the party, speaking at a meeting of Moscow propagandists, called Lysenko a pseudoscientist. The following Monday the AS praesidium discussed the improvements necessary in the leadership of its Institute of Genetics, and the question of Lysenko's dismissal was raised.

On October 31, 1964, a large group gathered at Astaurov's to mark his sixtieth birthday, and to congratulate a colleague who had spent more than half his life battling pseudoscience, and who, in spite of persecution, had made so significant a contribution to science as to be recognized by the whole world. In raising a toast, Astaurov said:

We have survived till the hour when real biologists finally feel relief. There is yet nothing concrete, but it is already possible to say that each of us has the kind of feeling experienced by a fisherman when the fish is on the hook and all that is needed is to reel it in. We are here today on the occasion of my anniversary. This is but an excuse; the real cause goes deeper. The hour each one present has done so much to bring about has finally arrived. But a not inconsiderable number of our dear comrades who also awaited this hour did not live to see it. And they also have done much, perhaps more than we have, toward its arrival, so that we and you should see the end of the long and difficult road down which our battle was fought. I ask you to rise in memory of our comrades.

I shall read their names in alphabetical order. It is not a full list, and perhaps each of you can add your comrades-at-arms who no longer exist, but who are still with us.

Dudintsev replied to the toast:

Genetics for a long time was sick, ever ready to draw its last breath. But fortunately it did not die, and the crisis has now passed. Now it reminds me of the patient who, while still in bed, is beginning to take an interest in life, and is looking at the window and the door. Soon the patient will arise and leave the ward, but his wardmates are still lying there, and he must not forget them.

One fish is on the hook, but how many more are still on the loose. . . .

THE PROCESS BEGINS TO BE IRREVERSIBLE

November, 1964, was a period of broad advance against Lysenkoism and a clear unmasking of its pseudo innovations. But this advance was largely in newspapers; the journals were lagging behind the events. Nor were any organizational measures in science taken in November: there were enough problems with the liquidation of the experimental forms of administrative and party leadership introduced by Khrushchev and with a return to the tested methods of management of the national economy and agriculture. But the broad wave of genetics articles (most of which were anti-Lysenkoist) in all the newspapers was commented on throughout the world. I shall note here only some of those appearing in the central press, without reference to provincial papers, which tried to keep up with the Moscow press.

Komsomol'skaya Pravda published an article by Vorontsov, "Life is pressing," about defective biology textbooks and the urgent need for preparing new ones for secondary and higher education.[2] The article also took apart the pedagogical journal, *Biologiya v Shkole.* The same day, *Izvestiya* carried an article by Alikhanyan, "Genetics: science and practice," mainly on the advances and prospects of genetics in the study of variation. On November 17 still another article, by Efroimson and R. A. Medvedev, "The criterion is practice," appeared in

Komsomol'skaya Pravda, describing the fate of a number of Lysenko's pseudo innovations. On the same day the *Literaturnaya Gazeta* contained a long essay by Pisarzhevsky, "Let the scientists debate." Two days later *Sel'skaya Zhizn'* published a vivid article by Zhukovsky, "On some new methods of applied genetics," which canceled the previous publicity given by the same newspaper to frost-resistant varieties produced by Lysenkoites.

The same day (November 19) *Komsomol'skaya Pravda* ridiculed the petty tyranny of Ol'shansky in his position as the LAAAS president. *Pravda* came out with an article on genetics on November 22, written by Belyaev, director of the Siberian Institute of Cytology and Genetics. In it he severely criticized the 1948 LAAAS session:

It is no secret that the backwardness of genetics in our country is to a considerable degree connected with the negative influence of the Stalin personality cult, and with arbitrary rule in science. This was particularly evident in 1948. After the notorious August session of the LAAAS, genetics was declared to be a bourgeois pseudo-science, idealism, metaphysics, and so forth. There is nothing more erroneous than such assertions. A science studying material structures, phenomena, and processes, discovering the laws that govern them, utilizing these laws in practice, cannot be either idealistic or metaphysical.

On November 24 the *Literaturnaya Gazeta* published a report on a conference of biologists and physicists which it had organized. Lysenkoites were represented only by Studitsky who was countered by weighty arguments from more than ten noted scientists. Finally, toward the end of November, the newspapers got to examining the question of raising butterfat content by Lysenko's method.

Sel'skaya Zhizn' on November 25, 1964, carried a detailed article, "About butterfat," written by Voronov, formerly with the Institute of Genetics. The article clearly demonstrated, on the basis of extensive data from farms neighboring on Lysenko's Gorki Leninskie, and which had followed his recommendations and had bought purebred bull calves from him, that high butterfat content was not retained in hybrids, but was proportional to the percentage of Jersey genes. On top of that, milk yield had also dropped in the hybrids.

Another critical analysis of Lysenko's experiments on butterfat was provided by Gorodinsky in an article with the clear-cut title, "Facts versus fabrication."[3] It contained conclusions and computations of many aspects of the activities at Lysenko's experimental farm, and pointed to the obvious scientific fraud by Lysenko. In part, Gorodinsky wrote: "As may be seen from reports of accountants, Lysenko exaggerated the butterfat percentage figures by at least 0.29–0.45. More than that, compared with 1954, the milk yield per cow dropped by 2660 kilograms." The author then gives numerous examples of the losses in yield, size, and development of animals, etc., from the use of Jersey crosses in different areas of the U.S.S.R.

On November 16, 1964, another plenary session of the CC was held which, in addition to dealing with the important question of the unification of previously separated party and Soviet agencies, took up matters of personnel. In particular, Polyakov was relieved of his post as CC secretary and director of its Section of Agriculture. Previously he had been editor-in-chief of *Sel'skaya Zhizn'*, and now he was transferred to the *Ekonomicheskaya Gazeta* as deputy editor. In his capacity as CC secretary, he had aided in creating the Lysenko monopoly and had personally intervened in all sorts of petty problems outside the sphere of his competence, in Lysenko's defense. Together with Khrushchev's assistant, Shevchenko, he had prepared many of Khrushchev's reports and speeches on agriculture. His removal from the CC deprived Lysenko of serious support in the leading party organ.

The newspaper offensive against Lysenko continued throughout the country in 1964. But its organizational effects, except for the removal of Ol'shansky from the post of LAAAS

president, were not very significant. The new president was
Lobanov, a more nearly neutral and objective person, but
still, however, incapable of a decisive cleanup of the LAAAS.
Although he was basically an administrator and not a scientist,
much in his past linked him to Lysenko. He had been appointed to the LAAAS on Lysenko's recommendation, and
presided at the 1948 session. As Minister of State Farms, he
opened and closed the session in the full spirit of Lysenko
and Prezent, then regarded as the official government position.

It is remarkable that neither Lysenko nor his associates, who
had previously reacted so tempestuously to even indirect criticism, wrote a single reply to the great number of exposés and
critical articles published. It might be thought that they were
refused publication, but this was not the case. There just were
no replies. I have especially checked with a number of editorial
boards, and it is clear that the staff of Lysenko's army kept
silent. These were sensible tactics. The fish was on the hook
or, more precisely, in the net, and it waited to see whether
or not it would be pulled ashore. Or, possibly, it might be
transferred to a smaller pond and allowed a peaceful existence.

RE-ESTABLISHMENT OF GENETICS, BIOLOGY,
AND THE AGRICULTURAL SCIENCES

The rapid liquidation of the monopoly of Michurinist biology
and the obvious bankruptcy of the various advertised schemes
and scientific propositions of Lysenkoism soon posed many
different problems for Soviet science. Restoration of a large
and necessary branch of the natural sciences is a very complex
and long affair. It will be years and years before Soviet biological and agricultural sciences, and especially genetics, can
reach the level of world science, and assume the significance
they should have in the development of a society, in agriculture, industry, public health, and education. In considering
only genetics, which suffered thirty years of persecution, the

Above: left, Vil'yams Museum; right, U.S.S.R. Ministry of Agriculture, site of the 1948 session of the LAAAS.

Center: left, Lenin All-Union Academy of Agricultural Sciences; right, Timiryazev Agricultural Academy.

Below: All-Union Institute of Plant Breeding.

successful solution of the problem calls for large-scale and varied measures. Let us note some of them:

1. Reform of secondary biological education. New curricula in biology. New textbooks. Reorganization of the pedagogical journal *Biologiya v Shkole*. Retraining of tens of thousands of schoolteachers.

2. Reform of higher education in universities and medical and agricultural schools. Preparation of new programs, new textbooks and laboratory guides in general biology and genetics. Retraining and renewal of teaching staffs.

3. Replacement of the leadership of many scientific establishments, institutes, laboratories, departments.

4. Changes in editorial boards of biological and agricultural journals.

5. Organization of new research establishments in genetics, medical genetics, biometry, biochemistry, molecular biology, and other modern disciplines.

Thus it was necessary to restore the situation of 1935–1936, but to restore at the level of 1965–1966 science. In 1948, when a reform on the same scale was undertaken, the Lysenkoites had it easy: they largely wrecked things. Now a constructive process was called for, involving millions of students. And all this had to be done fast and in the face of the opposition of numerous Lysenkoites, most of whom retained their posts.

Some who had previously been collaborators of Lysenko rapidly broke away from Lysenkoism and actively began to participate in the renaissance of biology. Among these, for instance, was Stoletov, professor of genetics at Moscow University, and the R.S.F.S.R. Minister of Higher Education. Others, remaining in their posts (e.g., Feiginson, Platonov, Studitsky, Nuzhdin, and Sizov), actively opposed reorganization, wrote complaints to the CEC, memoranda to ministries, and, mobilizing all their supporters, used their administrative power to interfere with the reforms being carried out.

LYSENKO'S DISMISSAL

In the beginning of February, 1965, foreign newspapers carried stories of Lysenko's dismissal from the post of the director of the AS Institute of Genetics. No news of this event appeared in the Soviet press, but it soon became widely known. The dismissal followed the annual meeting of the AS on February 1-2, at which the situation in biology was subjected to a series of analyses in a number of sharply critical speeches.[4] In his speech the AS president, Keldysh, softened the criticism somewhat. Improvement of the situation without overly inflaming the passions was accepted as an official directive. Keldysh said:

I think that in condemning the monopolistic position that Lysenko occupied, and while denying his erroneous views on many most important questions of biology, we must not indiscriminately deny all he did. In particular, in the view of some prominent scientists, his theory of phasic development of plants has a scientific significance and, according to some breeders, the methods he proposed had some application. . . .

We now have all the possibilities for normalization of the situation in biology. It is essential to carry out a number of further measures to help its development in our country. And here I wish to emphasize that we must concentrate on scientific and organizational problems and exclude all possibilities of administration by injunction, pressure, and sticking labels on one or another side.[5]

But, in spite of some disagreements in the evaluation of the theory of phasic development, the opinions of most members of the Academy about Lysenko's remaining as director of the Institute of Genetics coincided, and the decision was made to remove him from the post. This was done in a mild manner by accepting his resignation. The mildness was due to the indecisiveness of the scientific administrators. On the one hand, it was clear that Lysenkoites must be removed from leading posts. On the other, this decision had to be made independently since there were no special party or government directives on these issues.

On January 23, 1965, a long article by the noted journalist and publicist, Agranovsky, appeared under the title "Science accepts nothing on faith" in the *Literaturnaya Gazeta*. It was a result of several visits to Gorki Leninskie following the protests of the senior animal husbandman, Moskalenko, against Pisarzhevsky's essay (see p. 228). Moskalenko's letter, published together with Agranovsky's article, addressed itself to Pisarzhevsky:

Enough abstract arguments, comrade Pisarzhevsky! One should work in shirt sleeves, day and night. In your article you subjected Michurin's teaching to an unjust critique and defended the reactionary teaching of Weismann and Morgan which was rejected by agricultural practice and routed as unnecessary in 1948. Who gave you, a scribbler, the right to call the 1948 LAAAS session the beginning of an administrative rout of genetics? . . . If you really want to resolve a scientific debate as fast as possible, come to the farm in Gorki Leninskie and we'll acquaint you in detail with the latest advances of Michurin biology in animal husbandry.

When this letter was received, Pisarzhevsky was no longer alive (he died suddenly two days after his article appeared). Hence his close friend Agranovsky accepted the invitation in his stead.

His visits to Lysenko's experimental farm were very thorough. Not only did he look at the herd of Jersey crosses and taste the milk, but he also investigated in detail the history of its formation, the stability of various traits, the economics of milk and beef production, and the financial accounts. The outcome of this work was not very flattering to Lysenko. It was obvious that the herd was merely a showpiece and a result of concealed culling, with the selected animals being on a highly intensive regimen. Adoption of Lysenko's breeding methods on neighboring collective and state farms did not lead to repetition of Lysenko's results. In fact, those farms suffered financial losses by using second- and third-generation hybrids for reproduction. Agranovsky also found evidence of an analogous situation in many of the other publicized investigations of the farm.

His article sharply indicated the need for serious government control of three series of studies in Gorki Leninskie that were being adopted on a large scale in practice. Suffice to say that, by then, thousands of farms were transforming animals according to Lysenko's method, the 1962 governmental decision and wide propaganda about the method through the "Exposition of Advances in the State Economy" having aided the further spread of this process.

A state review commission was created at the end of January by the AS praesidium and the U.S.S.R. Ministry of Agriculture.[6] The composition of the commission was not fully representative, and its mandate was greatly circumscribed. Neither genetics nor agricultural chemistry was represented, although essentially what was reviewed was work in applied genetics and fertilizer use. The commission worked for several months, and its conclusions were discussed at a joint meeting of the AS praesidium, the board of the Ministry of Agriculture, and the LAAAS praesidium.[7]

Because of lack of scientific representation on the commission, its work was largely directed toward analysis of the purely managerial and financial-economic aspects. The commission, however, uncovered a large number of deceitful and fraudulent scientific methods used in the evaluation of experimental results and in the experimental design of tests of practical application, both in agricultural chemistry and in animal husbandry. Its report showed, in great detail, deliberate falsification of data. In particular it was found that, even under ideal nutritional conditions, the yield of the hybrid cows dropped as butterfat percentages went up, so that the amount of butterfat per cow was lowered. This was also true of protein and of beef production (the weight of the cows dropped by an average of 140 kilograms). Thus, even according to his own data, the methods recommended by Lysenko for application throughout the country were economically unsound and by 1965 were causing serious losses.

Together with the commission's report, a memorandum containing Lysenko's rebuttal, a re-rebuttal by the commission, and the proceedings of the debate on the report were published. Lysenko did not attend the discussion. The resolution unanimously adopted after the discussion found Lysenko's recommendations to be erroneous and economically harmful. Previous resolutions concerning them and various orders of the Ministry which called for their adoption were rescinded.

THE REFORM OF BIOLOGICAL EDUCATION

The nationwide pedagogical periodical, *Uchitel'skaya Gazeta*, immediately after October, 1964, published a series of articles about the necessity for reform of biological education in schools. Indeed, this was essential. In 1964–1965, instruction in the fundamentals of biology was based on old textbooks in which the bases of genetics, cytology, and Darwinism were recounted in the spirit of Lysenko's views and Michurinist biology in general. At the same time, many pupils reading the *Komsomol'skaya Pravda* and popular science magazines could clearly see the discrepancy between their textbooks and modern biology. These observations placed teachers, most of whom had also been educated along Michurinist lines, in a difficult situation.

In the beginning of 1965 the R.S.F.S.R. Ministry of Education created a commission on curricula, headed by Gunar, a well-educated physiologist and strong opponent of Lysenkoism. A majority of the members were regular biologists. As a result of the commission's work, a new, full-fledged program in general biology emerged and was approved. In addition, it was decided to suspend the teaching of biology in schools for one year (1965–1966) in order to provide time for retraining of teachers and the writing of a textbook. So that there should be no gap in the biological training of a generation of pupils, the biology course was moved from the ninth to the tenth grade. As a result of a competition, a new textbook of biology, compiled by a group headed by Polyansky, was adopted. It gave a comprehensive understanding of contemporary biology, but perhaps overemphasized general and molecular genetics.

Simultaneously, many programs and courses were being modified in agricultural and educational institutes and in biology faculties. For the course in genetics, Lobashev's book, *Genetika*, was adopted as well as a number of supplementary translated manuals. Seminars were organized at the universities of Moscow and Leningrad for retraining instructors at other universities. Noted scientists were enlisted to give lectures at these seminars: Astaurov, Timofeev-Resovsky, Prokof'eva-Bel'govskaya, Alikhanyan, Dubinin, Efroimson, and others.

From 1966, instruction in biological science in the system of higher education became full-fledged, although qualitatively, because of the acute shortage of qualified teaching personnel in many cities, it is still far from perfect.

THE CELEBRATION OF THE
MENDEL CENTENNIAL

More people in the U.S.S.R. than anywhere else in the world (except, perhaps, his birthplace, Czechoslovakia) knew of the existence of Gregor Mendel, the monk from Brno. After 1948 the terms "Mendelism," "Mendelist," "Morganist-Mendelist," and so forth, were disseminated by the popular press, satirical journals, the radio, variety shows, and the cinema. The hundredth anniversary of Mendel's first communication (1865) on the laws of heredity could not have come at a more opportune time. Mendel had been rehabilitated, and the centenary of his discovery was celebrated by Soviet science not only as a triumph of Mendelian laws, but also as a victory of real science over pseudoscience. Nearly all central papers carried articles on and portraits of Mendel.[8] A solemn, very high-level meeting of the AS was held in the festively decorated Moscow House of the Scientists.

A group of some seventy geneticists traveled to Brno, Czechoslovakia, to attend the memorial international symposium honoring Mendel. The Soviet delegation laid a wreath on the beautiful monument to Mendel in the monastery courtyard plots where once he conducted his experiments. This monument of white marble, which was removed from its pedestal in 1949 and which remained for about ten years in some barn, was now restored to its former place, and the Czechs, who once followed us in the persecution of their compatriot, could now see how unjust his long oblivion had been.

During the symposium the Czechoslovak Academy of Sciences awarded personal silver medals to twenty outstanding geneticists of the world. Among the Soviet scientists receiving medals were Astaurov, Dubinin, Lobashev, Timofeev-Resovsky, Tsitsin, and Rapoport.

ORGANIZATIONAL CHANGES IN SOVIET BIOLOGY

The changes occurring in biology naturally called for a number of organizational measures to reinforce the progress attained. Under pressure from the scientific community these measures were undertaken both in 1965 and 1966. We shall enumerate some of them:

1. The most active Lysenkoites occupying posts of institute directors (Sizov of the AIPB, Vsyakikh of the Animal Husbandry Institute, and others) were replaced, although they re-

mained in charge of departments and laboratories. On the basis of a competition, Feiginson and Dvoryankin were dismissed from Moscow University. Lysenko failed to be re-elected as Professor of Genetics and Breeding in the TAA.

2. The AS Institute of Genetics, consisting in the main of Lysenkoites, was disbanded at the beginning of 1966, and in its place an Institute of General Genetics, headed by Dubinin, was created. However, the laboratories of the previous institute were preserved and transferred, together with their leaders, to other AS and LAAAS institutions.

3. The Lysenko-edited journal, *Agrobiologiya*, which until the end of 1965 attempted to voice opposition to the general trend of Soviet biology, ceased to exist after 1966. In September, 1965, a new monthly journal, *Genetika*, appeared, with Zhukovsky as editor-in-chief, and Alikhanyan and Belyaev as deputy editors. Its editorial board included many other Soviet geneticists.

4. In 1966 the Committee on Awards of Scientific Degrees was reconstituted, and many deserving geneticists were awarded the degree of Doctor of Biological Sciences without defending a dissertation.

5. The composition of some editorial boards of biological and agricultural journals was modified, although not very radically. Thus the notorious Lysenkoite and scientific falsifier, Studitsky, who at one time headed the journal *Uspekhi Sovetskoy Biologii*, remained its deputy editor.

6. On May 30–31, 1966, a constituent meeting of the new Vavilov All-Union Society of Geneticists and Breeders was held, and Astaurov was elected its president.

HAS LYSENKOISM BEEN LIQUIDATED?

As a result of the processes and measures described, the position of Lysenkoism was weakened. Its influence on Soviet biology dropped sharply, and the number of people considering themselves to be representatives of Michurinist biology fell considerably. But Lysenkoism is far from having been liquidated; nor has it lost its aggressiveness. Neither has it lost from its midst people capable of grasping and comprehending modern biology, biochemistry, and genetics, and capable of real education, yet unwilling to relinquish the primitive collection of dogmas they have so firmly mastered and held for so long. What is more to the point, they were also unwilling to relinquish the high posts they had occupied for so long (by no means because of their high qualifications). The philosophical ideologists of Lysenkoism did not disappear either, and some of them (e.g., Platonov) continue to be publicly active in its support. Lysenkoism also did not lose many administrative opportunities in science—the full renovation of scientific institutions will still take many years. The causes for this are numerous, and explicable to a degree.

It is by now apparent that Lysenkoism, long masquerading under the designation "Michurinist biology," is a pseudoscience. It was a pseudoscience in the form in which it appeared in 1936, in 1948, and in 1958, and in the form in which it appears in 1966. Lysenkoism is not only a pseudoscience and scientific falsification, it is also undoubtedly a harmful practical tendency which has caused, and in many instances still does cause, grave damage to the national economy. And yet the active leaders of this trend still occupy important posts and professorial chairs and are in charge of many departments and laboratories (Shlykov, Sizov, Teterev, Studitsky, Platonov, Kushner, Glushchenko, and others). They have a public forum (e.g., the journal *Oktyabr'*); they enjoy many privileges and opportunities and actively support each other. No small number of them are still included in the Committee on Awards of Scientific Degrees, and on various editorial boards, soviets, and committees. They also still own the experimental farm at Gorki Leninskie, directed by our old friends Lysenko, Prezent, and Ol'shansky.

What are the reasons for this paradox, and what is the prognosis? There are many reasons, only some of which will be cited. First of all, there is the general democratization of scientific and social life. The constant struggle over many years, by scientists, against repressions and administration by injunction in science makes a new, radical cleanup of scientific establishments difficult now, when truth has triumphed. A cleanup is going on, but by legal means of competition and recertification. It is a *gradual* selective process.

It is apparent that since October, 1964, interference in scientific discussions by higher political and administrative organs has sharply dropped. Their resolutions are basically left to scientists, as they should be. In 1948 the Lysenkoites achieved a rapid rout of scientific institutions and replacement of editorial boards, academic councils, and so forth, by the basic methods of decrees from ministries, government departments, and boards, and by creation of special plenipotentiary commissions—in other words, by a coup. Today these methods are inapplicable; hence the reverse process is proceeding at a much slower pace.

It should also be pointed out that the general scientific isolation of Lysenkoites, the derision and lack of respect on the part of the majority of the scientific community, which they constantly feel, force them to this day to band into more or less homogeneous groups, maintaining mutual support and preserving caste.

They have also been able to utilize the principles brought forward in the struggle against them, and above all the principle of freedom of speech. This permits them now and again, in one form or another, to propagandize their erroneous, false dogmas, to criticize their opponents, and to falsify the real situation in biology.

There is no danger in these activities, which are unavoidable in a democratically structured science. In the main, publication of this type of material is carried on in *Oktyabr'*.[9] It may also be found in purely scientific journals in the form of various reviews and tendentious generalizations.

Such clamant obstacles exist in the scientific life of any country. In ours they are still at a higher level than is generally found internationally, but they are gradually being reduced. Resistance to such hindrances has been established, and this is the most important thing.

Preservation of Lysenkoism is aided by still another circumstance—the excessive importance, in our science, of various degrees and titles. These (candidate, doctor, professor, corresponding member, academician) are awarded for life by strict international tradition. And no matter how strange it seems that even now, for instance, Prezent is a professor and a full member of LAAAS, or that Lysenko belongs to three academies, is a laureate of many prizes, a Hero of Socialist Labor, and bearer of nine orders of Lenin, nonetheless these are lifetime privileges and they cannot be revoked without making such high titles and awards appear worthless. The interconnections among these titles and awards and the positions occupied are such that a bearer of a title also has a lifetime income independent of his scientific reputation. The latter could be very low or even negative—the income still continues. Furthermore, the strict official and unofficial regulations concerning corresponding positions and titles, especially in the academies of science and the universities of the capital, create great difficulties in the promotion of young, capable scientists to the posts now occupied by the members of the old Lysenko guard, richly equipped with titles.

And, finally, the controversy described was so prolonged, so deep are the roots of Lysenkoism in secondary and higher education, for so long has it been instilled into the minds of the youth, beginning with 1937, that our population of scientists has become far too heterogeneous in its attitudes toward Lysenkoism. A large number of persons, now good and capable scientists, went through a stage in their development at which they trusted Michurinist biology. This is especially true of those who received their secondary and higher education between 1948 and 1960. Many, not having proper guidance, published mistaken works. Not a small number of mature scientists were also in error during that period, and gradually discovered the truth for themselves. The transition of biologists into ceaseless and uncompromising fighters against Lysenkoism and its unprincipled and dogmatic representatives went through many intermediate stages, and varied widely in the different periods of the controversy. And how many journalists, essayists, publicists, writers, philosophers were there who first praised and later abused Lysenko! To disentangle the shades of guilt and innocence, of lack of principles and sincere delusions, of trust and deception is now very difficult. And there is hardly need to do so. The important thing is that Lysenkoism has now been unmasked forever as a pseudo-science, and recognized as a shameful stain on our history. And this was accomplished by the whole collective of Soviet scientists which was finally able to rid itself in the main from this far-flung, false doctrine.

CHAPTER 11

How Did It Happen?

IN RECENT YEARS the question of the prolonged dominance of Lysenkoism in our country (and its export to other socialist states in 1948–1955) has often been raised and discussed. This question has undoubtedly occurred to the reader of this book, in which we have shown the methods used by Lysenko and his group to secure their domination of our science. No single answer can be given to explain how an obvious pseudoscience could maintain a monopoly for so long, nor how clearly harmful and absurd recommendations could be adopted into the national economy. Among the many attempts to provide solutions in recent years, two serious works may be noted. In contrast to many other works, which only examine and criticize one or another of Lysenko's false dogmas and practical recommendations, these two analyze the causes of the phenomenon.

The first article is by Semenov,[1] and the second by Frolov.[2] The first analyzes the subjective-philosophical causes of the origin of false doctrines in natural science. The second demonstrates how such false doctrines, under the conditions of the personality cult, can apparently be amalgamated with a dominant, dogmatic philosophy and thus receive the strongest support from influential ideological circles. These articles analyze two very important, but far from most essential, conditions required for the possible domination of a false doctrine.

The false doctrine of Lysenko is by no means an isolated instance. Such domination has occurred in various countries in the last two or three hundred years. In the more remote past these situations arose frequently—suffice it to mention alchemy, which lasted for centuries. Even today, such instances are not too rare. Many theoretical branches of science and the well-known and flourishing system of homeopathy fall, no doubt, into the category of false doctrine, not to mention various religious and sectarian systems.

In science, appearance of false doctrines is a natural process: they are the extreme variants of essential hypotheses, assumptions, and theories. The majority of hypotheses, by the very nature of things, must be incorrect and incomplete reflections of actual phenomena, since they are proposed on the basis of insufficient facts and require further verification, refutation, or elaboration. In our daily theoretical and experimental work we propose and reject hypotheses, and consider it absurd to criticize a scientist who advances a hypothesis for discussion and examination which turns out to be wrong. Constant rejection of transient hypotheses and theories is mandatory in the process of scientific cognition. The author of a hypothesis is always more pleased if it is confirmed, becomes a theory, a trend, a branch of science: this is the road to achievement, fame and, often, glory. It is less pleasant to have a hypothesis rejected. The later one or another theoretical construct is refuted on the road toward apparent recognition, the more painful it is for its author.

Thus false doctrines are extreme manifestations of the natural process of constant origin and disappearance of erroneous explanations and concepts, but, for the prolonged existence of such doctrines, additional factors are required.

First of all, any false doctrine is, beyond question, a product of fanaticism. As indicated, the theoretical constructs of false doctrines are extreme manifestations in the spectrum of normal hypothetical constructs. In essence, they are hypertrophied and dogmatized hypotheses lying somewhere on the border between science and antiscience. And in most cases their creators are also extremist representatives of the heterogeneous world of science, whose scientific thinking lies somewhere on the border between the normal and the pathological. The world of science, as represented by its human diversity, is no more uniform than any other part of our society. The human psyche in science runs the full gamut of expression from total mediocrity to absolute genius, and includes a range of psychopathic deviations, often more dangerous in the area of talent than of mediocrity. To create a false doctrine, all that may be required is a fanatical person who has faith in the products of his own fantasy and who assumes the function of an infallible, scientific prophet. But, for false doctrines to succeed and for their creators to achieve a scientific monopoly, still other special conditions are necessary.

In the ancient and medieval worlds the origin of false doctrines was aided by ignorance, since only an insignificant amount of scientific information was available. In many cases the spread of false doctrines was secured through their defense by dominating groups, religious or political, whose interests they served. In more recent times the link between periodic monopolies by false doctrines and political alignments has become the main factor.

False doctrines, being an extreme product of the normal background of science, and having been created by extremist, fanatical representatives of the world of science, can achieve a monopolistic position only in state systems that are extremist in nature, as a particular manifestation of many other deviations from the reasonable norms of organized human society.

Monopoly in science by one or another false doctrine, or even by one scientific trend, is an external symptom of some deep-seated sickness of a society. In our concrete case the sickness is designated by the too-vague concept of "personality cult." Yet it is possible to point to the concrete causes which statistically guaranteed such fertile soil for fanatics (who appear everywhere and always) in our country between 1930 and 1964, and which left, in the form of Lysenkoism, an indelible mark on the history of human society.

While we can account for the development of the theoretical background of one or another unfounded complex of pseudoscience, it is somewhat more difficult to understand *the widespread adoption of its practical recommendations in the national economy, i.e., the coercion of wide masses of peasants and of agricultural and party leaders into putting into practice obviously ridiculous, harmful, or merely useless measures.*

The causes for this sort of situation may be examined both with reference to the concrete instance of Lysenkoism and with regard to broader aspects of the principles involved. They will not be discussed in order of importance, because the significance of the different factors varied in the different periods in which Lysenkoism flourished.

1. There was an erroneous tendency to classify sciences as bourgeois on the one hand, and proletarian or socialist on the other. This tendency, born in the areas of philosophy, political economy, and sociology, began to spread into the natural sciences in 1929-1931, and led to the struggle against "bourgeois" science and the creation of "Marxist" and "dialectical" concepts in many fields of knowledge. By and large these concepts were of a transient nature, but in a number of instances they proved to be enduring.

This tendency was decreed from above. It reached its first peak in 1929-1931 in the form of a campaign against bourgeois sciences and the "old" specialists, a campaign which had its psychological basis in this period in a series of falsified show-trials of experts (the "Promparty" case; "The Labor Peasant party"; "the Shakhtin affair"; and others). The second and higher peak was reached in 1946-1948 in the form of a drive against cosmopolitanism, "admiration of the West," and so forth, and was accompanied by extensive routs in the areas of literature, art, and nearly all sciences. The August, 1948, LAAAS session represented its culmination. Lysenkoism thus was undoubtedly induced by the political situation in the country, and its first heyday, when Lysenko was made president of the LAAAS, occurred at the time of mass repressions carried out by Stalin and the NKVD in 1936-1938, not by mere chance.

2. Constant difficulties and mistaken policies occurred in the country's agricultural production. For many years, beginning with the headlong collectivization and massive repressions against the more prosperous peasants, and ending with Khrushchev's decrees which limited the possibilities of individual livestock rearing, agricultural policy was based not so much on concern for an all-around development of agricultural production and an increase in soil productivity, but rather on achieving maximum agricultural output at minimum budgetary cost. The forms that organization of agricultural production took in the years of the personality cult—the rural population deprived of elementary civil rights (the passportless regime), management based on coercion and endless decrees—all were factors in the suppression of serious agricultural science, represented in those days by such men as Pryanishnikov, Vavilov, Doyarenko, Tulaikov, and Konstantinov. This science, having international bases and traditions, could not serve as a theoretical foundation for the ceaseless political experimentation in agriculture, which reached unprecedented proportions under Khrushchev. To counterbalance the genuine science, an agricultural science of a different style was being created, one which cynically used the weapon of promise and deceit, an opportunistic science which accepted the paragraphs of countless decrees as axioms of its logical structure, a science which recognized, in the first place, not the laws of nature or production, but the laws and decisions made by government organs. It was just such a "progressive" science that Lysenkoism, existing only through the support of political and state authorities, became. State agrobiology, deprived of international traditions and objective criteria and ideals, developed on the same principles as state philosophy, political economy, sociology, etc.

The practical measures in agriculture initiated by Lysenko

were only weak companions of the fundamental and even more groundless measures carried out in this area by Stalin and especially by Khrushchev, and which led to more serious damage. The conflict with serious science (not only in agriculture) did not originate with Lysenko. It originated with Stalin and was continued later under Khrushchev. Lysenko was a consequence of this conflict; he was the surrogate of a science which satisfied the political aims and tactics of both leaders. Under normal democratic conditions, Lysenko would have remained an ordinary provincial experimenter and a theoretical individualist expressing elements of fanaticism and obscurantism. We have many such people today, and there are many in other countries, but there they are not normally placed at the head of science.

3. The peculiarities of our press after the end of the twenties made possible popular support for one or another scientific trend selected by the political leadership, and complete suppression of the opposition. Although great diversity of newspapers and magazines exists, there is a clear-cut centralization and hierarchy, with *Pravda* the main lawgiver. Criticism by other papers of any articles published in *Pravda* is practically impossible. Beyond this, censorship stood guard over all officially supported concepts, and even matchbox labels had to pass through it. I know dozens of instances in which censorship stopped articles prepared for the press or already in type which contained direct or indirect criticism of Lysenko. Until Stalin's death all published material was subjected to three stages of censorship: in manuscript, after typesetting, and after publication before release. Since 1956, manuscripts have no longer been subjected to censorship, and only the last two stages remain.

From about 1934 until October, 1964—that is, for thirty years—the central press (*Pravda* and *Izvestiya*) did not allow any serious articles criticizing Lysenkoism (with the exception of Stankov's brief note in *Pravda* in 1954 criticizing the Lysenko theory of the origin of species), although many such manuscripts were being submitted. Meanwhile, during this period, these papers published hundreds of articles by Lysenko and his followers, criticizing classical biology and advertising various practical proposals, which, because of the special role of these newspapers, became directives for all the rest of the press.

Criticism of Lysenko in the three active periods of the controversy (1935-1938, 1946-1947, 1953-1958) was to be found only in specialized scientific journals. Several times, however, and for long periods, strict censorship bans on all criticism of Lysenko and Michurinist biology extended to all publications. Between 1948 and 1952, even any positive descriptions of genetical experiments were forbidden by the censorship. In 1958-1964, only direct criticism of Lysenko was prohibited, and papers on experimental genetics were published without great difficulty, but only in a small number of scientific journals. Of course, under a free exchange of opinion, Lysenkoism could not have lasted one or two years, and in any case his practical recommendations would not have been mandatory. Thus this favorable condition for the flowering of Lysenkoism is also linked to the political situation in the country.

4. An important factor in the prolonged domination of Lysenkoism was the protracted practical isolation of Soviet scientists and the Soviet intelligentsia from world science, foreign scientific institutions, and colleagues abroad. Beginning with 1933-1934, possibilities for Soviet scientists to participate in international conferences, congresses, and symposia abroad became sharply limited. Correspondence and exchange of manuscripts, reprints, and books began to fold up. Geographical and plant-breeding expeditions stopped. By 1937-1938, the natural and common desire of any scientist for interchange with foreign colleagues, for discussion of current and prospective scientific problems—a desire which meets no serious obstacles in any civilized country—had come to be looked on,

with respect to Soviet scientists, only as a political crime and proof of unreliability. Even ordinary scientific correspondence could be cause for arrest, and a prolonged earlier stay abroad, a threatening issue in filling out questionnaires. Happy were those who, with pride in their political innocence, could enter in the proper place in the questionnaire: "Have not been abroad" or "Never have been." This isolation reached its height in 1946 after the notorious affair of Kliueva and Roskin, who published simultaneously in the U.S.S.R. and abroad[3] a paper with preliminary data on cancer antibiotics. By special decree of higher authorities this normal act was classified as the gravest crime. Publication in the foreign scientific press by Soviet scientists came to a virtual halt. Traditional foreign-language résumés of papers in Soviet journals no longer appeared. The personal participation of Soviet scientists in scientific events of international significance was reduced to a minimum. It was at this particular time that the notion of the Iron Curtain appeared in foreign propaganda.

The situation began to change in 1955 after the first Geneva U.N. Conference on Peaceful Uses of Atomic Energy. We began to rediscover other countries. But progress was slow, and even now free interchange between Soviet scientists and their foreign colleagues meets many serious obstacles.

Such prolonged isolation of Soviet scientists from the outside world undoubtedly contributed much to the origin and protracted flourishing of various kinds of false doctrines. They were fully protected against the external criticism (let us say from England or France) which, through international public opinion, could have guaranteed a normal situation and prevented the spread of pseudoscience.

5. In conjunction with the factors previously discussed, the general system of rigid centralization in the U.S.S.R. of administration of science, of higher education, and of scientific publication, and the machinery for awarding scientific degrees and titles, had an exceptionally baleful effect on attempts to

withstand the spread and dominance of Lysenkoism and other false doctrines.

In the majority of economically developed countries the funding and administration of scientific laboratories are decentralized. Institutes, colleges, laboratories, and universities, sometimes entering into voluntary associations, are independent, and no administrative power can dismiss the founder of one or another productive laboratory or revoke the award of a scientific degree by an academic senate of a university. Academies of science are usually voluntary organizations and do not fall within the governmental administrative apparatus.

Under such a system it would be impossible for some single administrative organ to impose a mandatory curriculum in biology for all institutions of higher learning, or a single, obligatory textbook for all professional faculties (e.g., agriculture). Individual differences always exist among courses, and there is a variety of texts. The award of degrees is also decentralized, and a decision of an academic senate is not, as in the U.S.S.R., merely a petition to the Committee on the Award of Higher Degrees, but a definitive step. The direction of research is also guaranteed by establishment of foundations, so that a scientist receiving financial support from such a source to work, for instance, in genetics, can work independently of any government administrative organs.

This kind of system insures against the spread, especially by coercion, of false doctrines such as Lysenkoism. In contrast, with the extreme centralization of administration of science and education prevailing in the U.S.S.R., the periodic, prolonged capture of key administrative posts (the LAAAS praesidium, the Ministry of Agriculture, the agricultural section of the CC, the degree-awarding commission, the Ministry of Education, etc.) by Lysenkoites secured for them full control over virtually all biological and agricultural science and education, and placed in their hands factual power on a nationwide scale.

These are the basic causes and factors that created the conditions for and stimulated the shameful and painful phenomenon that Lysenkoism in our country is now seen to have been.

It can in no way be concluded, however, that Lysenkoism was vanquished in the end because all these factors and causes ceased to exist. Since October, 1964, the popular support which Lysenko and his followers received from state and political authorities disappeared, and this fact is important. Yet both the cessation of support by the country's new leadership and the subsequent gradual elimination of Lysenkoism in our country are connected with the mighty scientific patriotism of public opinion, which little by little was formed among Soviet scientists of all disciplines, among journalists and writers, and among public figures and directors of the national economy. No methods of administrative suppression managed to stop the discussion. Only the forms and methods of debate changed. The open fight became concealed and semi-legal in the difficult times, but the fight never stopped. And the victory won in the end by true science did not come about by happenstance.

NOTES

The variable style of the notes reflects the state of the original manuscript. Citations are, in some instances, less complete than is normally desirable. Some have been expanded from the original when missing information could be supplied. For obvious reasons, in many cases the original sources could not be consulted.

Dates in brackets at the end of some citations indicate author's additions to the original version.

Only major abridgments and modifications are indicated.

(*Transl.*)

Chapter 1. *The Historical Background of the Controversy*

1. *Estestvoznanie i Marxizm* for 1931.
2. A detailed analysis of the problems then discussed may be found in two books: P. P. Bondarenko et al., *Protiv Mekhanisticheskovo Materializma i Men'shevistviushchego Idealizma v Biologii* (eds.; Moscow-Leningrad: Medgiz, 1931); and D. Joravsky, *Soviet Marxism and Natural Science* (New York: Columbia University Press, 1961).
3. *Priroda* (1930), no. 9: 927–28.
4. "Klassovaya bor'ba na estestvenno-nauchnom fronte" (1932), Uchpedgiz.
5. August 7, 1927, no. 178/3710.
6. November 13, 1929, no. 212.

   Popovsky, in his "1000 days of Academician Vavilov" [*Prostor* (1966), no. 7: 13–14, Alma-Ata], described the meetings of Vavilov and Lysenko in Gandzha in 1926–1928, and Vavilov's alleged interests in Lysenko's experiments with peas and subsequently with wheat. These meetings of Lysenko and Vavilov in this period are, however, a complete literary fabrication. For details, see note 2, Chapter 2. [1966]
7. January 16, 1929, no. 13.
8. November 19, 1929.

9. *Trudy po Prikladnoy Botanike, Genetike i Selektsii* (1930), vol. 24.
10. Shock collective farmers were the equivalent, in Russian agriculture, of the stakhanovites in industry. (Transl.)
11. *Pravda*, February 15, 1935.
12. March 13, 1931.
13. *Pravda*, August 3, 1931, no. 212/5017.

Chapter 2. The Struggle Begins

1. The list of names given parenthetically in the text is accompanied by titles (professor or academician) with an explanatory note indicating the proper use of the term "academician" as a member of the U.S.S.R. Academy of Sciences as opposed to the practice, in the agricultural press, of applying the title to members of the LAAAS. The names cited are Vavilov, Meister, Konstantinov, Serebrovsky, Kol'tsov, Sapegin, M. S. Navashin, Pisarev, Kostov, M. M. Zavadovsky, Lisitsyn, Rudnitsky, Zhebrak, Dubinin, Shekhurdin, Karpechenko, Filipchenko, Levitsky, Levit, Pangalo, Govorov, and Flyaksberger. (Transl.)
2. Popovsky (see note 6, Chapter 1), citing some favorable statements by Vavilov on Lysenko's theory of phasic development, deduces that there was a friendship between them and that it was Vavilov who boosted Lysenko into his orbit of glory and fame. Popovsky interprets this as Vavilov's fundamental fatal mistake. Yet the favorable view of this theory taken by Vavilov and many other scientists in 1932–1934 was fully justified, since Lysenko's studies of temperature and light conditions for plant development fell within the plan for investigating the world collection of domesticated plants and thus could be useful and necessary for the AIPB. By his positive attitude Vavilov did not promote Lysenko but rather, for a time, kept him within the framework of a cooperative scientific endeavor. There was never any personal friendship between the two, and Vavilov's attitude, as the director of the LAAAS, toward Lysenko cannot be viewed as an error of

judgment. Vavilov's real possibilities of influencing the course of events connected with Lysenko's activities were very severely limited. The revolutionary innovators of "common folk" origin were becoming the official fashion. [1966]

3. The following thirteen pages of the original typescript, under the title "The positions of classical genetics," give a brief account of simple Mendelian genetics and the theory of the gene as it stood in 1936. They would be essential for Russian readers who have been denied acquaintance with these matters under Lysenko. For an English translation, however, they are superfluous and are hence omitted. (Transl.)

4. In: *Spornye Voprosy Genetiki i Selektsii* (LAAAS, 1937), p. 47.

5. *Ibid.*, pp. 61–62.

6. *Ibid.*, p. 71. According to eyewitnesses, in one of the discussions of this period, Lysenko expressed himself more simply: "Just what is this gene? Who has seen it? Who has felt it? Who has tasted it?"

7. The adjective "pea" in Russian has a derisory connotation. "Pea laws" was a favorite pun of anti-Mendelians in the U.S.S.R. (Transl.)

8. This section has been abridged on the grounds given in note 3 to this chapter. (Transl.)

9. In: *Spornye Voprosy Genetiki i Selektsii* (LAAAS, 1937), pp. 392–93.

10. T. D. Lysenko, *ibid.*, p. 455.

11. H. J. Muller, *ibid.*, pp. 143–44.

12. Published in *Pamyati V. I. Lenina* (AS, 1934), pp. 565–92.

13. *Izvestiya*, December 14, 1948.

14. H. J. Muller, in: *Spornye Voprosy Genetiki i Selektsii* (LAAAS, 1937), pp. 136–37.

15. *Ibid.*, p. 57.

16. W. S. Harwood, *The New Earth: A Recital of the Triumphs of Modern Agriculture in America* (New York: The Macmillan Company, 1906).

17. Ten pages of the original text containing excerpts from the report in *Spornye Voprosy Genetiki i Selektsii* are also omitted. (Transl.)

Chapter 3. The First Phase Climax

1. The "annihilation" of Darwinism in the Leningrad University consisted of closing the halls of the Museum of Darwinism (which were standing empty) to alleviate an acute shortage of space for new professorial chairs. The Darwin Museum organized by Prezent consisted of but two rooms, one of which was devoted to Darwin and the other exclusively to Lysenko and Prezent himself.

2. The reference is to the now rehabilitated Professor Uranovsky, a Darwinist and historian of natural science. Wood's article did not contain anything frightening. The editor-in-chief of the journal was the noted physicist, S. I. Vavilov.

3. Agol was executed on a false accusation of Trotskyism and later was posthumously rehabilitated. Before his arrest he was the academician-secretary of the Ukrainian Academy of Sciences. The communication about his arrest was published on the opening day of the December, 1936, session of the LAAAS.

4. Levit, who died in prison, was the outstanding U.S.S.R. specialist in medical genetics. He was the founder and leader of the Medico-Genetic Institute which enjoyed worldwide fame. At the time of publication of Prezent's article, Levit had not yet been arrested. The accusations advanced against him by Prezent began the persecution of this scientist, who was arrested one or two months after the cited article was published. Later, Levit was posthumously rehabilitated.

5. *Yarovizatsiya* (1937), no. 3: 49–66.

6. *Ibid.*, with citations from pp. 71–83.

7. *Sotszemledelie*, April 12, 1937.

8. The quotation cited on p. 47 is given here again. (Transl.)

9. *Sotszemledelie*, June 6, 1937.

10. *Yarovizatsiya* (1937), no. 2: 15.

11. That is, *Pravda* or *Izvestiya*, April 12, 1937. (Transl.)

12. *Selektsiya i Semenovodstvo* (1937), nos. 4–12.

13. Muralov was later fully rehabilitated. In connection with his eightieth birthday, his biography appeared in the newspaper *Sovetskaya Rossiya* (June 21, 1966). He was Commissar of

Agriculture for the R.S.F.S.R. from 1930 to 1933, and Deputy Commissar for the U.S.S.R. from 1933 to 1935. He replaced Vavilov as president of the LAAAS in June, 1935, in connection with the reorganization and expansion of that institution, and held the post until July 4, 1937, when he was arrested. His successor, Meister, was arrested at the beginning of 1938. Lysenko was appointed to the post of LAAAS president by a decree of the U.S.S.R. Council of Commissars on February 28, 1938. Thus Lysenko could consider himself the heir of three presidents who had been subjected to repression.

14. Biulleten' VASKHNIL (1937), no. 4.
15. *Pravda*, October 4, 1937, no. 274/7240.
16. January 11, 1938.
17. The protocol of the conference is preserved in the LAAAS archives.
18. *Pravda*, April 9, 1938.
19. September 12, 1938.
20. The reference here is to an abstract by Vavilov in the *Proceedings of the 3rd All-Russian Breeding Conference*, held in Saratov (1920). Later (1922) the article was published in English in the *Journal of Genetics*, vol. 12: 47–89. (Transl.)
21. *Yarovizatsiya* (1939), nos. 2 and 3.
22. It may be asked how a group of young scientists with such strong anti-Vavilov sentiments could appear in the institute. After all, Vavilov was always careful and thorough in the recruitment of personnel, and successfully attempted to concentrate the best specialists in the AIPB. The inroduction of the illiterate opposition to the institute was not Vavilov's fault. At the end of the twenties and beginning of the thirties, postgraduate students were not, as now, members of the different departments or institutes; rather, they were under the jurisdiction of independent graduate faculties. This system was reorganized in 1931, and all students were assigned to different scientific institutions and faculties. The Leningrad Agricultural graduate faculty was abolished at the beginning of 1931, and all seventy of its students were assigned to the AIPB. It was among this motley group that the later attitude of nihilism toward AIPB traditions arose.
23. *Sovetskie Subtropiki* (1939), no. 16: 57–61.

24. In the course of examining the Leningrad party archives, a copy of a memorandum by Shlykov, dated March 2, 1938, and addressed to the CEC scientific section, was found. In it, Shlykov proposed the appointment of Shundenko, already deputy director of the AIPB, as director. Shundenko's scientific worthlessness was completely apparent, and Vavilov, who had originally opposed his appointment as deputy, later completely ignored him in that post. The memorandum (a copy of which was provided me by N. I. Ivanov) read in part: "It would be over-optimistic, as I see it, to view the appointment of comrade Shundenko as Vavilov's deputy as providing realistic prospects of a genuine theoretical and practical reconstruction of the institute. But the same Shundenko, freed from the constant and very artful suppression of his initiative by Vavilov, invested with trust, and given full responsibility for the institute as director and not as deputy, could realize a more rapid, fuller, and better reconstruction of the institute in the direction of practical and strictly purposeful work of plant breeding." [1966]

25. Sizov, who persistently fought Vavilov for a long time, and later (1952–1961) Zhukovsky—who became head of the institute in 1951—himself became director. He was not appointed to the post immediately, but came to it in 1961, when Lysenko returned to the leadership of the LAAAS and Ol'shansky became Minister of Agriculture for the U.S.S.R. After becoming director, Sizov began energetically to liquidate the remnants of Vavilov traditions.

26. Abridged from the original. (Transl.)

27. This participant in the discussion is not identified in the original beyond the initial L. (Transl.)

28. A two-page memorandum by an outstanding plant breeder, Konstantinov, later dismissed from the Timiryazev Academy, is omitted. It contains some specific recommendations for the reform of the AIPB consonant with Vavilov's approach to his tasks. (Transl.)

29. "Za peredovuyu sovetskuyu geneticheskuyu nauku," *Pod Znamenem Marksizma* (1939), no. 10: 148–49.

30. *Pod Znamenem Marksizma*, no. 11: 127–40.

31. *Ibid.*, p. 139.
32. The original includes the full text of the letter. Of nine specific points of complaints, four are given in translation here. A copy of the letter is in Vavilov's archives. (Transl.)
33. Doctor and Candidate are higher degrees in Soviet science. (Transl.)
34. It should be noted that a night telephone call by Vavilov to Stalin in March, 1939, and their alleged ensuing dialogue (Popovsky in the newspaper *Sovetskaya Rossiya*, November 27, 1964) are invented. The episode derives from non-authenticated reminiscences of an acquaintance of Vavilov. None of his close friends or relatives confirms any meeting between Stalin and Vavilov in 1939. [1966]
35. The first most detailed and factual public description of the last expedition and arrest of Vavilov was given by Bakhteev at an anniversary meeting of the Moscow Society of Naturalists on November 24, 1964. He kindly gave the text of his talk to the author. The description given here is, to a great extent, based on a discussion with Bakhteev in 1962.

It seems to me that the fact that Vavilov was arrested under such extraordinary circumstances, when he was near the state border, is no coincidence. Apparently somebody in Moscow obtained sanction for his arrest precisely because of Vavilov's proximity to the border. At the end of 1940, persistent rumors were circulated that the main motivation for the arrest was Vavilov's attempt to cross the border. According to Bakhteev, the emissaries who arrested Vavilov arrived from Moscow by plane, and he was flown back there. The arrest was made so carefully that the rest of the expedition assumed that he was merely being urgently recalled.

In 1965 and 1966, Popovsky, who studied the files on Vavilov in detail, read excerpts from the resolution for Vavilov's arrest at public meetings. Together with absurd accusations of spying, of being the leader of the "Labor Peasant Party," etc., the resolution also said that AIPB, under Vavilov's instructions, carried out special studies merely to controvert the data of Lysenko which had a decisive significance in the economy of the U.S.S.R. In Vavilov's file there is also a letter from the NKVD chief, Beria, to Molotov, who was in charge of science in the CC Politbureau, requesting permission for Vavilov's arrest. [1966]

36. Karpechenko was arrested soon after the newspaper *Leningradsky Universitet*, on the editorial board of which Prezent played a leading role, published an editorial on December 13, 1940. In it, Karpechenko's lecture course on genetics was criticized in familiar tones, and demands were made that he, as well as his collaborators, be removed from the university, on the grounds that they had turned the department into "a stronghold of reactionary teachings representing, for all practical ends, the extremist theories of biology."

37. In the period of Vavilov's rehabilitation, and more recently, many were able to see the NKVD files on Vavilov. It has been definitely established that Shundenko was indeed the leader of the agricultural section of the NKVD, and headed the investigation of Vavilov's case. The direct interrogator was a certain Khvat. During the eleven months òf the investigation, Vavilov was summoned for questioning over one hundred times. [1967]

38. Popovsky reported publicly the existence of a 1954 letter from Yakushkin to the Procurator's Office in which he repudiates his original testimony. Yakushkin states that the "experts" were forced to sign previously prepared documents. He himself had been recruited into the NKVD after his arrest in 1929, as a condition of freedom. Hence he considers that he was not to be regarded as an independent expert, since in fact he was an NKVD agent. Nor were the other members of the expert commission independent. Zubarev was another agent; Mosolov, a deputy to Lysenko at the LAAAS; Chuenkov, the U.S.S.R. Deputy Commissar of Agriculture. In the period of rehabilitation all the experts repudiated their conclusions and testified that the commission never met as a body and each expert was "processed" individually.

39. Vavilov's arrest also apparently required higher approval and hence cannot be imputed to any single person. During the rehabilitation, many accusing statements, beginning with 1933, were discovered in his file. They did not serve as the imme-

diate cause of Vavilov's arrest, nor were they returned as slanderous, as used sometimes to be the practice in 1938–1939. They were accumulated in preparation for approval of arrest. In 1937–1938, Vavilov's arrest would have met an unfavorable reaction abroad and thus raised a question about the other trials. The higher authorities understood this. But by the end of 1940, when all Europe was enveloped in the flames of World War II, his arrest passed relatively unnoticed. [1966] (Abridged by Transl.)

40. Added in 1967. See Chapter 5.
41. Nemchinov, director of the Timiryazev Agricultural Academy, knew of Vavilov's evacuation to Saratov. According to his wife, in the course of evacuation to Central Asia, Nemchinov sent her to the Saratov prison with a food parcel for Vavilov. The parcel was refused and Nemchinov got a severe reprimand. Ternopol'sky, a prison mate of Vavilov, in both Moscow and Saratov, tells me that, in the latter prison, cells designed to hold one or two men were usually overcrowded with about ten inmates. (Abridged by Transl. from a 1966 note.)
42. A personal reminiscence by Baranov is omitted. (Transl.)
43. A three-page letter written from South America on the fifteenth anniversary of the October revolution, giving personal details and accounts of collecting activities and of the obstacles put in the way by the "sons of bitches" terrified of Russians, as if they were devils incarnate, is omitted. (Transl.)
44. In 1967 Bakhteev, with the help of former personnel of the Saratov prison and cemetery, succeeded in finding the probable site of Vavilov's interment. [1967]

Chapter 4. Medical Genetics in 1937–1940

1. *Organizatsiya Kletki* (Biomedgiz, 1936), 652 pp.
2. Two teams of scientists, Watson, Crick, and Wilkins, and Kornberg and Ochoa, received Nobel prizes for their work on self-reproduction of genetic material.
3. *Yarovizatsiya* (1939), no. 2: 109.
4. January 11, 1939.

5. This book, which contained a number of unverified and later disproved hypotheses, nevertheless was, for its time, a highly interesting and original attempt at a theoretical analysis of evolution.
6. In the same election, Prezent, whose only scientific contribution consisted of purely polemical articles, was nominated by the Odessa Institute of Plant Breeding and Genetics. Of course, he was not elected. Only in 1948 did he become a member of the LAAAS and, at that, without election.
7. *Pod Znamenem Marksizma* (1939), no. 5: 146–53.
8. Similar attacks are to be found in books by N. D. Ivanov (*Darvinism i Teoriya Nasledstvennosti*, AS Press, 1960), and the philosopher, Platonov (*Dialektichesky Materializm i Sovremennaya Genetika*, Sotsekgiz, 1961), and in the pamphlet by Kuroedov and Dryagina ("Sotsial'nye i gnoseologicheskie korni Weismannizma-Morganizma," Moscow State University, 1961), etc.
9. *Russky Evgenichesky Zhurnal* (1922), 1 (1): 9–10.
10. *Pod Znamenem Marksizma* (1936), no. 11: 64–72. The Black Hundred was the Russian political pogrom, reactionary, anti-Semitic group. (Transl.)
11. *Priroda* (1941), no. 5.
12. N. K. Kol'tsov, *Pamyati Pavshykh* (1906). (A copy is to be found in the Lenin State Library.)
13. The first favorable article about Kol'tsov since 1941 appeared in 1965 in the journal *Khimiya i Zhizn'*, no. 5. A more detailed biographical sketch is to be found in *Znamya* (1966), no. 8.

Chapter 5. *The Agronomy Debate of 1935–1938*

1. *Collected Works* (1953), pp. 413–42.
2. April 20, 1962.
3. General P. Skoropadsky was appointed ruler of the Ukraine after the German occupation in 1918. (Transl.)
4. *Works*, vol. 7, p. 119.
5. *Front Nauki i Tekhniki* (1935), no. 2: 61.
6. The sections on the controversies in which Vil'yams was involved are somewhat abridged and rearranged. (Transl.)

7. According to Pryanishnikov's computations in 1934–1935, production of mineral fertilizers had to be raised to 24 million tons by 1943. This would have satisfied only the minimal requirements of agriculture and prevented the progressive losses in soil fertility. Yet, before the war, in 1941, production was only 3 to 3.5 million tons, and even by 1961 had risen to only 15.3 million (*Pravda*, January 24, 1962).

8. *Pravda*, May 9, 1937.

9. *LAAAS Biulleten'* (1937), no. 4: 22.

10. *Pravda*, September 4, 1937. Analogous accusations appeared in *Sotszemledelie*, September 21, 1937.

11. *Sotszemledelie*, November 16 and 20, 1937.

12. *Ibid.*, January 11, 1938.

13. *Front Nauki i Tekhniki* (1938), no. 3: 129–31.

14. January 6, 1937.

15. Later president of the AS. (Transl.)

16. January 6, 1962.

17. April 15, 1937.

18. See the anonymous article, "Razgromit' do kontsa chuzhdye teorii v agronomii," in the Saratov newspaper, *Kommunist*, April 18, 1937.

Chapter 6. The Postwar Period

1. *Selektsiya i Semenovodstvo* (1946), nos. 1–2.

2. T. D. Lysenko, *Agrobiologiya* (Sel'khozgiz, 1949), pp. 602–606.

3. *Leningradskaya Pravda*, March 6, 1947.

4. T. D. Lysenko, *Agrobiologiya* (6th ed.; 1952), p. 482.

5. Two pages of quotations from Sabinin's article in *Vnutrividovaya Bor'ba Zhivotnykh i Rastenii* (Moscow University Press, 1947), pp. 41–43, are omitted. (Transl.)

6. Lysenko, Prezent, Ol'shansky, Avakyan, Glushchenko, Vlasiuk, Dolgushin, Stoletov, Zhukov-Verezhnikov, Greben', Dvoryankin, Nuzhdin, and others.

7. After Stalin's approval of Lysenko's article, Yuriy Zhdanov had to confess his sins in a special letter to Stalin dated July 7, 1948, but published in *Pravda* on the concluding day

of the LAAAS session. In particular, he wrote: "From the first day of my work in the Science Section, representatives of formal genetics came to me with complaints that the new varieties of useful plants (buckwheat, kok-sagyz, geraniums, hemp, citrus fruit) with improved qualities are not being adopted in practice and meet the opposition of the followers of Lysenko . . . My mistake was that, having decided to defend these practical attainments, which happened to be 'gifts from the Greeks,' I did not subject the basic methodological vices of Mendelist-Morganist genetics to merciless criticism. I realize that this is a utilitarian approach to practice, a chase after pennies . . ."

8. *LAAAS Archives*, bundle no. 1, folder no. 3.
9. See *Pravda*, July 27, 1948.
10. *Ibid.*, March 8, 1953.
11. I. I. Prezent, Stenographic report of the LAAAS session (1948), p. 510.
12. N. I. Nuzhdin, *ibid.*, p. 99. From 1941, Nuzhdin was Lysenko's personal theoretician. Before that he worked under Vavilov's direction in the AS Institute of Genetics and was a typical "formal geneticist" working on *Drosophila*. While Vavilov was still alive, Nuzhdin persistently attempted to become his deputy. Every time that Vavilov came from Moscow to Leningrad, he would find on the top of accumulated material on his desk a draft of Nuzhdin's appointment as deputy director. Vavilov would sigh with resignation and consign it to the wastepaper basket. This went on for several years. When, after Vavilov's arrest, Lysenko took possession of the institute, he signed the long-awaited appointment. Nuzhdin was also made editor-in-chief of the *Zhurnal Obshchei Biologii*.
13. M. B. Mitin, Stenographic report of the LAAAS session (1948), p. 233.
14. *Ibid.*, p. 10.
15. *Ibid.*, p. 227.
16. I. E. Glushchenko, *Michurinskaya Agrobiologicheskaya Nauka i ee Osnovnye Printsipy* (Sel'khozgiz, 1949), p. 27.
17. I. A. Polyakov, *Nauka i Zhizn'* (1948), no. 9: 12–21.
18. *Protiv Reaktsionnogo Mendelizma-Morganizma* (AS Press,

1950), p. 350. Studitsky had previously been a collaborator of Shmal'gauzen who, in 1948, was declared to be a leader of the Morganists, and subjected to the most violent hounding. After 1948 he was the first to bait his former teacher, and occupied himself in elaboration and "proof" of the ideas of Lysenko, Lepeshinskaya, and others. He was rewarded by appointment to a number of key posts: head (as deputy scientific director) of the Institute of Morphology, where he replaced the dismissed Shmal'gauzen; the chair of Histology at Moscow University, replacing the dismissed Roskin; and the deputy editorship of the journal *Uspekhi Sovremennoi Biologii*. More than that, soon after the LAAAS session, Studitsky became science editor of *Pravda*, in which position he was engaged for many years in tendentiously misinforming the Soviet public in matters of biology.

19. A. N. Studitski, "Fly-lovers and man-haters," *Journal of Heredity* (1949), vol. 40: 307–14. (Transl. from the Russian.)

20. V. P. Bushinsky, *Nauka i Zhizn'* (1948), no. 10: 36–39.

21. O. B. Lepeshinskaya, *Soveshchanie po Probleme Zhivogo veshchestva* (AS Press, 1951), p. 13.

22. D. M. Troshin, *Filosofskie Voprosy Sovremennoi Biologii* (Moscow University Press, 1951), p. 296.

23. *Mesto i Rol' Estestvoznaniya v Razvitii Obshchestva* (1961).

24. See *Izvestiya*, August 27, 1948.

25. *Pravda*, August 28, 1948.

26. *Meditsinskii Rabotnik*, September 15, 1948.

27. "Za bezrazdel'noe gospodstvo michurinskoi biologicheskoi nauki" (1948).

28. Subsequently, expulsion of Lobashev and his Leningrad University colleagues from the party was attempted. Prezent demanded this at a party meeting of the Faculty of Biology. The stenographic report which has been preserved records an interesting dialogue. One party member interrupted Prezent, who was proving that the University Morganists were abetting fascism. "How can it be" (a listener could not contain himself) "that these comrades of which you speak spent nearly the whole war under arms, fighting fascists, and were decorated with military awards?" "This is no argument," replied

Prezent, "they fought fascism only empirically." It should be noted, by the way, that Prezent himself, and many of his friends, avoided precisely such an empirical fight against fascism during the war.

29. List of examples of other directives omitted. (Transl.)

30. Abridged. (Transl.)

31. Zhebrak, known to geneticists throughout the world for his classical experiments in production of polyploids (largely in wheat), was one of the first in 1935–1936 to criticize the scientific nihilism and obscurantism of Prezent and Lysenko. Because of this the Lysenkoites continuously attempted to defame him and his work. They succeeded in subjecting him to an ignominious "Court of honor" only because, in his article on Soviet genetics in the American journal, *Science,* he failed to describe Lysenko's achievements. After Zhebrak's dismissal, Lysenko and his cohorts actually destroyed the most valuable collection of polyploids, created by Zhebrak and his co-workers.

32. Paramonov was the Professor of Darwinism and Zoology, and one of the best lecturers in the Academy. His post (in addition to other positions) was given to Lysenko's collaborator, Nuzhdin, under whom the department deteriorated very badly.

33. *Filosofskie Voprosy Sovremennoi Fiziki* (AS Press, 1952).

34. T. D. Lysenko, "Stalin i michurinskaya biologiya," in *Works* (1953), p. 9. Lysenko's fundamental article which first described extensively his idea of a saltatory transformation of species was entitled "Species," and was written by him for the *Great Soviet Encyclopedia.* I recently came into possession of the covering letter, on LAAAS stationery, submitting the article. It reads: "The facts set forth in the submitted article 'Species' are correct. I take full scientific responsibility for it. However, because the thoughts expressed in the article are at complete variance with the concepts of species and speciation as generally accepted in biology, I cannot make bold to recommend it for publication myself. Hence I request preliminary approval by the CC Section on Propaganda." [1966]

35. *Meditsinsky Rabotnik,* March 10, 1953.

36. *Uspekhi Sovremennoi Biologii* (1953), vol. 35: 161–67.

37. *Works*, vol. 1, p. 30.
38. December 12, 1948. Translation of the letter omitted. (Transl.)
39. *Agrobiologiya, Zhurnal Obshchei Biologii, Uspekhi Sovremennoi Biologii.*
40. P. Baranov, "O vidoobrazovanii," *Botanichesky Zhurnal* (1953), no. 5; B. M. Kozo-Polyansky, "Voprosy novogo ucheniya o vide," *ibid.*, no. 6; E. V. Bobko, "K voprosu o metodike izucheniya obrazovaniya novykh vidov," *ibid.*, no. 3; and others.
41. *Botanichesky Zhurnal* (1953), no. 1.
42. Stenographic report (Gospolitizdat, 1958), p. 235.
43. Sukachev, Baranov, Zhukovsky, Lipshits, Takhtadzhyan, Turbin, Fedorov, Tikhomirov, and many other noted botanists were removed and replaced by Avakyan, Vlasiuk, Genkel', Razumov, and other Lysenko followers. The reorganization of the board was undertaken in accordance with a personal directive by Khrushchev. In the second issue of the journal for 1959, prepared for press by the new Michurinist board, an editorial justifying the changes appears. It also contains a comment of Khrushchev at the December CC plenary sessions. The following dialogue is quoted from the stenographic account (Gospolitizdat, 1958, p. 233): *"Mustafaiev:* ... Especially bad is the situation in biology, as was pointed out in *Pravda* of December 14, where the inexplicable behavior of the *Botanichesky Zhurnal* and some of our scientists is discussed. Instead of criticizing each other in a businesslike scientific fashion, and pointing out defects, insulting tones and humiliation are resorted to. *Khrushchev:* The cadres must be reviewed. Apparently people have been selected for the editorial board who are against Michurinist science. Nothing will change so long as they are there. They must be replaced by others, by real Michurinists. This is the radical solution of the problem."

It is important to note that the disbandment of the board was carried out by the AS praesidium and Biological Section, albeit following a directive from above. Yet only two and one-half months earlier the Biological Section reviewed and approved the activities of the journal (special resolution of September 23, 1958). Other resolutions of approval were passed by the All-Union Botanical Congress in May, 1957, and by the Council of the All-Union Botanical Society on December 17, 1957. They were printed in the *Botanichesky Zhurnal* (1958, no. 2), but the issue was withheld before distribution, and their texts were removed before the journal went into circulation. [1966]

44. A chapter on the resurrection of Vil'yamsism in 1948 and the spread of the grassland system of agriculture throughout the nation is omitted. Its subsection titles are: "A theoretical analysis of soil formation concepts developed by Vil'yams," "The flowering of Vil'yamsism after the 1948 LAAAS session and the general adoption of the grassland system in the guise of the 'Stalin plan for transforming nature,'" "The new wave of persecution of the representatives of Pryanishnikov's school of agricultural chemistry," "The role of Lysenko in the support and spread of Vil'yams' system." (Transl.)

Chapter 7. The Two Trends up to 1963

1. This chapter was written in 1962 and augmented in 1963. Today, naturally, much more could be said. But it seems advisable to me to leave the original text in order to show the situation as it was in 1962–1963, i.e., at the last stage of the monopoly of Lysenkoism protected from criticism. This statement applies equally to Chapter 8. [1966]

2. A thirteen-page section describing the state of genetical knowledge in the West in 1962–1963 is omitted. Its contents may be judged from the subsection headings: "The discovery of the biochemical structure and function of genes," "How genes control protein synthesis," "The molecular mechanism of mutation," "Cracking the genetic code," "The mechanism of exact self-replication of the genetic material of the chromosomes," "The volume of genetic information for individual development," "The molecular mechanism of reproduction of viruses, phages, and bacteria." (Transl.)

3. *Nauka i Zhizn'* (1962), no. 4, and *Izvestiya*, July 26, 1962, respectively.

4. I. I. Prezent, Stenographic report of the LAAAS session (1948).

5. K. Y. Kostriukova, *ibid.*, p. 272.

6. N. G. Belen'ky, *ibid.*, p. 73.

7. N. M. Sisakyan, *Biokhimiya Obmena Veshchestv* (AS Press, 1954). It should be noted that Sisakyan has now completely reversed his attitude toward molecular genetics and published a number of articles in which high appraisal of the genetic code and template molecules is made.

8. No. 6, December, 1961.

9. K. Y. Kostriukova, "Nauchnye doklady vysshei shkoly," *Seriya Filosofii* (1962), no. 1.

10. V. M. Kaganov, *Zhurnal Obshchei Biologii* (1962), vol. 23, no. 1.

11. *Dialektichesky Materializm i Voprosy Genetiki* (Sotsekgiz, 1962), p. 27.

12. *Ibid.*, pp. 140–41.

13. *Ibid.*, pp. 49–50.

14. On personal direction of Khrushchev, transmitted by telephone from Kiev where he, together with Lysenko, attended an agricultural conference. [1967]

15. A two-page discussion of the interpretation of environment-genotype relationships is omitted. One of the two pages was missing from the original manuscript. (Transl.)

Chapter 8. Lysenko's Agrobiology

1. In the original text, twenty pages are devoted to a review of the practical contributions of genetics. As this seems superfluous for a Western reader, the titles of the sections will suffice to indicate the nature of the material discussed: "Genetics as the basis of selection," "Increase in variability by artificial mutagenesis," "Practical application of polyploidy," "New methods of hybridization and utilization of heterosis," "Regulation of sex in animals," "Medical and cancer genetics, and the genetics of aging," "Radiation genetics." (Transl.)

2. I have been aided in writing this section by extensive unpub-

lished manuscripts on the history of Lysenko's agronomic proposals by A. A. Liubishchev and by V. P. Efroimson. I am grateful to both for placing the material at my disposal.

3. J. H. Klippart, "An essay on the origin, growth, diseases, varieties, etc., of the wheat plant," *12th Annual Report of Ohio State Board of Agriculture, 1857* (Columbus, 1858), p. 757.

4. See Konstantinov's speech at the 1936 session of the LAAAS.

5. *Pravda*, December 14, 1958.

6. *Biulleten' Yarovizatsii* (1932), nos. 2–3.

7. In: *Spornye Voprosy Genetiki i Selektsii* (LAAAS, 1937), pp. 162–63.

8. No. 1 (1935).

9. *Sotsrekonstruktsiya Sel'skogo Khozyaistva* (1936), no. 10: 128.

10. In: *Spornye Voprosy Genetiki i Selektsii* (LAAAS, 1937), pp. 56–57.

11. *Michurinskie Printsipy Selektsii i Semenovodstva Kul'turnykh Rasteniy* (1949), pp. 22–33.

12. *Sel'skoe Khozyaistvo*, August 6, 1954.

13. For example, A. E. P. de Gasparin, *Course d'Agriculture* (Paris: Bureau de la Maison Rustique, 1848), IV, chap. 12.

14. G. N. Linnik, "O prichinakh vyrozhdeniya kartofelya," *Bottanichesky Zhurnal* (1955), 40 (4): 528–41.

15. *Partiynaya Zhizn'* (1956), no. 9: 29–30.

16. *Raboty v Dni Otechestvennoy Voiny.*

17. *Chastnoe Zemledelie.*

18. *Podarok Molodoy Khozyaike* (part 2), recipe no. 4029, pp. 189–90.

19. N. M. Nikiforov, *Okul'tivirovanie Khlopchatnika v Tashkentskom Rayone* (Tashkent, 1896) and the pamphlet by M. Bushuev (Glvakhlopok, 1926).

20. A pun on the world *lyset'*, "to become bald." (Transl.)

21. *Lesnoie Khozyaistvo* (1955), no. 3: 49.

22. The article cited first appeared in *La Pensée* (1957, no. 72, pp. 23–26), and is quoted here from a translation in the *Botanichesky Zhurnal* (1957), 42 (10): 1517.

23. *Botanichesky Zhurnal* (1958), no. 8.

24. See the Moscow papers for July 12, 1962.

25. *Agrobiologiya* (1952), no. 6: 27.

26. "O filosofskikh osnovakh biologicheskoy teorii vida," *Voprosy Filosofii* (1957), no. 4.

27. The original contains four single-spaced pages from a stenographic report of Sokolov's speech. In it are given a very detailed technical description and criticism of the reports of Lysenko and his supporters who claimed high yields from the use of his methods. In general, the so-called small doses turned out to be massive. The excerpts from Sokolov's speech included here are designed to indicate the tone of the attack on Lysenko and to illustrate his experimental methodology. (Transl.)

28. Nitrogen, phosphorus, and potassium. (Transl.)

29. *Timiryazevets*, March 5, 1955.

30. H. Stubbe, *Botanichesky Zhurnal* (1958), vol. 43: 1362–77; A. R. Zhebrak, *ibid.* (1956), vol. 41: 358–60.

31. The original, curiously enough, makes no mention of the extensive experiments on vegetative hybridization of animals carried out by the Lysenko school, and even less susceptible of verification than such hybridization of plants. (Transl.)

32. *Agrobiologiya* (1948), no. 1: 47–77.

33. *Problemy Botaniki* (1950), vol. 1, p. 367.

34. "Chto my videli v Anglii" (1956).

35. *Yarovizatsiya* (1935), no. 1: 45–46.

36. *Ibid.*

37. Stenographic account of the LAAAS session (1948), p. 316.

38. *Michurinskie Printsipy Selektsii i Semenovodstva Kul'turnykh Rasteniy* (1949), p. 19.

39. A documentary account is to be found in P. A. Baranov, N. P. Dubinin, and M. I. Khadzhinov, *Botanichesky Zhurnal* (1955), vol. 10: 481–507. An accurate popular version by M. Popovsky appears in *Novy Mir* (1961), no. 8.

40. *Vozniknovenie Kletok iz Zhivogo Veshchestva.*

41. August 13, 1952, no. 1338.

42. *Sel'skaya Zhizn'*, June 20, 1962; *Izvestiya*, June 19, 1962; *Pravda*, July 13, 1962; etc.

43. For example, the article "Stepnoi kolos" in *Pravda*, September 3, 1962.

44. *Vestnik Sel'skokhozyaistvennoi Nauki* (1962), no. 6: 45.

45. T. D. Lysenko, *Agrobiologiya* (1957), no. 6, and (1958), no. 6.

46. *Izvestiya*, August 8, 1962.
47. *Agrobiologiya* (1957), no. 6: 9.
48. Four pages of the original dealing with the incompleteness of Lysenko's results and the technical dangers in applying his methods in the country at large are omitted. (Transl.)
49. *Tsel' Zhizni* and "Akademik iz Askanii," respectively.
50. From Pushkin's "Bacchic Song." (Transl.)

Chapter 9. The Events of 1962–1964

1. *Izvestiya AS, Seriya Biol.* (1962), no. 5.
2. *Pravda*, July 12, 1962.
3. See *Pravda* and other newspapers for January 25, 1963.
4. *Pravda* and *Izvestiya*, January 28, 1963.
5. *Vestnik Sel'skokhozyaistvennoi Nauki* (1963), no. 5.
6. Eikhfel'd, Vysokos, Musiyko, Remeslo, Sizov, Vsyakikh, Greben', Kuperman, Krasota, and others.
7. The composition of the committee on Lenin prizes was confirmed by the U.S.S.R. Council of Ministers in January, 1963 (see *Izvestiya*, January 17, 1963). It consisted of 120 scientists, but agriculture in the main was represented by Lysenko supporters: Ol'shansky, Luk'yanenko, Eikhfel'd, Pustovoit, Stoletov, and Sisakyan.
8. The author of this book. (Transl.)
9. *Zhivotnovodstvo* (1963), no. 6: 3–8.
10. Resolution of the TAA party committee of July 30, 1962.
11. Published in an English translation by Ann Synge under the title *Protein Synthesis and Problems of Heredity, Development, and Aging* (Edinburgh: Oliver and Boyd, 1966). (Transl.)
12. *Moskovskaya Pravda*, June 20, 1963, no. 145, and *Vechernyaya Moskva*, June 19, 1963, no. 144.
13. *Meditsinskaya Gazeta*, October 4, 1963.
14. Pavlenko also produced a popular pamphlet on the subject: "Estestvenno-nauchnye osnovy meditsinskoy genetiki" (Medgiz, 1963).
15. *Pravda*, February 11, 1964.
16. *Izvestiya* and *Pravda*, February 14, 1964.

17. Considerably abridged. (Transl.) *Pravda* and *Izvestiya*, February 15, 1964.
18. *Pravda* and *Izvestiya*, March 7, 1964.
19. *Sel'skaya Zhizn'*, March 10, 1964.
20. 1964, no. 8. Among the twelve authors were Musiyko, Mel'nik, Dolgushin, Vorob'ev, Kirichenko, and Khitrinsky.
21. *Sel'skaya Zhizn'*, August 29, 1964, no. 204 (9989).

Chapter 10. The End of Lysenkoism

1. *Komsomol'skaya Pravda*, October 23, 1964.
2. *Ibid.*, November 11, 1964, no. 266.
3. *Ibid.*, November 29, 1964.
4. See *Vestnik Akademii Nauk S.S.S.R.* (1965), no. 3.
5. *Pravda*, February 4, 1965.
6. Its chairman was the agricultural economist, Tulupnikov. The most competent animal husbandman was Kravchenko. Others included the specialists in animal husbandry, Guneeva and Krynkina, the agronomist Lesik, the accountant Popok, and two staff members of the AS praesidium.
7. The protocols appear nearly in full in the *Vestnik Akademii Nauk S.S.S.R.* (1965), no. 11, and in *Vestnik Sel'skokhozyastvennoi Nauki* (1965), no. 12.
8. *Pravda*, June 24, 1965; *Izvestiya*, June 25, 1965; *Sovetskaya Rossiya*, June 25, 1965, etc.
9. 1965, no. 8; 1966, nos. 2 and 12.

Chapter 11. How Did It Happen?

1. N. N. Semenov, "Nauka ne terpit subiektivizma," *Priroda* (1965), no. 4.
2. I. T. Frolov, "Genetika i dialektika," *Voprosy Filosofii* (1967), no. 1.
3. G. Roskin, "Toxin therapy of experimental cancer. The influence of protozoan infections upon transplanted cancer," *Cancer Research* (1946), 6 (7): 363–65.

Well-known political and scientific figures (e.g., Stalin, Beria, Pavlov) and non-Soviet scientists are merely listed. Others are identified as far as possible.

284

Index of Names

Vol'f, opponent of Vil'yams, 88, 92
Volkov, student, 84
Volovchenko, I. P., Minister of Agriculture, 212
Vorob'ev, A. I., supporter of Lysenko, 275
Voronin, S. A., editor-in-chief, Neva, 204
Voronov, V., animal breeder, 228
Vorontsov, N., critic of Lysenkoite textbook, 227
Vsyakikh, A. S., animal husbandman, 193, 205, 238, 274
Vyshinsky, A. I., 66
Vysokos, G. P., supporter of Lysenko, 274

Watson, J. D., 263
Weismann, A., in passim
Wells, H. G., 82
Wilkins, M., 263
Wood, E., 47, 118

Yakovlev, P. P., supporter of Lysenko, 49-51, 160
Yakovlev, Y. A., Commissar of Agriculture, 15, 155

Yakushkin, I. V., NKVD agent, 71-72, 262
Yudintsev, S. D., dean, Biology Faculty, Moscow University; member, LAAAS, 124
Yur'ev, V. Y., plant breeder, 161, 184

Zaporozhets, director, Fertilizer Institute, 92
Zavadovsky, B. M., biologist, 21
Zavadovsky, M. M., developmental biologist, 7, 52, 124, 178
Zelikman, A., assistant professor, Moscow University, 124
Zhdanov, A. A., secretary, CEC, 112-13
Zhdanov, Y. A., head, Science Department, CEC, 112, 265
Zhebrak, A. R., geneticist, 125-26, 132, 157, 256, 268, 273
Zheltikov, S., pupil of Vil'yams, 88
Zhukovsky, P. M., botanist, 68-69, 105-6, 129, 228, 239, 260, 269
Zhukov-Verezhnikov, N. N., microbiologist, 181, 209, 265
Zosimovich, V. P., plant breeder, 185
Zubarev, NKVD agent, 262